"I believe in memory not as a place of arrival, but as point of departure—a catapult throwing you into present times, allowing you to imagine the future instead of accepting it. It would be absolutely impossible for me to have any connection with history if history were just a collection of dead people, dead names, dead facts. That's why I wrote *Memory of Fire* in the present tense, trying to keep alive everything that happened and allow it to happen again, as soon as the reader reads it."

EDUARDO GALEANO

Praise for

EDUARDO GALEANO AND *MEMORY OF FIRE*

"Who else can make skeletons dance the way Galeano does?"

—*The New Yorker*

"A Uruguayan journalist forced most of his life to leave town a step ahead of coups and dictatorships, Galeano on the road and on the lam turned himself into an historian and an anthropologist, a three-ring circus and a one-man band. In *Memory of Fire*, his three-volume prestidigitation of the history of the Americas, he manages marvels of juxtaposition, from Pancho Villa reading *The Three Musketeers* to Superman flunking the Bay of Pigs."   —John Leonard, *Harper's*

"I really like this book."   —Doris Lessing

"Among Latin American literary giants, Gabriel Garcia Marquez is known for mesmerizing, Pablo Neruda for wooing. Mario Vargas Llosa educates. Jorge Luis Borges captivates. Then there is Eduardo Galeano, the galvanizer, firebrand, a writer who tells readers about history that other, more powerful people don't want them to know or understand."

—Marie Arana, *Washington Post*

"This is an epic book that will destroy your preconceptions."

—Ariel Dorfman

"The speculum, *espéculo* or mirror, understood as a sort of whimsical anthology or commonplace book, is a literary genre of venerable antiquity. In Spanish, one of the earliest of these exemplary works is a 14th-century version of the *Speculum laicorum* attributed to the English divine John of Howden, translated under the title *El espéculo de los legos,* in which brief factual chronicles are interspersed with gossip on various subjects, mini-biographies of heroes and saints, and legends culled from various sources. Among speculum authors, the most distin-

guished is the Uruguayan Eduardo Galeano, who has made the genre his trademark, notably in his three-volume masterpiece, *Memory of Fire*."
—Alberto Manguel, *The Guardian*

"The Uruguayan author's vignettes stitch together tales of wonder and terror, love and war, and just about everything in between. Are these koans, fables, experiences, or testimonials? Galeano, author of the groundbreaking *Memory of Fire* trilogy, is a collector of stories, a clairvoyant reared in the cafés of Montevideo who, like [Roberto] Bolaño, carries with him a multitude. He, too, sings of the dead, the tortured, the brutalized; like Bolaño, he resuscitates an endless array of friends, comrades, and fellow travelers."
—Anderson Tepper, *Village Voice*

"An extraordinary canter through the history of the Americas."
—Isabel Fonseca

"Unquestionably Galeano's masterwork, *Memory of Fire* is a kind of secret history of the Americas, told in hundreds of kaleidoscopic vignettes that resurrect the lives of campesinos and slaves, dictators and scoundrels, poets and visionaries."
—Scott Sherman, *The Atlantic*

"A massive fresco of Latin American history since the pre-Columbian era to modern times."
—Isabel Allende

"He has merged Homer and Herodutus and, like them, has demonstrated that a tale well told, particularly a collective one, is an oracle that we could do well to heed."
—Gregory Rabassa

"Passionate and lyrical, lucidly visual . . . Galeano parades the subjects of history before us in a dazzling frieze."
—*New Statesman*

"[A]n epic work of literary creation . . . there could be no greater vindication of the wonders of the lands and people of Latin America."
—*Washington Post*

"Galeano's outrage is tempered by intelligence, an ineradicable sense of humor, and hope. . . . [A] compelling book."
—*Los Angeles Times*, front-page review

Eduardo Galeano

MEMORY OF FIRE

II. FACES AND MASKS

Part Two of a Trilogy

Translated
by Cedric Belfrage

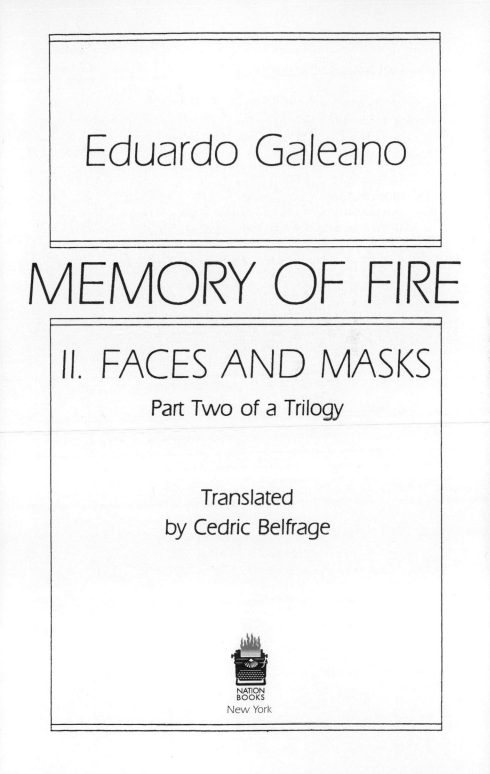

NATION
BOOKS
New York

Translator's Acknowledgment

Translation is a field in which two heads are better than one. I am grateful to Mark Fried for making himself so freely available to cooperate in this work.

Translation copyright© 1987 by Cedric Belfrage
First published as a Norton paperback 1998,
reprinted by arrangement with Pantheon Books
Paperback reprinted in 2010 by Nation Books,
A Member of the Perseus Books Group

Nation Books is a co-publishing venture of the Nation Institute and the Perseus Books Group.

Books published by Nation Books are available at special discounts for bulk purchases in the United States by corporations, institutions, and other organizations. For more information, please contact the Special Markets Department at the Perseus Books Group, 2300 Chestnut Street, Suite 200, Philadelphia, PA 19103, or call (800) 810-4145, ext. 5000, or e-mail special.markets@perseusbooks.com.

Text design by Marsha Cohen

Originally published in 1984 in Spain as *Memoria del fuego, II. Las caras y las máscaras*, by Siglo Veintiuno de España Editores, S.A. Copyright © 1984 by Siglo Veintiuno de España Editores, S.A; copyright © 1984 by Siglo Veintiuno de España Editores, S.A; copyright © 1984 by Eduardo Galeano.

Cataloging-in-Publication data for this book are available from the Library of Congress.

ISBN 0-393-31806-0 (v. 2)
Nation Books paperback ISBN 978-1-56858-445-4

Contents

Preface

This book

is the second volume of the trilogy *Memory of Fire*. It is not an anthology, but a work of literary creation. The author proposes to narrate the history of America, and above all the history of Latin America, reveal its multiple dimensions and penetrate its secrets. In the third volume this vast mosaic will reach to our own times. *Faces and Masks* embraces the eighteenth and nineteenth centuries.

At the head of each text is indicated the year and place of occurrence of the episode. The numbers in parentheses below show the principal works consulted by the author in his search for information and points of reference. Documentary sources are listed at the end of the book.

Literal transcriptions are italicized.

Acknowledgments

In addition to the friends mentioned in *Genesis*, who continued collaborating through this second volume, many others have facilitated the author's access to the necessary bibliography. Among them, Mariano Baptista Gumucio, Olga Behar, Claudia Canales, Hugo Chumbita, Galeno de Freitas, Horacio de Marsilio, Bud Flakoll, Piruncha and Jorge Galeano, Javier Lentini, Alejandro Losada, Paco Moncloa, Lucho Nieto, Rigoberto Paredes, Rius, Lincoln Silva, Cintio Vitier, and René Zavaleta Mercado.

This time the following nobly undertook to read the first draft: Jorge Enrique Adoum, Mario Benedetti, Edgardo Carvalho, Antonio Doñate, Juan Gelman, María Elena Martínez, Ramírez Contreras, Lina Rodríguez, Miguel Rojas-Mix, Nicole Rouan, Pilar Royo, César Salsamendi, José María Valverde, and Federico Vogelius. They suggested several changes and caught foolish and silly mistakes.

Once again Helena Villagra accompanied the work step by step, sharing tailwinds and setbacks, to the last line with mysterious patience.

This book

is dedicated to Tomás Borge, to Nicaragua.

I don't know who I am,
nor just where I was bedded.
Don't know where I'm from
nor where the hell I'm headed.

I'm a piece of fallen tree,
where it fell I do not know.
Where can my roots be?
On what sort of tree did I grow?
                    (Popular verses
                of Boyacá, Colombia)

FACES AND MASKS

Promise of America

The blue tiger will smash the world.

Another land, without evil, without death, will be born from the destruction of this one. This land wants it. It asks to die, asks to be born, this old and offended land. It is weary and blind from so much weeping behind closed eyelids. On the point of death it strides the days, garbage heap of time, and at night it inspires pity from the stars. Soon the First Father will hear the world's supplications, land wanting to be another, and then the blue tiger who sleeps beneath his hammock will jump.

Awaiting that moment, the Guaraní Indians journey through the condemned land.

"Anything to tell us, hummingbird?"

They dance without letup, ever lighter and airier, intoning the sacred chants that celebrate the coming birth of the other land.

"Shine your rays, shine your rays, hummingbird!"

From the sea coasts to the center of America, they have sought paradise. They have skirted jungles and mountains and rivers in pursuit of the new land, the one that will be founded without old age or sickness or anything to interrupt the endless fiesta of living. The chants announce that corn will grow on its own and arrows shoot into the thickets all by themselves; and neither punishment nor pardon will be necessary, because there won't be prohibition or blame.

(72 and 232)*

1701: Salinas Valley

The Skin of God

The Chirigua Indians of the Guaraní people sailed down the Pilcomayo River years or centuries ago, and reached the frontier of the empire of the Incas. Here they remained, beneath the first of these Andean heights, awaiting the land without evil and without death.

The Chiriguans discover paper, the written word, the printed word, when after a long journey the Franciscan monks of Chuquisaca appear carrying sacred books in their saddlebags.

As they didn't know paper or that they needed it, the Indians

* These numbers refer to the documentary sources consulted by the author as listed on pages 261–76.

had no word for it. Today they give it the name *skin of God*, because paper is for sending messages to friends far away.

(233 and 252)

1701: São Salvador de Bahia
Voice of America

Father Antonio Vieira died at the turn of the century, but not so his voice, which continues to shelter the defenseless. The words of this missionary to the poor and persecuted still echo with the same lively ring throughout the lands of Brazil.

One night Father Vieira spoke about the ancient prophets. They were not wrong, he said, in reading destinies in the entrails of the animals they sacrificed. In the entrails, he said. In the entrails, not the heads, because a prophet who can love is better than one who can reason.

(351)

1701: Paris
Temptation of America

In his study in Paris, a learned geographer scratches his head. Guilla·ime Deslile draws exact maps of the earth and the heavens. Should he include El Dorado on the map of America? Should he paint in the mysterious lake, as has become the custom, somewhere in the upper Orinoco? Deslile asks himself whether the golden waters, described by Walter Raleigh as the size of the Caspian Sea, really exist. And those princes who plunge in and swim by the light of torches, undulating golden fish: are they or were they ever flesh and bone?

The lake, sometimes named El Dorado, sometimes Parima, figures on all maps drawn up to now. But what Deslile has heard and read makes him doubt. Seeking El Dorado, many soldiers of fortune have penetrated the remote new world, over there where the four winds meet and all colors and pains mingle, and have found nothing. Spaniards, Portuguese, Englishmen, Frenchmen, and Germans have spanned abysses that the American gods dug with nails and teeth; have violated forests warmed by tobacco smoke puffed by the gods; have navigated rivers born of giant trees the gods tore out by the roots; have tortured and killed Indians the gods created out of saliva, breath, or dream. But that fugitive gold has vanished and always vanishes into the air, the lake disappearing before anyone can reach it. El Dorado seems to be the name of a grave without coffin or shroud.

In the two centuries that have passed since the world grew and became round, pursuers of hallucinations have continued heading for the lands of America from every wharf. Protected by a god of navigation and conquest, squeezed into their ships, they cross the immense ocean. Along with shepherds and farmhands whom Europe has not killed by war, plague, or hunger, go captains and merchants and rogues and mystics and adventurers. All seek the miracle. Beyond the ocean, magical ocean that cleanses blood and transfigures destinies, the great promise of all the ages lies open. There, beggars will be avenged. There, nobodies will turn into marquises, scoundrels into saints, gibbet-fodder into founders, and vendors of love will become dowried débutantes.

(326)

Sentinel of America

Long, long ago in the Andean cordillera, the Indians lived in perpetual night. The condor, oldest of all flying creatures, was the one who brought them the sun. He dropped it, a little ball of gold, among the mountains. The Indians picked it up and, blowing as hard as they could, blew it up toward the sky where it remains suspended forever. With the golden rays the sun sweated, the Indians modeled the animals and plants that inhabit the earth.

One night the moon rose, ringed by three halos, to shine upon the peaks: the halo of blood announced war; the halo of flame, fire; and the black halo was the halo of disaster. Then the Indians fled into the cold, high wilderness and, carrying the sacred gold, plunged into the depths of lakes and into volcanos.

The condor, bringer of the sun to the Andeans, is the caretaker of that treasure. With great gliding wings he soars over the snowy peaks and the waters and the smoking craters. The gold warns him when greed approaches. The gold cries out, and whistles, and shouts. The condor swoops down. His beak picks out the eyes of the thieves, and his claws tear their flesh.

Only the sun can see the back of the condor, his bald head, his wrinkled neck. Only the sun knows his loneliness. Seen from the earth, the condor is invulnerable.

(246)

1701: Ouro Prêto

Conjuring Tricks

The silver mountain of Potosí is not an illusion, nor do the deep tunnels of Mexico contain only delirium and darkness; nor do the rivers of central Brazil sleep on beds of fool's gold.

The gold of Brazil is apportioned by lottery or by fists, by luck or by death. Those who don't lose their lives make immense fortunes, one-fifth of which is owed to the Portuguese king. Yet, when all's said and done, that royal fifth is but a fable. Heaps and heaps of gold escape as contraband, and even as many guards as the region's dense forests have trees could not stanch its flow.

The friars of the Brazilian mines devote more time to trafficking in gold than to saving souls. Hollow wooden saints serve as containers. For the monk Roberto way off by the coast, forging dies is as simple as telling his rosary, and so illicit gold bars come to sport the royal seal. Roberto, a Benedictine monk of the Sorocaba monastery, has also manufactured an all-powerful key that vanquishes any lock.

(11)

1703: Lisbon

Gold, Passenger in Transit

A few years ago a governor-general of Brazil made some prophesies that were as accurate as they were useless. From Bahia, João de Lencastre warned the king of Portugal that hordes of adventurers would turn the mining region into a sanctuary for criminals and vagabonds; and even graver, with gold the same might happen to Portugal as to Spain, which as soon as it receives its silver from America kisses it a tearful goodbye. Brazilian gold might enter by the Bay of Lisbon and, without ever stopping on Portuguese soil, continue its voyage up the River Tagus en route to England, France, Holland, Germany . . .

As if to echo the governor's voice, the Treaty of Methuen is signed. Portugal will pay with Brazilian gold for English cloth. With gold from Brazil, another country's colony, England will give its industrial development a tremendous push forward.

(11, 48, and 226)

1709: The Juan Fernández Islands

Robinson Crusoe

The lookout reports distant gunfire. To investigate it, the freebooters of the Duke change course and head for the coast of Chile.

The ship approaches the Juan Fernández Islands. From a string of bonfires, a canoe, a splash of foam comes toward it. Onto the deck climbs a tangle of hair and filth, trembling with fever, emitting noises from its mouth.

Days later, Captain Rogers has the story. The shipwrecked man is one Alexander Selkirk, a Scottish colleague well versed in sails, winds, and plunder. He arrived off the Valparaíso coast with the expedition of the pirate William Dampier. Thanks to Bible, knife, and gun, Selkirk has survived more than four years on one of those uninhabited islands. He has learned the art of fishing with goats' intestines, cooked with salt crystallized on the rocks, and lighted his world with seal oil. He built a hut on high ground and beside it a corral for goats. He marked the passage of time on a tree trunk. A storm brought him the remains of some wreck and also an almost-drowned Indian. He called the Indian Friday because that was the day of his arrival. From him he learned the secrets of the plants. When the big ship came, Friday chose to stay. Selkirk swore to him that he would return, and Friday believed him.

Within ten years, Daniel Defoe will publish in London his novel about the adventures of a shipwrecked sailor. Selkirk will be Robinson Crusoe, native of York. The expedition of the British pirate Dampier, who had ravaged the coasts of Peru and Chile, will become a respectable commercial enterprise. The desert island without a history will jump from the Pacific Ocean to the mouth of the Orinoco, and the shipwrecked sailor will live there twenty-eight years. Robinson will save the life of a savage cannibal. "Master" will be the first word he teaches him in English.

Selkirk marked with a knife-point the ears of each goat he caught. Robinson will undertake the subdivision of the island, his kingdom, into lots for sale; he will put a price on every object he gets from the wrecked ship, keep accounts of all he produces on the island and a balance of every situation, the "debit" of bad fortune and the "credit" of good. Robinson will endure, like Selkirk, the tough tests of solitude, fear, and madness; but at the hour of rescue Alexander Selkirk is a shivering wretch who cannot talk and is scared of everything. Robin-

son Crusoe, on the other hand, invincible tamer of nature, will return
to England with his faithful Friday, totting up accounts and planning
adventures.

(92, 149, and 259)

1711: Paramaribo
The Silent Women

The Dutch cut the Achilles tendon of a slave escaping for the first
time, and one who makes a second try gets the right leg amputated;
yet there is no way to stop the spreading plague of freedom in Surinam.

Captain Molinay sails downriver to Paramaribo. His expedition
is returning with two heads. He had to behead the captured women,
one named Flora, the other Sery, because after the torture they were
in no condition to walk through the jungle. Their eyes are still fixed
heavenward. They never opened their mouths in spite of the lashes,
the fire, and the red-hot pincers, stubbornly mute as if they had not
spoken a word since that remote day when they were fattened up
and smeared with oil, and stars or half-moons were engraved on their
shaven heads to fit them for sale in the Paramaribo market. Always
mute, this Flora and Sery, as the soldiers kept asking where the
fugitive slaves hid out: they stared upwards without blinking, following clouds stout as mountains that drifted high in the sky.

(173)

They Carry Life in Their Hair

For all the blacks that get crucified or hung from iron hooks stuck
through their ribs, escapes from Surinam's four hundred coastal plantations never stop. Deep in the jungle a black lion adorns the yellow
flag of the runaways. For lack of bullets, their guns fire little stones
or bone buttons; but the impenetrable thickets are their best ally
against the Dutch colonists.

Before escaping, the female slaves steal grains of rice, corn, and
wheat, seeds of bean and squash. Their enormous hairdos serve as
granaries. When they reach the refuges in the jungle, the women
shake their heads and thus fertilize the free land.

(173)

The Maroon

The crocodile, disguised as a log, basks in the sun. The snail revolves its eyes on the point of little horns. The male bird courts the female with circus acrobatics. The male spider climbs up the female's perilous web—bedsheet and shroud—where he will embrace and be devoured. A band of monkeys leaps to seize wild fruits in the branches. The monkeys' screams daze the thickets, drowning out the litanies of cicadas, the questionings of birds. But strange footsteps sound on the carpet of leaves and the jungle falls quickly silent. Paralyzed, it draws into itself and waits. When the first gunshot rings out, the whole jungle stampedes in flight.

The shot announces a hunt for runaway slaves: *cimarrones*, in the Antillean phrase meaning "arrow that seeks freedom." Used by Spaniards for the bull that takes off for the woods, it passes into other languages as *chimarrão, maroon, marron* to designate the slave who in every part of America seeks the protection of forests and swamps and deep canyons; who, far from the master, builds a free domain and defends it by marking false trails and setting deadly traps.

The maroon is the gangrene of colonial society.

(264)

1711: Murrí

They Are Never Alone

There are Indian maroons too. To shut them in under the control of friars and captains, prisons are built. The newly born village of Murrí, in the region of the Chocó, is one.

Some time back, huge canoes with white wings arrived here, seeking the rivers of gold that flow down from the cordillera; and since then, Indians have been fleeing. Countless spirits accompany them as they journey through forests and across rivers.

The witch doctor knows the words that call the spirits. To cure the sick he blows his conch shell toward the foliage where the peccary, the bird of paradise, and the singing fish live. To make the well sick, he puts into one of their lungs the butterfly of death. The witch doctor knows that there is no land, water, or air empty of spirits in the Chocó region.

(121)

1711: Saint Basil's Refuge
The Black King, the White Saint
and His Sainted Wife

More than a century ago, the Negro Domingo Bioho fled from the galleys in Cartagena of the Indies and became warrior-king of the swamplands. Hosts of dogs and musketeers went hunting for him, and Domingo was hanged several times. On various days of great public enthusiasm Domingo was dragged through the streets of Cartagena tied to the tail of a mule, and several times had his penis chopped off and nailed to a long pike. His captors were rewarded with successive grants of land and repeatedly given the title of marquis; but within the maroon palisades of the Dique Canal or of the lower Cauca, Domingo Bioho reigns and laughs with his unmistakable painted face.

The free blacks live on constant alert, trained from birth to fight, protected by ravines and precipices and deep ditches lined with poisonous thorns. The most important of the refuges in the region, which has existed and resisted for a century, is going to be named after a saint, Saint Basil, whose effigy is soon expected to arrive on the Magdalena River. Saint Basil will be the first white man authorized to enter here. He will arrive with mitre and staff of office and will bring with him a little wooden church well stocked with miracles. He will not be scandalized by the nudity, or ever talk in a master's voice. The maroons will provide him with a house and wife. They will get him a saintly female, Catalina, so that in the other world God will not wed him to an ass and so that they may enjoy this world together while they are in it.

(108 and 120)

The Maríapalito

There is much animal life in the region where Domingo Bioho reigns forever and a day within his palisades. Most feared are the tiger, the boa constrictor, and the snake that wraps himself around the vines and glides down into the huts. Most fascinating are the mayupa fish that shits through his head, and the maríapalito.

Like the spider, the female maríapalito eats her lovers. When the male embraces her from behind, she turns her chinless face to him, measures him with her big, protuberant eyes, fastens her teeth in him and lunches off him with absolute calm, until nothing remains.

The maríapalito is extremely devout. She always keeps her arms folded in prayer and prays as she eats.

(108)

1712: Santa Marta
From Piracy to Contraband

From the green foothills of the Sierra Nevada, which wets its feet in the sea, rises a belltower surrounded by houses of wood and straw. In them live the thirty white families of the port of Santa Marta. All around, in huts of reed and mud, sheltered by palm leaves, live the Indians, blacks, and mixtures whom no one has bothered to count.

Pirates have always been the nightmare of these coasts. Fifteen years ago the bishop of Santa Marta had to take apart the organ of the church to improvise ammunition. A week ago English ships penetrated the cannon fire of forts guarding the bay and calmly met the dawn on the beach.

Everybody fled into the hills.

The pirates waited. They didn't steal so much as a handkerchief or burn a single house.

Mistrustful, the inhabitants approached one by one; and Santa Marta has now become a pleasant market. The pirates, armed to the teeth, have come to buy and sell. They bargain, but are scrupulous in paying.

Far away over there, British workshops are growing and need markets. Many pirates are becoming contrabandists although not one of them knows what the devil "capital accumulation" means.

(36)

1714: Ouro Prêto
The Mine Doctor

This doctor does not believe in drugs, nor in the costly little powders from Portugal. He mistrusts bleedings and purges and has small use for the patriarch Galen and his tablets of laws. Luis Gomes Ferreira advises his patients to take a daily bath, which in Europe would be a clear sign of heresy or insanity, and prescribes herbs and roots of the region. Dr. Ferreira has saved many lives, thanks to the common sense and ancient experience of the Indians, and to the aid of the "white handmaiden," sugarcane brandy that revives the dying.

There is little he can do, however, about the miners' custom of disemboweling each other with bullet or knife. Here, every fortune is fleeting, and shrewdness is worth more than courage. In the implacable war of conquest against this black clay in which suns lie concealed, no science has any role to play. Captain Tomás de Souza, treasurer to the king, went looking for gold and found lead. The doctor could do nothing for him but make the sign of the cross. Everyone believed the captain had a ton of gold stashed away, but the creditors found only a few slaves to divide up.

Rarely does the doctor attend a black patient. In the Brazilian mines slaves are used and scrapped. In vain Ferreira recommends more careful treatment, telling the bosses they sin against God and their own interests. In the places where they pan for gold, and in the galleries below ground, no black lasts ten years, but a handful of gold buys a new child, who is worth the same as a handful of salt or a whole hog.

(48)

1714: Vila Nova do Príncipe
Jacinta

She hallows the ground she walks on. Jacinta de Siquiera, African woman of Brazil, is the founder of this town of Príncipe and of the gold mines in the Quatro Vintens ravines. Black woman, verdant woman, Jacinta opens and closes like a carnivorous plant swallowing men and birthing children of all colors, in this world still without a map. Jacinta advances, slashing open the jungle, at the head of the scoundrels who come on muleback, barefoot, armed with old rifles, and who, when they enter the mines, leave their consciences hanging from a branch or buried in a swamp: Jacinta, born in Angola, slave in Bahia, mother of the gold of Minas Gerais.

(89)

1716: Potosí

Holguín

The viceroy of Lima, Don Rubico Morcillo de Auñón, enters Potosí beneath a hundred and twenty triumphal arches of tooled silver, through a tunnel of canvases depicting Icarus and Eros, Mercury, Endymion, the Colossus of Rhodes, and Aeneas fleeing from Troy.

Potosí, poor Potosí, is not what it once was. Its population down by half, the city receives the viceroy on a street of wood, not of silver. But as in the days of wonder and glory, trumpets and drums resound: pages in gallant liveries light up with wax torches the parade of captains on horseback, governors and judges, magistrates, ambassadors . . . With nightfall comes the radiant masquerade: the city offers the dust-covered visitor the homage of the twelve heroes of Spain, the twelve peers of France, and the twelve Sibyls. In garish costumes the valiant Cid and Emperor Charles salute him, plus as many nymphs and Arab princes and Ethiopian kings as ever existed in the world or in dreams.

Melchor Pérez Holguín depicts this day of prodigies. One by one, he paints the thousand personages, and Potosí, and the world's most generous mountain, in earth and blood and smoke hues lustered with silver, and paints his own image at the foot of the vast canvas: Holguín, eagle-nosed mestizo in his fifties, long black hair streaming from beneath his slouch hat, palette raised in one hand. He also paints two old characters leaning on canes, and writes the words coming from their mouths:

"So many marvels all at once, who ever did see?"

"Never saw nothing this grand in a hundred and some years."

Perhaps Holguín doesn't know that the marvel is the thing he is creating, believing he is just copying; nor does he know that his work will remain alive when the pomp of Potosí has been blotted from the face of the earth and no one can remember any viceroy.

(16 and 215)

1716: Cuzco

The Image Makers

Holguín's mentor, Diego Quispe Tito, died shortly after his eyes died. In the initial fog of blindness he managed to paint his own likeness en route to Paradise, with the imperial tassel of the Incas on his forehead. Quispe was the most talented of the Indian artists of Cuzco. In his works, parrots soar among the angels and alight on a Saint Sebastian riddled with arrows. American faces, birds, and fruits appear smuggled into landscapes of Europe or of Heaven.

While the Spaniards burn flutes and ponchos in the Plaza Mayor, the image makers of Cuzco find a way to paint bowls of avocados, rocoto chilis, chirimoyas, strawberries, and quinces on the table of the Last Supper, and to paint the Infant Jesus emerging from the belly of the Virgin and the Virgin sleeping on a bed of gold, in the embrace of Saint Joseph.

The people raise crosses of corn, or adorn them with garlands of potatoes; and at the foot of the altars there are offerings of squashes and watermelons.

(138 and 300)

Mary, Mother Earth

In churches hereabouts it is common to see the Virgin crowned with feathers or protected by parasols, like an Inca princess, and God the Father in the shape of a sun amid monkeys holding up columns and moldings adorned with tropical fruits, fish, and birds.

An unsigned canvas shows the Virgin Mary in the silver mountain of Potosí, between the sun and the moon. On one side is the pope of Rome, on the other the king of Spain. Mary, however, is not on the mountain but *inside* it; she *is* the mountain, a mountain with woman's face and outstretched hands, Mary-mountain, Mary-stone, fertilized by God as the sun fertilizes the land.

(137)

Pachamama

In the Andean highlands, the Virgin is *mama* and the land and time are also *mama*.

Earth, mother earth—the Pachamama—gets angry if someone drinks without inviting her. When she is extremely thirsty, she breaks the vessel and spills out its contents.

To her is offered the placenta of the newly born, which is buried among flowers so that the child may live; and so that love may live, lovers bury their knotted hair.

The goddess earth takes into her arms the weary and the broken who once emerged from her, opens to give them refuge at the journey's end. From beneath the earth, the dead make her flower.

(247)

Mermaids

In the main portico of the cathedral of Puno, Simón de Asto will carve two mermaids in stone.

Although mermaids symbolize sin, the artist will not sculpt monsters. He will create two handsome Indian girls, gay charango-players who will love without a shadow of guilt. These Andean mermaids, Quesintuu and Umantuu, in ancient times rose from the waters of Lake Titicaca to make love with the god Tunupa, the Aymara god of fire and lightning, who in passing left a wake of volcanos.

(137)

1717: Quebec
The Man Who Didn't Believe in Winter

The way Rabelais told it and Voltaire repeats it, the cold of Canada is so cold that words freeze as they emerge from the mouth and are suspended in midair. At the end of April, the first sun cleaves the ice on the rivers and spring breaks through amid crackings of resurrection. Then, only then, words spoken in the winter are heard.

The French colonists fear winter more than the Indians, and envy the animals that sleep through it. Neither the bear nor the marmot knows the ills of cold: they leave the world for a few months while winter splits trees with a sound like gunshots and turns humans into statues of congealed blood and marbleized flesh.

The Portuguese Pedro da Silva spends the winter carrying mail in a dog sled over the ice of the Saint Lawrence River. In summer he travels by canoe, and sometimes, due to the winds, takes a whole month coming and going between Quebec and Montreal. Pedro carries decrees from the governor, reports by monks and officials, offers by fur traders, promises from friends, secrets of lovers.

Canada's first postman has worked for a quarter of a century without asking winter's permission. Now he has died.

(96)

1717: Dupas Island

The Founders

The map of Canada fills a whole wall. Between the east coast and the great lakes, a few cities, a few forts. Beyond, an immense space of mystery. On another wall, beneath the crossed barrels of muskets, hang the scalps of enemy Indians, darkened by tobacco smoke.

Seated on a rocking chair, Pierre de La Vérendrye bites his pipe. La Vérendrye doesn't hear the bawlings of his newly born son as he squints at the map and lets himself go down the torrential rivers that no European has yet navigated.

He has returned alive from the battlefields of France, where they had given him up for dead from a shot in the breast and various saber wounds. In Canada he has plenty to eat, thanks to the wheat in his fields and his wounded lieutenant's pension; but he is bored to delirium.

His wounded legs will travel farther than his wildest daydreams. La Vérendrye's explorations will make this map look foolish. Heading west in search of the ocean that leads to the China coasts, he will reach places to the north where the musket barrel explodes from the cold when fired, and farther south than the unknown Missouri River. This child who is crying beside him in his wooden cradle will be the discoverer of the invincible wall of the Rocky Mountains.

Missionaries and fur traders will follow in his footsteps. So it has ever been. So it was with Cartier, Champlain, and La Salle.

Europe pays good prices for the skins of beavers, otters, martens, deer, foxes, and bears. In exchange for the skins, the Indians get weapons to kill each other, or die in the wars between Englishmen and Frenchmen who dispute their lands. The Indians also get firewater, which turns the toughest warrior into skin and bone, and diseases more devastating than the worst snowstorms.

(176 and 330)

Portrait of the Indians

Among the Indians of Canada there are no paunches nor any hunchbacks, say the French friars and explorers. If there is one who is lame, or blind, or one-eyed, it is from a war wound.

They do not know about property or envy, says Pouchot, and call money *the Frenchmen's snake*.

They think it ridiculous to obey a fellow man, says Lafitau. They elect chiefs who have no privilege whatsoever; and if one gets bossy, they depose him. Women give opinions and decisions on par with men. Councils of elders and public assemblies have the final word; but no human word has precedence over the voice of dreams.

They obey dreams as Christians do the divine mandate, says Brébeuf. They obey them every day, because the soul speaks through dreams every night; and when winter comes to an end and the ice of the world is broken, they throw a big party dedicated to dreams. Then the Indians dress up in costumes and every kind of madness is permitted.

They eat when they are hungry, says Cartier. Appetite is the only clock they know.

They are libertines, Le Jeune observes. Both women and men can break their marriage vows when they like. Virginity means nothing to them. Champlain has found women who have been married twenty times.

According to Le Jeune, they do not like working, but they delight in inventing lies. They know nothing of art, unless it be the art of scalping enemies. They are vengeful: for vengeance they eat lice and worms and every bug that enjoys human flesh. They are incapable, Biard shows, of understanding any abstract idea.

According to Brébeuf, the Indians cannot grasp the idea of hell. They have never heard of eternal punishment. When Christians threaten them with hell, the savages ask: *And will my friends be there in hell?*

(97)

Songs of the Chippewa Indians in the Great Lakes Region

Sometimes
I go about pitying myself
while I am carried by the wind
across the sky.

• • •

The bush
is sitting under a tree
and singing.

(38 and 340)

1718: São Jose del Rei

The Pillory

The horde of adventurers level forests, open mountains, divert rivers; and as long as fire evokes a sparkle in the rusty stones, the pursuers of gold eat toads and roots, and found cities under the double sign of hunger and punishment.

Erection of the pillory marks the birth of each city in the Brazilian gold region. The pillory is the center of everything, and around it will be the houses, and on the hilltops, churches: the pillory, with a crown on top and two iron rings to bind the hands of slaves deserving the lash.

Raising his sword before it, the count of Assumar is giving official birth to the town of São Jose del Rei. The journey from Rio de Janeiro has taken him four months and on the way he has had to eat monkey meat and roast ants.

This land makes the count of Assumar, governor of Minas Gerais, panicky and sick. He considers the spirit of revolt second nature for these intractable and rootless people. Here the stars induce disorder, he says; the water exhales uprisings and the earth gives off tumultuous vapors; the clouds are insolent, the winds rebellious, the gold outrageous.

The count has every runaway slave beheaded and organizes militias to put down black subversion. The *raceless ones*, neither white nor black, wretched offspring of master and slave, or mixtures of a thousand bloods, are the hunters of fugitive slaves. Born to live outside the law, all they are good for is dying as killers. They, the mulattos and mestizos, are abundant. Here, with no white women, there is no way of complying with the will of the king, who has ordered from Lisbon the avoidance of *defective and impure offspring*.

(122 and 209)

1719: Potosí

The Plague

Three years ago heaven sent a warning, *horrendous fire, presaging calamity*. The comet—maverick sun, crazy sun—pointed its accusing tail at the mountain of Potosí.

At the beginning of this year a child with two heads was born in the San Pedro barrio and the priest wondered whether to do one or two baptisms.

Despite comet and monster, Potosí persists in its French styles, clothing, and customs *reproved by God, shameful to sex, offensive to nature and a scandal to civic and political decency*. The city celebrates the Shrovetide carnival as usual, binge and uproar *very contrary to honesty*; and when six lovely damsels proceed to dance in the nude, the plague strikes.

Potosí suffers a thousand ills and deaths. God is merciless with the Indians, who shed rivers of blood to pay for the city's sins. According to Don Matías Ciriaco y Selda, *scientific and highly qualified physician*, to avenge himself God has used the evil influence of Saturn to turn the blood into urine and bile.

(16)

1721: Zacatecas
To Eat God

Bells ring out summoning all to the celebration. The mining center of Zacatecas has signed a peace pact with the Huichol Indians.

Long ago having fallen back into the Nayarit mountains, the Huichols have defended their independence for two centuries, invulnerable to constant assault. Now they are submitting to the Spanish crown. The pact guarantees that they will not be forced to serve in the mines.

On pilgrimages to their sacred lands, the Huichols have had no alternative but to pass through the region of mines, which is always hungry for hands. Grandfather Fire protects them from scorpion and snake, but can do little against the Indian-hunters.

The long trek to the Viricota plateau through an endless stony wilderness is a journey to their place of origin along the road of the gods. In Viricota the Huichols relive the ancestral deer hunt; they return to the eternal moment when the Lord of the Deer raised his horns to the newly risen sun, when he sacrificed himself so that human life would be possible, when he fertilized the corn with his own blood.

The deer, god of gods, inhabits a cactus, the peyote, which is extremely hard to find. The small and ugly peyote conceals itself among the rocks. When the Huichols discover it, they shoot arrows at it; and when they trap it, it weeps. Then they bleed it and skin it and cut the flesh into strips. Around the campfire, the Huichols eat the sacred cactus and then the trance sets in. At the edge of madness, in the ecstasy where all is forever and all is never, they are gods— while the communion lasts.

(31)

If You Inadvertently Lose Your Soul

That Huichol Indian woman about to give birth, what is she doing? She is remembering. She remembers intensely the night of love from which comes the child about to be born. She thinks about it with all the strength of that memory, that happiness, her body opening, joyful with that joy she had, sending forth a good Huichol who will be worthy of the joy that made him.

A good Huichol takes care of his soul, shining life force, but everyone knows that soul is smaller than an ant, softer than a whisper, a little nothing, a puff of wind. In any careless moment it can be lost.

A young lad trips and rolls down the mountainside. The soul, tied to him by no more than a silken spider's thread, detaches as he falls. The young Huichol, dizzy, sickening, calls haltingly to the guardian of the sacred songs, the wizard-priest.

That old Indian scratching at the mountainside, what is he looking for? He retraces the sick lad's trail. He climbs, silently, among the sharp rocks, searching the foliage leaf by leaf, looking under little stones. *Where did life fall? Where does it lie in fright?* He walks slowly, listening alertly because lost souls weep or sometimes whistle like the breeze.

When he finds the missing soul, the wizard-priest lifts it with the tip of a feather, wraps it in a tiny ball of cotton, and carries it in a little hollow reed back to its owner, who will not die.

(124)

1726: Montevideo Bay
Montevideo

East of the bend in the Uruguay River, the rolling prairie nurtures more cows than clover. The *bandeirantes* of Brazil, swallowers of frontiers, covet this enormous mine of meat and hides; and now the Portuguese flag flutters on the River Plata coast, over the Colonia del

Sacramento fortress. To stop their onslaught, the king of Spain orders a town built on Montevideo Bay.

Under the protection of cannon and cross, the new city emerges. It blooms on a point of earth and rock beaten by the wind and threatened by Indians. From Buenos Aires come the first settlers, fifteen young people, nineteen children, and a few slaves who do not figure on the list—black hands for the ax, the hoe, and the gallows, breasts to give milk, a voice to cry wares.

The founders, almost all illiterate, get knightly privileges from the king. They try out the right to call themselves "Don" over rounds of maté, gin, and cigars:

"Your health, Don."

"Here's to yours."

The general store smells of maté and tobacco. It is the first house to have a wooden door and adobe walls among the cowhide huts scattered in the shadow of the fort. The store offers drinks, talk, and guitars, and also sells buttons and frying pans, biscuits and what-have-you.

Out of the general store, the cafe will be born. Montevideo will be the city of cafes. No corner will be a corner without a cafe as an accessory for secrets and noise, a little temple where all loneliness can take refuge, all encounters be celebrated, with cigarette smoke serving as incense.

(278 and 315)

1733: Ouro Prêto

Fiestas

Arches of flowers span the streets of Ouro Prêto, and in their shade the Holy Sacrament parades between walls of silks and damasks. The Four Winds and the Seven Planets come and go on horses sheathed with jewels, and on lofty thrones gleam the Moon and the Nymphs and the Morning Star, with their corteges of angels. After a week of fireworks and continuous celebration, the procession chants thanksgivings to Gold, hallelujahs to the Diamond, and devotions to God.

Diamonds are a novelty in the region. Until recently they were used to keep score in card games. When it was discovered what these little crystals were, the king of Portugal presented the first ones to

God and the pope and then bought from the Vatican the very costly title of Most Faithful King.

The streets of Ouro Prêto rise and fall steeply like knife blades, its people divided between summits and abysses. The fiestas of those at the top are displays of obligatory celebration, but the fiestas of those at the bottom provoke suspicion and punishment. Dark skins conceal threats of witchcraft and dangers of rebellion. The songs and music of the poor are a sin. The mulatta who likes to laugh risks prison or banishment, and on a Sunday of merriment a black slave can lose his head.

(209)

1736: Saint John's, Antigua
Flare-ups

They sealed their oath drinking from the same earthenware bowl a mixture of rum, grave dirt, and rooster's blood, and an earthquake of drums exploded. They had the powder ready to blow up the governor and all the chief gentry of the British island of Antigua. So the prosecutor told it. So the judges believed.

Six black slaves die of hunger, lashed to the stake, and another five are broken to pieces. Seventy-seven are burned alive. Two others save themselves by telling lies that condemn their fathers to the fire.

The conspirators are charcoal or putrid meat, but they wander along the beach at dawn. While the low tide bares marvels in the sand, fishermen cross paths with the dead, who are seeking water and food to continue their journey to the beyond.

(78)

1738: Trelawny Town
Cudjoe

Plants and people stream with sweat in the hairy mountains of western Jamaica. Even the sun hides itself when the long wail of the horn announces that the enemy chief has arrived at the pass.

This time Colonel Guthrie does not come to fight. The English slavers offer peace to the maroons. They promise to respect the freedom they have won in long years of war and recognize their ownership of the lands they live on. In exchange, the maroons turn themselves into gendarmes of their imprisoned brothers: from now on, they will help punish slave rebellions on the sugar plantations and will return fugitives who come here seeking refuge.

Chief Cudjoe goes out to meet Colonel Guthrie. Cudjoe wears a brimless hat and a jacket that once was blue and had sleeves. The red dust of Jamaica imparts one color to skin and clothing, but not even a button is missing on the colonel's vest and the whiteness of his rolled wig can still be discerned. Cudjoe falls to the ground and kisses his boots.

(78, 86 and 264)

1739: New Nanny Town
Nanny

After dealing with Cudjoe, chief of the Leeward maroons, Colonel Guthrie marches east, but some unknown hand slips a deadly poison into his rum, and he falls like lead from his horse.

Some months later, at the foot of a very high mountain, Captain Adair secures peace in the east. Sporting a ceremonial sword and a silvery hat, Quao, chief of the Windward maroons, accepts his conditions. But on these eastern cliffs Nanny has more power than Quao. The scattered Windward bands obey her, as do the squadrons of mosquitos. Nanny, a large woman of fiery clay, mistress of the gods, wears nothing but a necklace of English soldiers' teeth.

No one sees her, everyone sees her. They say she is dead, but she hurls herself naked, a black bombshell, into the center of the battle. She squats with her back to the enemy, and her magnificent ass catches the bullets. Sometimes she sends them back with interest and sometimes she turns them into balls of cotton.

(78 and 264)

Pilgrimage in Jamaica

They come from holes in the trees, holes in the ground, chinks between rocks.

Rains and rivers do not hold them back. They cross marshes, ravines, forests. Neither fog nor the fierce sun sidetracks them. Slowly, implacably, they descend from the mountains. They march in profile, on a straight course, without deviations. Their shells gleam in the

sun. Battalions of warrior males head the pilgrimage. At any sign of
danger they raise their weapons, their claws. Many die or lose an
arm opening the way. The soil of Jamaica creaks, covered by this
immense army of crabs.

The journey to the sea is long. After two or three months they
arrive exhausted—those that arrive. Then the females come forward
and let themselves be covered by the waves, and the sea pulls out
their eggs.

Of the millions that began the journey to the sea, few return.
But the sea incubates, beneath the sand, a new crab people. And
before long this new people sets out for the mountains whence came
their mothers; and there is no one to stop them.

The crabs have no heads. They arrived late at the distribution
of heads that was made by the god king in his cotton and copper
palace back in Africa. Crabs have no heads, but they dream and know.

(86)

1742: Juan Fernández Islands
Anson

The Chileans believe that the waves of this ocean are horses with
foaming mouths that witches ride with reins of gulfweed. The waves
hurl their assault upon the boulders which do not believe in witches,
and the rocky castles submit to the beating with remote disdain. High
above, dignified as a king, a billy goat with venerable beard contemplates the spray. Few goats remain on the Juan Fernández Islands.
Years ago the Spaniards brought from Chile a pack of dogs to seize
this easy food, thus denying it to the pirates.

Commander Anson's men vainly hunt the shadows of horns among
rocks and precipices, and think they recognize the mark of Alexander
Selkirk on the ears of a goat they catch. The English flag flies intact
from the ships' masts. Lord George Anson's fleet will return to London
devastated by hunger and scurvy, but the booty will be so splendid
that forty ox-carts will not suffice to haul it from the port. In the name
of perfecting Cartography, Geography, Astronomy, Geometry and
the Art of Navigation, scientist Anson has hunted down various Spanish ships with his guns and set fire to several towns, taking everything,
down to wigs and embroidered underwear.

In these years the British Empire is coming to birth in the trans-

lation from piracy to contraband; but Anson is a pirate of the old
school.

(10)

1753: Sierra Leone River
Let Us Praise the Lord

The revelation of God came in the flashes of lightning. Captain John
Newton was converted to Christianity on a night of blasphemy and
drunkenness when a sudden storm was on the point of sending his
ship to the bottom of the ocean.

Since then he is one of the Lord's elect. Every evening he preaches
a sermon. He says grace before each meal and starts every day singing
psalms which the crew hoarsely repeat in chorus. In Liverpool, at
the end of each voyage, he pays for a special ceremony of thanksgiving
to the All-Highest.

While awaiting a cargo at the mouth of the Sierra Leone River,
Captain Newton puts fears and mosquitos to flight and beseeches God
to protect the ship *African* and all her crew, and to ensure that the
merchandise he is about to load reaches Jamaica intact.

Captain Newton and his numerous colleagues are engaged in a
triangular trade between England, Africa, and the Antilles. At Liverpool they load cloth, rum, rifles, and knives which they exchange
for men, women, and children on the African coast. The ships steer
a course for the Caribbean islands, and there exchange the slaves for
sugar, molasses, cotton, and tobacco which they take to Liverpool to
start the cycle again.

In his leisure hours the captain contributes to the sacred liturgy
by composing hymns. On this night, shut up in his cabin, he begins
to write a new one as he waits for the slave caravan, delayed because
a few slaves tried to kill themselves by eating clay on the way. He
already has the title. The hymn will be called "How Sweet the Sound
of Jesus' Name." The first verses are done, and the captain hums
possible melodies beneath the accomplice lamp that swings from the
upper deck.

(193)

1758: Cap Français

Macandal

Before a large assembly of runaway slaves, François Macandal pulls a yellow handkerchief out of a glass of water.

"First it was the Indians."

Then a white handkerchief.

"Now, whites are the masters."

He shakes a black handkerchief before the maroons' eyes. The hour of those who came from Africa has arrived, he announces. He shakes the handkerchief with his only hand, because he has left the other between the iron teeth of the sugar mill.

On the plains of northern Haiti, one-handed Macandal is the master of fire and poison. At his order cane fields burn; and by his spells the lords of sugar collapse in the middle of supper, drooling spit and blood.

He knows how to turn himself into an iguana, an ant, or a fly, equipped with gills, antennae, or wings; but they catch him anyway, and condemn him; and now they are burning him alive. Through the flames the multitude see his body twist and shake. All of a sudden, a shriek splits the ground, a fierce cry of pain and exultation, and Macandal breaks free of the stake and of death: howling, flaming, he pierces the smoke and is lost in the air.

For the slaves, it is no cause for wonder. They knew he would remain in Haiti, the color of all shadows, the prowler of the night.

(63 and 115)

1761: Cisteil

Canek

The Maya Indians proclaim the independence of Yucatán and announce the forthcoming independence of America.

"Spanish power has brought us nothing but troubles. Nothing but troubles."

Jacinto Uc, who makes trumpets sound by caressing the leaves of trees, crowns himself king. Canek, *black snake*, is his chosen name. The king of Yucatán ties around his neck the mantle of Our Lady of the Conception and harangues the other Indians. They have rolled grains of corn on the ground and sung the war chant. The prophets, the men with warm breasts enlightened by the gods, have said that he who dies fighting will reawaken. Canek says he is not king for love of power, that power craves more and more power, and that when the jug is full the water spills out. He says he is king against the power of the powerful, and announces the end of serfdom and whipping posts and of Indians lining up to kiss the master's hand.

"They won't be able to tie us up: they'll run out of rope."

In Cisteil and other villages the echoes multiply, words become screams; and monks and captains roll in blood.

(67 and 144)

1761: Merida

Fragments

After much killing, they have taken him prisoner. Saint Joseph has been the patron saint of this colonial victory. They accuse Canek of scourging Christ and of stuffing Christ's mouth with grass. He is convicted. He is to be broken alive with iron bars in the main square of Merida.

Canek enters the square on muleback, his face almost hidden by an enormous paper crown. On the crown his infamy is spelled out: *Risen against God and against the King.*

They chop him up bit by bit, without permitting him the relief of death, worse than an animal's fate in a slaughterhouse; then they throw the fragments of him into the bonfire. A prolonged ovation punctuates the ceremony. Beneath the ovation, it is whispered that the serfs will put ground glass in the masters' bread.

(67 and 144)

1761: Cisteil

Sacred Corn

The executioners throw Canek's ashes into the air, so that he won't revive on the day of the Last Judgement. Eight of his chiefs die by garroting and two hundred Indians have an ear cut off. Hurting what is most sacred, soldiers burn the rebel communities' seedcorn plantings.

The corn is alive. It suffers if it is burned; its dignity is hurt if it is trodden on. Perhaps the corn dreams about the Indians, as the

Indians dream about the corn. It organizes space and time and history for the people made of corn flesh.

When Canek was born, they cut his navel cord over a corncob. In the name of the newly born, grains of corn stained with his blood were planted. From this cornfield he fed, and drank clear water containing the light of an evening star, and so grew up.

(1, 67, 144, and 228)

1763: Buraco de Tatú
The Subversives Set a Bad Example

The guides, who can see as well on a moonless night as by day, elude the traps. Thanks to them, the soldiers are able to cross the labyrinth of treacherous sharpened stakes, and swoop down at dawn on the free blacks' village.

Smoke of gunpowder, smoke of flames: the air is thick and sour down by the beach at Itapoã. By midday nothing remains of the Buraco de Tatú, the fugitive slaves' refuge which for twenty years has been such an offense to the nearby city of São Salvador de Bahia.

The viceroy has sworn to cleanse Brazil of runaway slaves, but they sprout up on all sides. In vain Captain Bartolomeu Bueno lops off four thousand pairs of ears in Minas Gerais.

Rifle butts force into line those who did not fall in defense of the Buraco de Tatú. All are branded on the chest with the letter F for fugitive, and returned to their owners. Captain Joaquim da Costa Cardoso, who is short of cash, is selling children at bargain prices.

(264 and 284)

Communion

History, the pink-veiled lady offering her lips to those who win, will have much to hide. She will feign absent-mindedness or sicken with fake amnesia; she will lie that the black slaves of Brazil were meek and resigned, even happy.

But plantation owners oblige the cook to sample each dish before their eyes. Among the delights of the table lurk poisons that promise long agonies. Slaves kill; and they also kill themselves or flee, which are their ways of robbing the master of his chief wealth. Or they rise up, believing and dancing and singing, which is their way of redemption and resurrection.

The smell of cut sugarcane inebriates the plantation air, and fires burn in the earth and in human breasts: the fire tempers the whips, drums rumble. The drums invoke the ancient gods, who fly to this land of exile in response to the voices of their lost children, enter them, make love to them, and, pulling music and howls from their mouths, give them back their broken life intact.

In Nigeria or Dahomey, the drums ask fecundity for the women and the fields. Not here. Here the women bear slaves and the fields crush them. The drums do not ask for fecundity, but vengeance; and Ogum, the god of iron, sharpens daggers instead of plows.

(27)

Bahia Portrait

Those in command in Bahia say that *the black man does not go to Heaven, pray as he might, because he has rough hair that pricks Our Lord*. They say he does not sleep: he snores. That he does not eat: he swallows. That he does not talk: he mumbles. That he does not die: he comes to an end. They say that God made the white man and painted the mulatto. The black man, the Devil shat.

Any black fiesta is suspect of homage to Satan, that atrocious black with tail, claws, and trident, but those in command know that if the slaves amuse themselves from time to time, they do more work, live more years and have more children. Just as the *capoeira*—ritual and mortal hand-to-hand combat—purports to be a colorful game, the *candomblé* pretends to be nothing but dance and noise. Furthermore, Virgins or saints to lend a disguise are never lacking. No one stops Ogum from turning into Saint George, the blond cavalier, and the mischievous black gods even conceal themselves in the wounds of Christ.

In the slaves' Holy Week, it is a black that administers justice to the traitor, blowing up the white Judas, a puppet painted with lime; and when the slaves parade the Virgin in procession, the black Saint Benedict is at the center of all homage. The Church does not recognize this saint. According to the slaves, Saint Benedict was a slave like themselves, a cook in a monastery, and angels would stir the pot while he said his prayers.

Anthony is the saint preferred by the masters. Saint Anthony sports military stripes, draws a salary, and specializes in policing blacks. When a slave escapes, the master throws the saint into the corner with the trash. Saint Anthony remains in penitence, face down, until the dogs catch the runaway.

(27 and 65)

Your Other Head, Your Other Memory

From the sundial of the San Francisco monastery, a lugubrious inscription reminds passersby how time flies: *Every hour that passes wounds thee and the last will kill thee*.

The words are written in Latin. The black slaves of Bahia do not know Latin or how to read. From Africa they brought happy and scrappy gods: the blacks are with them, to them they go. Whoever dies, enters. The drums beat so that the deceased will not get lost and will arrive safely in Oxalá. There, in the house of the creator of creators, awaits his other head, the immortal head. We all have two heads and two memories. A head of clay, which will turn to dust; and another, forever invulnerable to the gnawings of time and of passion. One memory that death kills, a compass that expires with the journey; and another memory, the collective memory, which will live as long as the human adventure in the world lives.

When the air of the universe first stirred and breathed, and the god of gods was born, there was no separation between earth and heaven. Now they seem to be divorced; but heaven and earth join again each time someone dies, each time someone is born, and each time someone receives the gods in a throbbing body.

(361)

1763: Rio de Janeiro
Here

A quarter of a century ago, Luis da Cunha proposed to the king of Portugal that he move with all his court from Lisbon to Rio de Janeiro, and that in this city he proclaim himself Emperor of the West. The capital of the empire should be here, at the center of abundance, because Portugal could not live without the riches of Brazil but Brazil, Luis da Cunha warned, could easily live without Portugal.

For the time being the throne remains in Lisbon, but the center of the colony is displaced from north to south. Bahia, the sugar port, yields to Rio de Janeiro, port of gold and diamonds. Brazil is growing southward and westward, beating against Spanish frontiers.

The new capital occupies the most beautiful spot in the world. Here the mountains look like pairs of lovers, the air has aromas that make you laugh, and a warm breeze excites the birds. Things and people are made of music, and the sea so sparkles before your eyes that it would be a pleasure to drown yourself.

(48)

1763: Tijuco

The World Inside a Diamond

Among lofty red rocks which look like dragons undulates the red earth hurt by man's hand. The region of diamonds exhales a fiery dust that reddens the walls of the city of Tijuco. A stream flows at its side and in the distance are mountains the color of the sea or of ashes. From the bed of the river come diamonds which will cross the mountains, and sail from Rio de Janeiro to Lisbon and from Lisbon to London, where they are cut, their price multiplying several times over, later to lend brilliance to the whole world.

Many diamonds escape as contraband. Although the corpus delicti may be the size of a flea's eye, clandestine miners who have been caught lie without graves, meat for crows; and the slave suspected of swallowing what he shouldn't gets a violent purge of hot chili.

Every diamond belongs to the king of Portugal and to João Fernandes de Oliveira, who reigns here by right of the king's contract. Beside him is Chica da Silva, also known as Chica Who Commands. A mulatta, she wears European clothes barred to the dark-skinned, and shows off by going to Mass on a litter followed by a cortege of black women decked out like princesses. In the church, she occupies the place of honor. There is no noble hereabouts who does not bend his spine before her hand covered with gold rings, and none who misses her gatherings at the mansion in the mountains. There, Chica da Silva throws banquets and theater parties—performances of *The Charms of Medea* or some other fashionable play—and afterwards takes her guests for a sail on the lake that Oliveira had dug for her because she wanted ocean and there was no ocean. They mount a gilded stairway to the dock and cruise in a grand vessel crewed by ten sailors.

Chica da Silva wears a wig of white rolls. The rolls cover her forehead and hide the mark left by the branding iron when she was a slave.

(307)

1763: Havana

Progress

A year ago the English arrived at Cojímar beach with guns blazing.

While Havana signed the surrender, after a long siege, the slave ships waited outside the port. When they anchored in the bay, buyers grabbed up their merchandise. Merchants customarily follow warriors. A single slave trafficker, John Kennion, sold seventeen hundred slaves during the British occupation. He and his colleagues doubled the work force on the plantations, which were so antiquated that they still grew all kinds of food and had only one machine, the mill that crushes sugarcane, turning at the pace of circling oxen.

British dominion over Cuba hardly lasts ten months, but the Spaniards scarcely recognize the colony they get back. The English have given it such a shaking that Cuba awakens from its long agrarian siesta. In times to come this island will turn into an immense sugar factory, grinding up slaves and ravaging everything else. Tobacco farms, cornfields, and vegetable patches will be razed. Forests will be devastated and streams dried up. Each black slave will be squeezed out in seven years.

(222)

The Slaves Believe:

The gods move blood and sap. In every blade of Cuban grass breathes a god, and that's why the forest is alive. Temple of African gods, home of African ancestors, the forest is sacred and keeps secrets. If anyone fails to greet it, its anger rises and it denies health and fortune. One must offer it a gift to receive the leaves that heal wounds and ward off misfortune. One must greet it with ritual words—or whatever words come out. Everyone talks with the gods as he feels or is able.

No god is all good or all bad. The same one may save or kill. The breeze refreshes and the hurricane destroys, but both are air.

(56)

The Ceiba Tree

"Good evening, mother Ceiba. Bless you."
The imposing ceiba is a tree of mystery. The ancestors and the gods favor it. The flood respected it. It is secure from lightning and hurricanes.

One may not turn one's back on it or walk in its shade without permission. Anyone striking an ax to its sacred trunk feels the ax-blow on his own body. They say that at times it consents to die by fire, fire being its favorite son.

It opens when you ask it for shelter, and to defend the fugitive it covers itself with thorns.

(56)

The Royal Palm

In this haughty palm lives Shangó, the black god who calls himself Saint Barbara when he disguises himself as a Christian woman. The leaves of its crest are his arms. From on high he fires his heavenly artillery. Shangó eats fire, wears lightning, talks thunder, and shakes the earth with his rays. He turns enemies into ash.

Warrior and satyr, Shangó never tires of joking and loving. The gods hate him; the goddesses are crazy about him. He took his brother Ogum's woman Oyá, who is said to be the Virgin of Candelaria and fights at Shangó's side with two swords. In the rivers he makes love to Oshún, and together they eat delicacies of sugar and cinnamon.

(28 and 56)

1766: The Fields of Areco
The Wild Horses

In Buenos Aires, the twenty Indian children from the Jesuits' San Javier mission choir have sung in the cathedral and in several full churches; and the public has shown its gratitude for these voices from heaven. The Guaraní orchestra of violins and one-stringed *trompas marinas* has also worked miracles.

The musicians set out on their return journey, led by Fray Hermann Paucke. Two weeks' traveling separates them from their homes on the coast. On the way, Paucke collects and sketches all he sees: plants, birds, customs.

In the fields of Areco, Paucke and his Guaraní musicians witness the sacrifice of maverick horses. Peons bring these wild horses to the corrals mixed in with domesticated ones, and there they halter them and take them out one by one into open country. Then they turn them over and with a single slash, open their bellies. The mavericks still gallop, treading on their entrails, until they roll on the grass; and the next day dawns on bones whitened by dogs.

The wild horses wander through the pampa in troops that are more like shoals, flying fish slithering between air and grass, and spread their contagion of freedom among the domesticated horses.

(55)

1767: Misiones

The Story of Seven Villages

The king of Spain had made his father-in-law, the king of Portugal, a present of seven villages. He offered them empty, but they were inhabited. Those villages were seven missions founded by Jesuit fathers, for Guaraní Indians, east of the upper Uruguay River. Like many other missions of the Guaraní region, they had served as bulwarks for the constantly assaulted frontier.

The Guaranís declined to get out. Change their pasturelands, like a flock of sheep, because the man said so? The Jesuits had taught them to make clocks, plows, bells, clarinets, and books printed in their Guaraní language; but they had also taught them to make guns to defend themselves against the slave hunters.

Portuguese and Spanish soldiers chase the Indians off and the Indians slip back by night. Again they are chased off and again they return, but this time transformed into thunderous winds, a storm of lightning that sets fortresses afire.

Everyone knows the monks are on their side. *The will of the king is the will of God,* say the superiors of the Order of Loyola, *an impenetrable will that puts us to the test: When Abraham obeyed the divine voice, and raised the sword against the neck of his own son Isaac, God sent an angel to stay the blow at the critical moment.* But the Jesuit priests refuse to immolate the Indians. To no avail the archbishop of Buenos Aires threatens to excommunicate both Indians and priests. In vain the Church hierarchy orders the burning of the gunpowder and destruction of the guns and lances with which the missions have a thousand times stopped Portuguese attacks against the Spanish frontier.

Long is the war of the seven villages against the two crowns. In the battle of Caybaté hill, fifteen hundred Indians fall. The seven missions are razed, but the king of Portugal cannot enjoy the king of Spain's gift.

The kings never forgive the offense. Three years after the battle of Caybaté, the king of Portugal expels the Jesuits from all his dominions. And now the king of Spain follows suit.

(76 and 189)

1767: Misiones

The Expulsion of the Jesuits

The instructions arrive from Madrid in envelopes sealed with wax. Viceroys and governors execute them immediately throughout America. They seize the Jesuit fathers at night by surprise and immediately ship them to far-off Italy. More than two thousand priests go into exile.

The king of Spain punishes the sons of Loyola, who have become such sons of America, for repeated disobedience and the suspected planning of an independent Indian kingdom.

No one weeps for them as do the Guaranís. The Jesuits' many missions in the Guaraní region announced the promised land without evil and without death; and the Indians called the priests *karaí*, a name reserved for their prophets. From the wreckage of the San Luis Gonzaga mission, the Indians send a letter to the governor of Buenos Aires. *We are not slaves*, they say. *We don't like your custom of every man for himself instead of helping one another*.

Soon all is broken up. Common property and the communal system of production and life disappear. The best missionary estancias are sold to the highest bidder. Churches, factories, schools fall apart. Undergrowth invades pastures and wheat fields. Pages are torn from books to make cartridges for gunpowder. The Indians flee into the forest or stay to become vagabonds, whores, and drunks. To be born Indian is once again an insult or a crime.

(189)

1767: Misiones

They Won't Let Their Tongues Be Torn Out

In the print shops of the Paraguay missions some of the best books of colonial America have been published, religious books in the Guaraní language, with typefaces and engravings carved in wood by Indians.

Guaraní was the spoken and written language of the missions. After the expulsion of the Jesuits, Castilian is imposed as the obligatory and only language.

No one resigns himself to becoming dumb and without memory. No one pays any attention.

(117)

1769: London

The First Novel Written in America

Ten years ago the bells of London wore themselves out celebrating the victories of the British Empire. The city of Quebec had fallen after intense bombardment, and France had lost her dominions in Canada. The young general James Wolfe, who commanded the English army, had announced that he would crush *the Canadian plague*, but died before seeing it happen. According to the gossip, Wolfe would measure himself when he awoke and find himself a bit taller each day, until a bullet interrupted his growth.

Now Frances Brooke publishes a novel in London, *The History of Emily Montague*, which depicts Wolfe's officers conquering hearts in the land conquered by their guns. The author, a plump and pleasant Englishwoman, lives and writes in Canada. In the form of two hundred and twenty-eight letters, she relates her impressions and experiences in the new British colony and weaves in some romances between uniformed English gallants and the breathless young ladies of Quebec high society. Their well-educated passions lead to matrimony, via the fashion house, the ballroom, and picnics on the islands. The magnificent waterfalls and noble lakes provide a fitting backdrop.

(50, 52, and 176)

Indians and Dreams in
the Novel of Frances Brooke

*The Indians retain most of their ancient superstitions. I should par-
ticularize their belief in dreams, of which folly even repeated dis-
appointments cannot cure them . . . As I happened to smile at the
recital a savage was making of a prophetic dream, from which he
assured us of the death of an English officer whom I knew to be alive,
"You Europeans," said he, "are the most unreasonable people in the
world; you laugh at our belief in dreams, and yet expect us to believe
things a thousand times more incredible."*

(50)

1769: Lima
Viceroy Amat

At the hour when families kneel to say the rosary, the holy, holy,
holy, the novena, and prayers for the dead, the trot of the viceroy's
carriage heading for the theater is heard. A murmur of scandal echoes
through half-open Venetian blinds. Prayers stop short. Gossip breaks
forth. The brusque viceroy of Lima, a rascal, rogue, and knave, has
lost his head to a small-time comedienne.

Night after night, Don Manuel de Amat y Junyent attends any
zarzuela, farce, mystery or comedy in which Micaela Villegas waggles
her hips and stomps her heels on the stage. He doesn't care about
the plot. When Micaela, that exquisite pure cinnamon, that cinnamon
in flower starts singing her cajoleries, the old viceroy's wig flies off.
He applauds madly and punches holes in the floor with his cane. She
answers him rolling her eyes, smiling beneath the indispensable beauty
spot, and offering her breasts in sequined curtsies.

The viceroy has been a man of the barracks, not of parties and
balls. A scowling bachelor with five big scars won in the North African
wars, he came to Lima to clean horse- and cattle-thieves off the roads
and throw out idlers and loafers. Under this leaden sky, more roof
than sky, he wanted to kill himself, but conquered the temptation by
hanging people.

Eight years after his arrival the viceroy has learned to steal, to
eat rocote chilis and spicy guinea pig, and to study décolletages with

an opera glass. The ship that brought him from Valparaíso had a naked woman as figurehead on its prow.

(26 and 245)

1769: Lima

La Perricholi

Like all women of Lima, Micaela Villegas displays her bosom but hides her feet, protects them with tiny shoes of white satin. Like the others, she enjoys wearing rubies and sapphires even on her belly, be they only paste, as hers were.

Daughter of a poor provincial mestizo, Micaela made the rounds of this city's shops for the pure pleasure of seeing or feeling Lyons silks and Flanders woollens, and bit her lips when she discovered a gold and diamond necklace around the neck of a highborn lady's kitten.

Micaela got into the theater and was transformed into queen, nymph, fashion plate, or goddess as long as the performance lasted. Now she is First Courtesan all day and all night, too. A cloud of black slaves surrounds her, her jewelry is above suspicion and counts kiss her hand.

The ladies of Lima avenge themselves by calling her Perricholi. The viceroy himself had so baptized her, trying to say *perra chola* (mestizo bitch) with his toothless mouth. They say he put this curse on her, as a sort of exorcism, while carrying her up the steps to his lofty bed, because she stirred in him dangerous panics and burnings and wet and dry sensations that took him back trembling to his early years.

(95, 245, and 304)

The Snack Clock

With the milkwoman at seven o'clock begins the bustle of Lima. Behind her, in an odor of sanctity, comes the vendor of herb teas.

At eight the curds-seller passes.

At nine, a voice offers cinnamon candies.

At ten, tamales seek mouths to delight.

Eleven is the hour of melons and coconut candies and toasted corn.

At noon, bananas and passion fruit, pineapples, milky *chirimoyas* of green velvet, and avocados promising soft pulp promenade through the streets.

At one, come the cakes of hot honey.

At two, a hawker offers *picarones*, buns that invite choking; and behind her come the corn sugarcakes steeped in cinnamon that no tongue can forget.

At three, appears the vendor of *anticuchos*, roasted broken hearts, followed by the peddlers of honey and sugar.

At four, the chili-vendor sells spice and fire.

Cebiche, raw fish steeped in lime, marks five o'clock.

At six, nuts.

At seven, *mazamorra* pastries baked to a T on open tile roofs.

At eight, ice creams of many flavors and colors, fresh gusts of wind, push the doors of night wide open.

(93 and 245)

1771: Madrid
Royal Summit

Big crates arrive at the palace from the incandescent deserts of Peru. The Spanish monarch reads the report of the official who sends them: this is the complete tomb of a Mochica chief, much older than the Incas; the descendants of the Mochicas and of the Chimús now live in dire penury and there are ever fewer of them; their valleys are in the hands of a *few greedy Spaniards*.

The cases are opened. A seventeen hundred-year-old king appears at the feet of Charles III. He has teeth, nails and hair still intact, and flesh of parchment stuck to his bones, and his majestic raiment gleams with gold and feathers. His scepter, a god of corn garlanded with plants, accompanies the remote visitor; and the vases that were buried with him have also made the journey to Madrid.

The king of Spain, dumbfounded, contemplates the ceramics that surround his defunct colleague. The king of the Mochicas lies amid pleasures. The ceramics represent pairs of lovers embracing and entering each other in a thousand ways, ignorant of original sin, enjoying themselves without knowing that for this act of disobedience we have been condemned to live on the earth.

(355)

1771: Paris

The Age of Enlightenment

In Europe the venerable walls of cathedrals and palaces are cracking. The bourgeoisie is on the offensive, armed with steam engines and volumes of the *Encyclopedia* and other unstoppable battering rams of the industrial revolution.

Budding from Paris are defiant ideas which, flying over the heads of *hoi polloi*, set their seal on the century. A time of the *fury to learn* and the *fever of intelligence*, the Age of Enlightenment raises up human reason, the reason of the minority who think, against the dogmas of the Church and the privileges of the nobility. Condemnations, persecution, and exile only stimulate the learned sons of the English philosophers and of prolific Descartes, *he who started by doubting everything*.

No subject is out of bounds for the philosophers of the Enlightenment, from the law of gravity to ecclesiastical celibacy. The institution of slavery merits their constant attack. Slavery contradicts nature, says Denis Diderot, director of the *Encyclopedia, Reasoned Dictionary of the Sciences, Arts, and Professions*: a man cannot be the property of his master for the same reason that a child cannot be his father's property, nor a woman her husband's, nor a servant his employer's, nor a subject his king's, and anyone thinking the opposite is confusing persons with things. Helvetius has said that *no barrel of sugar reached Europe that is not stained with blood*; and Candide, Voltaire's character, meets in Surinam a slave missing a hand devoured by a sugar mill, and a leg cut off for trying to escape:

"At this price you eat sugar in Europe."

If we admit that blacks are human beings, we admit how little Christian we are, says Montesquieu. All religion that hallows slavery deserves to be prohibited, says the Abbé Raynal. For Jean-Jacques Rousseau, slavery makes him ashamed to be a man.

(95 and 98)

1771: Paris

The Physiocrats

More than a crime, slavery is an economic error, say the physiocrats. In the last issue of the *Citizen's Ephemerides* Pierre Dupont de Nemours explains that slavery perpetuates archaic methods of agriculture and slows the development of France's colonies in the Antilles and on the mainland of America. Despite continuous replacement of the spent labor force, slavery means waste and a depreciation of invested capital. Dupont de Nemours proposes that calculations should take into account losses incurred by the early death of slaves, fires set by runaways and the cost of the constant war against them, the appallingly bad preparation of harvests, and tools ruined by ignorance or ill will. Ill will and laziness, he says, are weapons that the slave uses to recover a part of his personality stolen by the master; and his ineptitude results from the absolute lack of incentive to develop his intelligence. It is slavery, not nature, that makes the slave.

Only a free labor force proves efficiently productive, according to the economist-philosophers of the Physiocrat school. They believe that property is sacred, but only in freedom can it fully achieve the production of value.

(98)

1771: Paris

The Minister of Colonies Explains Why Mulattos Should Not Be Freed from Their Congenital "State of Humiliation"

His Majesty has considered that such a favor would tend to destroy the differences that nature has placed between whites and blacks, and that political prejudice has been careful to maintain as a distance which people of color and their descendants will never be able to bridge; finally, that it is in the interest of good order not to weaken the state of humiliation congenital to the species, in whatever degree it may perpetuate itself; a prejudice all the more useful for being in the very heart of the slaves and contributing in a major way to the due peace of the colonies . . .

(139)

1772: Cap Français

France's Richest Colony

The monks have denied last rites to the diva of the Cape Comedy, Mademoiselle Morange, whose irreparable loss to Haiti is mourned in six theaters and more than six bedrooms. No dead artiste deserves to be prayed for, the theater being an infamous occupation eternally condemned; but one of the actors, bell in hand and crucifix on breast, in black cassock and shining tonsure, marches singing psalms in Latin at the head of the dead virtuosa's cortege.

Before it reaches the cemetery, the police are already chasing off the baritone and his accomplices, who vanish in a split second. But the people protect and hide them. Who does not feel sympathy for these show folk who fan the insufferable languors of Haiti with breezes of cultural madness?

On the stages of this colony, France's richest, plays just opened in Paris are applauded, and the theaters are like Paris's—or, at least, would like to be. Here, though, the public is seated according to color of skin: in the center, ivory; on the right, copper; and on the left, ebony, a few free blacks.

The affluent sail into the theaters in a flutter of fans, the heat releasing floods beneath their powdered wigs. Each white woman resembles a jewelry store: gold, pearls, and diamonds make a dazzling frame for damp breasts leaping out of silk, demanding obedience and desire.

Haiti's most powerful colonists live on guard against the sun and the cuckold's horns. They do not leave home until after dusk, when the heat is less punishing, and only then dare to show themselves in litters or carriages drawn by many horses. The ladies are notorious for indulging in much love and much widowhood.

(115 and 136)

1772: Léogane

Zabeth

Ever since she learned to walk she was in flight. They tied a heavy chain to her ankles, and chained, she grew up; but a thousand times she jumped over the fence and a thousand times the dogs caught her in the mountains of Haiti.

They stamped the fleur-de-lis on her cheek with a hot iron. They put an iron collar and iron shackles on her and shut her up in the sugar mill, where she stuck her fingers into the grinder and later bit off the bandages. So that she might die of iron they tied her up again, and now she expires, chanting curses.

Zabeth, this woman of iron, belongs to Madame Galbaud du Fort, who lives in Nantes.

(90)

1773: San Mateo Huitzilopochco

The Strength of Things

The church of this village is a sorry wreck. The priest, newly arrived from Spain, decides that God cannot go on living in such a miserable and broken-down house, and sets to work. To raise solid walls, he orders the Indians to bring stones from some nearby ruins from the times of idolatry.

No threat or punishment can make them obey. The Indians refuse to move those stones that still lie where the grandfathers of their grandfathers worshiped the gods. Those stones promise nothing, but they prevent forgetting.

(132 and 322)

1774: San Andrés Itzapan

Dominus Vobiscum

The Indians are forced to spit every time they mention one of their gods. They are forced to dance new dances, the Dance of the Conquest and the Dance of Moors and Christians, which celebrate the invasion of America and the humiliation of the infidels.

They are forced to cover up their bodies, because the struggle against idolatry is also a struggle against nudity, a dangerous nudity that, according to the archbishop of Guatemala, produces in anyone seeing it *much lesion in the brain.*

They are forced to repeat from memory the Praise Be to God, the Hail Mary, and the Our Father.

Have Guatemala's Indians become Christians?

The doctrinal friar of San Andrés Itzapan is not very sure. He says he has explained the mystery of the Holy Trinity by folding a cloth and showing it to the Indians: *Look, a single cloth folded into three. In the same way God is one in three.* And he says this convinced the Indians that God is made of cloth.

The Indians parade the Virgin on feathered platforms. Calling her Grandmother of the Light, they ask her each night that tomorrow may bring the sun; but they venerate more devoutly the serpent that she grinds underfoot. They offer incense to the serpent, the old god who gives a good corn crop and good deer hunting and helps them to kill enemies. More than Saint George they worship the dragon, covering it with flowers; and the flowers at the feet of the horseman

Santiago pay homage to the horse, not to the apostle. They recognize themselves in Jesus, who was condemned without proof, as they are; but they adore the cross not as a symbol of his immolation, but because the cross has the shape of the fruitful meeting of rain and soil.

(322)

1775: Guatemala City

Sacraments

The Indians only perform Easter rites if they coincide with days of rain, harvesting, or planting. The archbishop of Guatemala, Pedro Cortés Larraz, issues a new decree warning that forgetfulness may imperil salvation of the soul.

Nor do the Indians come to Mass. They do not respond to announcements or to the bell. They have to be sought out on horseback in villages and fields and dragged in by force. Absence is punished with eight lashes, but the Mass offends the Mayan gods and that has more power than fear of the thong. Fifty times a year, the Mass interrupts work in the fields, the daily ceremony of communion with the earth. For the Indians, accompanying step by step the corn's cycle of death and resurrection is a way of praying; and the earth, that immense temple, is their day-to-day testimony to the miracle of life being reborn. For them all earth is a church, all woods a sanctuary.

To escape the punishment of the pillory in the plaza, some Indians come to the confessional, where they learn to sin, and kneel before the altar, where they eat the god of corn by way of communion. But they only bring their children to the baptismal font after having offered them, deep in the forest, to the old gods. Before them they celebrate the joys of resurrection. All that is born, is born again.

(322)

1775: Huehuetenango

Trees that Know, Bleed, Talk

The monk enters Huehuetenango through mists of incense. He thinks the infidels are paying homage in this way to the true God. But the mothers cover their new babies with cloths, so that the priest may not make them sick by looking at them. The clouds of incense are not for gratitude or welcome, but for exorcism. The copal resin burns and the smoke drifts up in supplication to the ancient Maya gods to halt the plagues that the Christians have brought.

The copal, which bleeds incense, is a sacred tree. Sacred are the ceiba, which by night becomes a woman, and the cedar, and all the trees that know how to listen to human woes.

(322)

1775: Gado-Saby

Bonny

A hail of bullets opens the way for the eight hundred soldiers from Holland. The maroon village of Gado-Saby crackles and falls. Behind a curtain of smoke and fire, the traces of blood disappear at the edge of the forest.

Swiss colonel Fourgeaud, veteran of the European wars, decides to camp among the ruins. At dusk mysterious voices sound from the brush, and a whistling of shots obliges the soldiers to throw themselves on the ground.

The troop spends the night surrounded by shots, insults, and chants of defiance and victory. The maroons, invisible, burst out laughing when Colonel Fourgeaud, from the ground, promises freedom and food in return for surrender.

"Hungry dog!" cry a thousand voices from the foliage. "Scarecrow!"

The voices call the Dutch soldiers white slaves, and announce that chief Bonny will very soon be master of this whole land of Surinam.

When dawn breaks the siege, Colonel Fourgeaud discovers that his men have been wounded not by bullets but by little stones and buttons and coins. He also discovers that the maroons have spent the night carting into the forest sacks of rice, cassava, and yams, while the volleys of projectiles and words kept the Dutchmen immobilized.

Bonny has been responsible for the maneuver. Bonny, leader of the maroons, does not have the branding iron's mark on his body. His mother, a slave, fled from the master's bed and gave him free birth in the forest.

(264)

1776: Cape Coast Castle

Alchemists of the African Slave Trade

Captain Pegleg Clarke has spent a long time bargaining on the coast of Africa. The ship stinks. The captain orders his sailors to bring the already purchased slaves up on deck and give them a bath; but hardly have their chains been removed when the blacks jump into the sea and swim toward their land. The current devours them.

The loss of the merchandise hurts the honor of Captain Clarke, old-time shepherd of these flocks, and damages the prestige of the Rhode Island slave traders. North American shipyards take pride in building the most secure ships for the Guinea traffic. Their floating prisons are so effectively constructed that only one slave rebellion occurs in four and a half years, an average four times smaller than the French, and half as much as England's specialized enterprises can boast.

The thirteen colonies that will soon be the United States of America have much to thank their slave traders for. Rum, good medicine for the soul and for the body, is turned into slaves on the African coast. Then those blacks become molasses in the Antillean islands of Jamaica and Barbados. From there, the molasses heads north and becomes rum in the distilleries of Massachusetts, and then the rum crosses the ocean again to Africa. Each voyage is rounded off with sales of tobacco, lumber, ironware, flour, and salted meat, and with purchases of spices in the islands. The blacks left over go to the plantations of South Carolina, Georgia, and Virginia.

Thus the slave trade produces profits for seamen, merchants, moneylenders, and owners of shipyards, distilleries, sawmills, meat salting plants, flour mills, plantations, and insurance companies.

(77 and 193)

1776: Pennsylvania

Paine

Its title is *Common Sense*. The pamphlet was published early this year and has circulated through the North American colonies like water or bread. The author, Tom Paine, an Englishman who came to these lands a couple of years ago, pleads for declaring independence without further ado: *A government of our own is our natural right. Why do we hesitate?*

There is something exceedingly ridiculous, says Paine, *in the composition of a monarchy.* In the best of cases, Paine considers government a necessary evil; in the worst, an intolerable evil. And monarchy is the worst of cases. One honest man, he says, *is of more worth than all the crowned ruffians that ever lived,* and he calls George III *the Royal Brute of Great Britain.*

Throughout the world, he says, liberty is fiercely hunted down. In Europe it is regarded as a foreigner; Asia and Africa long since expelled it; and the English have warned it to get out. Paine exhorts American colonists to turn this soil into a refuge for free men: *O! receive the fugitive, and prepare in time an asylum for mankind.*

(243)

1776: Philadelphia

The United States

England has never paid too much attention to her thirteen colonies on North America's Atlantic coast. They have no gold, silver, or sugar. They were never indispensable to her; she never prevented them from growing. They have walked alone, so it has been since that remote time when the Pilgrims first trod the stony lands they called New England—and the soil was so hard that they had to plant seeds with bullets, or so it was said. Now well developed, the thirteen English colonies have to run away.

The thirteen colonies are hungry for the West. Many pioneers dream of taking off over the mountains, with rifle, ax, and a handful of corn as baggage; but the British crown has drawn the frontier on the crests of the Appalachians and reserved the lands beyond for Indians. The thirteen colonies are hungry for a world. Already their ships ride all the oceans; but the British crown forces them to buy what it wants them to buy and sell where it says they should sell.

With one jerk they break the ties. The thirteen colonies refuse to continue paying obedience and money to the king of such a remote island. They hoist their own flag, decide to call themselves the United States of America, reject tea, and proclaim that rum, a national product, is the patriotic drink.

All men are created equal, says the Declaration of Independence. The slaves, half a million black slaves, don't even hear about it.

(130 and 224)

1776: Monticello

Jefferson

The writer of the Declaration of Independence, the United States' birth certificate, is a man of a thousand talents and concerns.

Tireless reader of thermometers, barometers, and books, Thomas Jefferson seeks and finds, pursuing the revelations of nature and wanting to embrace all dimensions of human thought. He is assembling a fabulous library and a universe of stones, fossils, and plants; and he knows all that can be known about neoplatonic philosophy, Latin grammar, the structure of the Greek language, and the organization of society throughout history. He knows everything about his land of Virginia, every son and grandfather of every family, every blade of grass; and he is up-to-date on all the technical novelties in the world. He enjoys trying out steam engines, new types of plows, and original methods of producing butter and cheese. He imagined his mansion of Monticello and designed and built it faultlessly.

The Puritans counted the population by "souls." Jefferson counts it by "individuals of the human species." Within the species, blacks are almost equal. Black have fair memories and no imagination, and their poor intelligence could never understand Euclid. Aristocrat of Virginia, Jefferson preaches democracy, a democracy of proprietors, and freedom of thought and religion; but he defends the hierarchies of sex and color. His educational plans do not include women, or Indians, or blacks. Jefferson condemns slavery and is, and will continue to be, a slave owner. Mulattas attract him more than white women, but loss of racial purity panics him and he thinks the mixture of bloods is the worst of the temptations besetting the white colonist.

(41 and 161)

1777: Paris

Franklin

The most famous of North Americans arrives in France on a desperate mission. Benjamin Franklin comes to ask help against the English colonial troops, who have occupied Philadelphia and other patriot redoubts. Using all the weight of his personal prestige, the ambassador proposes to kindle fires of glory and revenge in French breasts.

There is no king or commoner on earth who hasn't heard of

Franklin, since he sent up a kite and and discovered that heavenly fires and thunders express not the wrath of God but electricity in the atmosphere. His scientific discoveries emanate from daily life. The most complicated resides in the most commonplace: dawn and its never-repeated patterns, oil that is thrown on water and calms its waves, the fly drowned in wine that revives in the sun. Observing that sweat keeps the body fresh on days of stifling heat, Franklin conceives a system for producing cold by evaporation. He also invents and produces stoves and watches and a musical instrument, the glass harmonica, which inspires Mozart; and since the constant changing of spectacles for reading or distant vision bores him, he cuts lenses and fits them in a single frame and thus gives birth to bifocals.

But Franklin makes himself most popular when he notices that electricity seeks out sharp points, and defeats lightning by placing a pointed iron rod on top of a tower. Franklin being the spokeman for the American rebels, the king of England has decreed that British lightning rods should have rounded tips.

(79)

If He Had Been Born a Woman

Of Benjamin Franklin's sixteen brothers and sisters, Jane is the one most resembling him in talent and strength of will.

But at the age when Benjamin leaves home to make his own way, Jane marries a poor saddler, who accepts her without dowry, and ten months later bears her first child. From then on, for a quarter of a century, Jane has a child every two years. Some of them die, and each death opens a wound in her breast. Those that live demand food, shelter, instruction, and consolation. Jane spends whole nights cradling those that cry, washes mountains of clothing, bathes stacks of children, rushes from market to kitchen, washes piles of dishes, teaches ABC's and chores, toils elbow to elbow with her husband in his workshop, and attends to the guests whose rent helps to fill the stewpot. Jane is a devoted wife and exemplary widow; and when the children are grown up, she takes charge of her own ailing parents and of her unmarried daughters and her orphaned grandchildren.

Jane never knows the pleasure of letting herself float in a lake, drifting over the surface hitched to the string of a kite, as Benjamin enjoys doing despite his years. Jane never has time to think, nor allows herself to doubt. Benjamin continues to be a fervent lover, but Jane doesn't know that sex can produce anything except children.

Benjamin, founder of a nation of inventors, is a great man of all the ages. Jane is a woman of her age, like almost all women of all the ages, who has done her duty on this earth and expiated her share of blame in the Biblical curse. She has done all she could to keep from going mad and sought, in vain, a little silence.

Her case will awaken no interest in historians.

(313)

1778: Philadelphia
Washington

The first among the soldiers is also the most prestigious among the farmers, the swiftest among the horsemen, the best marksman among the hunters. He gives no one his hand, nor lets anyone look him in the eye. No one calls him George. From his mouth come no eulogies, nor any complaints either; and he always sets an example of composure and bravery, no matter his sufferings from ulcers, toothaches, and fevers.

With the help of men and weapons from France, George Washington's army seizes the city of Philadelphia from British hands. The war for the independence of the United States, blackcoats against redcoats, becomes long and painful.

(224 and 305)

1780: Bologna
Clavijero Defends the Accursed Lands

One of the Jesuits expelled from America, Francisco Javier Clavijero, writes in Italy his *Ancient History of Mexico*. In four volumes the priest tells *the life of a people of heroes*, marking the dawn of national and historical consciousness in native-born people who are beginning to call New Spain "Mexico" and already speak the word "fatherland" with pride. The work assumes the defense of America, so much under attack in these years from Paris, Berlin, or Edinburgh: *If America had no wheat, neither did Europe have corn . . . If America had no pomegranates or lemons, now she has them; but Europe never had, has not, and cannot have chirimoyas, avocados, bananas, chicozapotes . . .*

With innocence and passion Clavijero attacks the Encyclopedists who describe the New World as an emporium of abominations. Count Buffon says that in America the skies are miserly and the rains rot the soil; that the lions are bald, small and cowardly and the tapir is a vest-pocket elephant; that over there horses, pigs, and dogs become dwarfs and that the Indians, cold as serpents, have no soul, nor fire for females. Voltaire, too, speaks of hairless lions and men, and Baron Montesquieu explains that warm countries produce despicable peoples. Abbé Guillaume Raynal is offended because in America mountain ranges extend from north to south instead of from east to west as they should, and his Prussian colleague Corneille de Pauw portrays the American Indian as a flabby, degenerate beast. According to de Pauw, the climate over there leaves animals sickly and without tails; the women are so ugly that they are confused with men; and the sugar has no taste, the coffee no aroma.

(73 and 134)

1780: Sangarara
America Burns from Mountains to Sea

Two centuries have passed since the executioner's blade cleaved the neck of Túpac Amaru, last of the Incas, in the Plaza Mayor of Cuzco. The myth born of his death is now fulfilled. The prophecy is coming to pass: the head rejoins the body and a reborn Túpac Amaru attacks.

José Gabriel Condorcanqui, Túpac Amaru II, enters the village of Sangarara to the music of giant seashells, *to cut off the bad government of so many thieving drones who rob the very honey from our combs*. Behind his white horse, a desperate army assembles. They fight with slingshots, sticks, and knives, these naked soldiers. They are mostly Indians who *spill out their lives in bloody vomit* in the depths of Potosí or burn themselves out in workshops and haciendas.

Thunder of drums, clouds of banners, fifty thousand men crowning the sierra: Túpac Amaru, liberator of Indians and blacks, scourge of *those who have put us in such a lamentable state of dying*, advances and destroys. Messengers at the gallop rouse whole communities to rebellion from the valley of Cuzco to the coasts of Arica and the frontiers of Tucumán, *because those who fall in this war are sure of resurrection later*.

Many mestizos join the rebellion. Also some Creoles, of European blood but American birth.

(183 and 344)

1780: Tungasuca

Túpac Amaru II

Antonio Oblitas, slave of the magistrate Arriaga, hoisted a strong rope, hangman's rope, mule's rope, in the plaza of this town of Tungasuca, and for a whole week the wind rocked the body of Arriaga, boss of Indians, owner of blacks, owner of Antonio.

This hand that paints is the hand that hanged. Antonio Oblitas is painting the portrait of the man who ordered the freedom of all the slaves in Peru. For lack of easel, the board rests against some sacks of corn. Creating color over the rough wood, come and go the brushes of Antonio, hangman of his master, nevermore a slave. Túpac Amaru poses on a horse, out in the open. He is not wearing his usual black velvet jacket or his three-cornered hat. The inheritor of the Incas wears the royal insignias of the son of the sun: like his forebears, on his head the feather headdress and triple crown and hanging tassel; on his breast the golden sun; and in one fist the scepter of authority bristling with barbs. Around the motionless horseman appear scenes of the recent victory against colonial troops. From Antonio's hand spring little soldiers and puffs of smoke, Indians at war, flames devouring the church of Sangarara and prisoners escaping from the jail.

The painting is born between two battles, during the armed truce. Túpac and his horse have been posing for some time. They are so stony that Antonio wonders if they are breathing. Bright colors spread across the board, very slowly. The painter immerses himself in this long moment of truce. Thus the artist and his model escape from time; stave off, while the work lasts, defeat and death.

(137, 183, and 344)

1780: Pomacanchi

The Workshop Is an Enormous Ship

that sails over American lands, a galley that never stops advancing, propelled night and day by Indians who row toward a port they will never reach. Toward the coast that retreats, the Indians row and row; and the whip wakes them up when sleep overcomes them.

Men and women, children and old people spin, weave, and elaborate cotton and wool in the workshops. The laws promise hours and wages, but the Indians, thrown into these great slave quarters or prisons, only leave them when their burial hour arrives.

South of Cuzco, Túpac Amaru goes about freeing Indians tied to the looms. The winds of the great rebellion deprive viceroys of sleep in Lima, Buenos Aires, and Bogotá.

(170 and 320)

A Colonial Poem: If the Indians Triumph . . .

. . . they will make us toil
the way they toil now
and to the extent we despoil now
they will despoil us back.
All of us can expect to lack
house, hacienda, or splendors,
nobody will win honors
and all will nobodies be:
we will belong to Indians free
and they'll ride herd upon us.

(183)

1781: Bogotá
The Commoners

The archbishop of Bogotá trembles with rage and the leather of his chair groans. His hands, sweetmeat hands, ornamented with rubies and emeralds, clutch his purple robe. The Most Illustrious Don Antonio Caballero y Góngora curses with his mouth full, although he is not eating, for his tongue is as fat as the rest of him.

Outrageous news has come from the town of Socorro. The commoners, people without rank, have risen against the new taxes, and have appointed rich Creoles as captains. Both rich and poor are hit by the taxes, which punish everything from tallow candles to honey, sparing not even the wind: the tax on transient merchants is called the *wind sales tax.*

In Socorro, city of rocks, the rebellion that the viceroy in Bogotá saw coming has come. It happened one market day, right in the plaza.

A plebeian woman, Manuela Beltrán, pulled the decree from the doors of City Hall, tore it to pieces and stamped on it; soon after, the people hurled themselves upon the stores and burned down the jail. Now thousands of commoners, armed with sticks and hoes, are heading for Bogotá beating drums.

Spanish arms collapse in the first battle. The archbishop, who commands more authority than the viceroy, decides to go out and meet the insurrectionists. To deceive them with promises he will march at the head of the court commission. His mule stares at him in panic.

(13 and 185)

1781: Támara

The Plainsmen

Yelling Túpac Amaru's name, fifteen hundred Indians come galloping from the plains east of the Andes. They seek to gain the cordillera, to join the tide of commoners marching on Bogotá. The governor of the plains flees and saves his neck.

These rebels are Indians of the savannas of rivers that flow into the Orinoco. On the beaches of the Orinoco, where turtles deposit their eggs, they once held their markets. There they gathered, since the remotest of remote times, with the Indians of Guyana and Amazonia, exchanging salt, gold, clay pots, baskets, nets, dried fish, turtle oil, arrow poison, and red dye to protect the naked body from mosquitos. Snail conches were the currency, until Europeans arrived eager for slaves and offered axes, scissors, mirrors, and brandy in exchange for men. Then the Indians began to enslave one another, and to sell their brothers, and every hunter was also hunted; and many died of measles or smallpox.

(121 and 185)

1781: Zipaquirá

Galán

In the village of Zipaquirá the peace treaty is signed. The archbishop dictates it, swears to it by the evangels and consecrates it with a high Mass.

The agreement justifies the rebels. Soon this piece of paper will be cinders, and the rich Creole captains well know it; but they too need to dispel as soon as possible the stunning storm, the *supreme disorder of the plebeians*, which grow constantly, darkening the skies of Bogotá and threatening wealthy Americans as much as the Spanish crown.

One of the rebel captains refuses to enter the trap. José Antonio Galán, who had his baptism of fire in the mulatto battalion of Cartagena, carries on the struggle. He marches from town to town, from one hacienda to another, freeing slaves, abolishing tribute and dividing up lands. *Union of the Oppressed Against the Oppressors*, proclaims his banner. Friends and enemies call him *the Túpac Amaru of Here and Now*.

(13 and 185)

Popular Ballad of the Commoners

Let the drumbeats stop
and you, lend an ear
for this is the true ballad
and voice of the commoner:
The goat is pulled toward the hills
and hills toward the sky;
the sky toward God knows where
and right now neither do I.
The rich pull at the poor.
The Indian, worth only a little,
gets pulled by both poor and rich
till he splits right down the middle . . .

(13)

1781: Cuzco
The Center of the Earth,
the House of the Gods

Cuzco, the sacred city, wants to be itself again. The black stones of ancient times, tightly pressed together in loving embrace, victors over the furies of the earth and of man, want to shake themselves loose of the churches and palaces which crush them.

Micaela Bastidas stares down at Cuzco and bites her lips. Túpac

Amaru's wife is looking at the center of the earth, the spot chosen by the gods, from the crest of a hill. Right there, the color of clay and smoke so close that one could touch it, waits the capital of the Incas.

A thousand times Micaela has insisted in vain. The new Inca will not attack. Túpac Amaru, son of the sun, refuses to kill Indians. Túpac Amaru, incarnation of the founder of all life, living promise of resurrection, cannot kill Indians. And it is Indians, under the command of chief Pumacahua, who defend this Spanish bastion.

A thousand times Micaela has insisted, and a thousand times insists, and Túpac is silent. She knows now that there will be a tragedy in the Plaza of Tears, and knows that no matter what, she'll go on to the end.

(183 and 344)

1781: Cuzco

Dust and Sorrow Are the Roads of Peru

Riddled with bullets, some seated and others prone, they still defended themselves and infuriated us by hurling many stones . . . Slopes of the sierras, a litter of corpses: among the dead and the spears and the broken banners, the victors pick up here and there a carbine.

Túpac Amaru does not enter the sacred city as a conqueror, heading his tumultuous troops. He enters Cuzco on the back of a mule, loaded with chains which drag over the pavestones. Between two files of soldiers, he goes to the prison. The church bells ring out in a frenzy.

Túpac Amaru had escaped by swimming across the River Combapata and was taken by surprise in an ambush in the town of Langui— sold out by one of his captains, Francisco Santa Cruz, who was also his compadre.

The traitor does not look for a rope to hang himself. He collects two thousand pesos and a title of nobility.

(183 and 344)

1781: Cuzco

Sacramental Ceremony
in the Torture Chamber

Bound to the rack, Túpac Amaru lies naked and bloody. The torture chamber of Cuzco's prison is gloomy and low-ceilinged. A shaft of light falls on the rebel chief, violent bruising light. José Antonio de Areche wears a rolled wig and military dress uniform. Areche, representative of the king of Spain, commanding general of the army, and supreme judge, is seated beside the crank. When he moves it, another turn of the rope convulses the arms and legs of Túpac Amaru and stifled groans are heard.

ARECHE: Ah king of kings, little king sold for a contemptible price! Don José I, agent in the pay of the British crown! Money married to the ambition for power . . . Who should be surprised by the wedding? It's normal enough . . . British arms, British money. Why don't you deny it, eh? Poor devil. (*He rises and strokes Túpac Amaru's head.*) The Lutheran heretics have thrown dust in your eyes and a dark veil over your brain. Poor devil. José Gabriel Túpac Amaru, absolute and natural lord of these dominions . . . Don José I, monarch of the New World! (*Unrolls a parchment and reads out loud.*) "Don José I, by the grace of God, Inca, King of Peru, Santa Fe, Quito, Chile, Buenos Aires and continents of the southern seas, duke of the Superlative, Lord of the Caesars and Amazons, with dominion in the great Paitití, Commissioner of divine mercy . . ." (*Turns suddenly toward Túpac Amaru.*) Deny it! We found this proclamation in your pockets . . . You promised freedom . . . The heretics have taught you the evil arts of contraband. Wrapped in the flag of freedom, you brought the cruelest of tyrannies. (*Walks around the figure bound to the rack.*) "They treat us like dogs," you said. "They skin us alive," you said. But did you by any chance even pay tribute, you and your fellows? You enjoyed the privilege of using arms and going on horseback. You were always treated as a Christian of pure-blooded lineage! We gave you the life of a white man and you preached race hatred. We, your hated Spaniards, have taught you to speak. And what did you say? "Revolution!" We taught you to write, and what did you write? "War!" (*Sits. Turns his back on Túpac Amaru and crosses his legs*.) You have laid Peru waste. Crimes, arson, robberies, sacrileges . . . You and your terrorist henchmen have brought hell to these provinces. So the Spaniards leave the Indians licking the dirt, do they? I have already ordered forcible sales stopped and workshops opened and fair wages paid. I have suppressed tithes and tariffs . . . Why did you continue the war, if good treatment has been reestablished? How many thousands of deaths have you caused, you sham emperor? How much pain have you inflicted on the invaded lands? (*Rises and leans toward Túpac Amaru, who does not open his eyes*.) So the labor draft is a crime and of every hundred Indians who go to the mines, twenty return? I have ordered an end to compulsory work. And anyway, wasn't the detestable labor draft invented by your forebears? The Incas . . . No one has treated the Indians worse. You blaspheme the European blood that runs in your veins, José Gabriel Condorcanqui Noguera . . . (*Pauses and speaks while encircling the body of the victim*.) Your sentence is ready. I conceived it, wrote it, signed it. (*His hand cuts the air over Túpac's mouth*.) They will haul you to the scaffold and the executioner will cut out your tongue. They will tie you to four horses by the hands and feet. You will be quartered. (*Passes his hand over the bare torso*.) They will throw your trunk on the bonfire on Mount Picchú and the ashes in the air. (*Touches the face*.) Your head will hang from a gallows for three days in the town of Tinta and afterwards will be nailed to a pole at the gate of the town, with a crown of eleven iron spikes, for your eleven titles of emperor. (*Strokes Túpac's arms*.) We will send one arm to Tungasuca and the other will be exhibited in the capital of Carabaya. (*And his legs*.) One leg to the town of Livitaca and the other to Santa Rosa de Lampa. The houses you have lived in will be obliterated. We will throw salt on your lands. Infamy will fall upon your descendants through all the centuries. (*Lights a candle and holds it over Túpac Amaru's face*.) You still have time. Tell me: who carries on the rebellion you started? Who are your accomplices? (*Wheedling*.) You have time. I offer you the gallows. You have time to avoid so much humiliation and suffering. Give me names. Tell me. (*Lowers his ear*.) You are your own hangman, Indian butcher! (*Again sweetens his tone*.) We'll cut out the tongue of your son Hipólito. We'll cut out the tongue of Micaela, your woman, and garrote her . . . All right, don't repent, but save her. Her. Save your wife from an infamous death. (*Moves nearer. Waits*.) God knows the crimes you must carry with you. (*Violently twists the torture crank, and a ghastly cry is heard.*) Silence won't get you anything before the tribunal of the All-Highest, arrogant Indian! (*Pityingly.*) Oh, it saddens me that a soul chooses to go like that to eternal condemnation . . . (*With fury.*) For the last time! Who are your accomplices?

TÚPAC AMARU: (*Raising his head with a tremendous effort, opens his eyes and finally speaks.*) Here there are no accomplices but you and me. You as oppressor, I as liberator, both of us deserve death.

(183 and 344)

1781: Cuzco

Areche's Order Against Inca Dress and to Make Indians Speak Spanish

Indians are forbidden to wear the dress of the gentry, and especially of the nobility, which serves only to remind them of what the ancient Incas wore, bringing back memories that merely cause them to feel more and more hatred for the ruling nation; apart from looking ridiculous and hardly in keeping with the purity of our religion, since it features in various places the sun which was their first deity; this order extends to all provinces of this Southern America, totally abolishing such clothing . . . and at the same time all paintings or portraits of the Incas . . .

And to the end that these Indians should rid themselves of the hatred they have conceived against Spaniards, that they should dress in clothing prescribed by law, and that they should adopt our Spanish customs and speak the Castilian language, schools shall be more vigorously encouraged than heretofore, with the most stern and just punishment for those who do not use them, after a due period of time for their enlightenment . . .

(345)

1781: Cuzco
Micaela

In this war, which has made the earth groan with birth pains, Micaela Bastidas has had neither rest nor comfort. This woman with the neck of a bird has traveled constantly from region to region *making more people*, and sending to the front new fighters, and a few rifles, and the telescope someone asked for, and coca leaves and ripe ears of corn. Horses galloped incessantly back and forth across the mountains with her orders, safe-conducts, reports, and letters. She sent many messages to Túpac Amaru urging him to hurl his troops upon Cuzco once and for all, before the Spaniards could fortify their defenses and dishearten and disperse the rebels. *Chepe*, she wrote, *Chepe, my dearest one: Enough warnings I've given you* . . .

Pulled by a horse's tail, Micaela enters the main plaza of Cuzco, which the Indians call the Plaza of Tears, inside a leather bag, the kind in which maté is brought from Paraguay. Horses are also dragging to the gallows Túpac Amaru and Hipólito, their son. Another son, Fernando, looks on.

(159 and 183)

1781: Cuzco
Sacred Rain

The boy wants to turn his head, but the soldiers force him to look. Fernando sees how the executioner tears out the tongue of his brother Hipólito and pushes him down the steps from the scaffold. The executioner hangs two of Fernando's uncles, and then the slave Antonio Oblitas, who had painted Túpac Amaru's portrait, and afterward he cuts him to bits with an ax; and Fernando sees. With chains on his hands and irons on his feet, between two soldiers who force him to look, Fernando sees the executioner apply the garrote to Tomasa Condemaita, the woman chief of Acos, whose women's battalion has dealt the Spanish army tremendous blows. Then Micaela Bastidas mounts the scaffold and Fernando sees less. His eyes cloud over as the executioner reaches for Micaela's tongue, and a curtain of tears covers the boy's eyes when they sit his mother down to finish off the torture: the iron collar does not quite strangle her fine neck and it is necessary to *fasten nooses around her neck and pull from different directions, finishing her off with kicks in the belly and breasts.*

Fernando, born of Micaela nine years ago, now sees nothing and hears nothing. He doesn't see that they are bringing in his father, Túpac Amaru, and lashing him to the cinches of four horses by the hands and feet, his face turned skyward. The horsemen dig in their spurs heading for the four points of the compass, but Túpac Amaru doesn't split. *They have him up in the air, looking like a spider*; spurs tear at the bellies of the horses, which rear up on their hind legs to muster all their forces, but Túpac Amaru doesn't split.

It is the season of long dryness in the Valley of Cuzco. Precisely at noon, as the horses struggle and Túpac Amaru doesn't split, a violent downpour bursts from the sky: drops fall heavy as clubs, as if God or the Sun or someone had decided that it was the moment for the kind of rain that leaves the world blind.

(183 and 344)

The Indians Believe:

Jesus has clothed himself in white to come to Cuzco. A child shepherd sees him, plays with him, follows him. Jesus is a child too, and runs between earth and air: he crosses the river without getting wet, and slips very softly through the sacred valley of the Incas, careful not to scrape these recently wounded lands. From the slopes of the peak Ausangate, whose icy breath radiates the energy of life, he walks toward Mount Coylloriti. At the foot of this mountain, shelter of ancient divinities, Jesus lets fall his white tunic. He climbs up the rock and stops. Then he enters the rock.

Jesus has wanted to give himself to the conquered, and for them he turns into stone, like the ancient gods of this region, stone that says and will say: *I am God, I am you, I am those who fell*.

Forever the Indians of the Valley of Cuzco will go up in procession to greet him. They will purify themselves in the waters of the torrent, and with torches in their hands will dance for him, dance to give him joy: so sad is Jesus, so broken, there inside.

(301)

The Indians Dance to the Glory of Paradise

Far from Cuzco, Jesus' sadness has also stricken the Tepehua Indians. Ever since the new god arrived in Mexico, the Tepehuas had been going to church with a musical band, offering him dances, costume games, tasty tamales, and good drink; but nothing gave him happiness. Jesus continued to grieve, his beard pressed against his breast, and so it went until the Tepehuas invented the Dance of the Old Ones.

It is danced by two men in masks. One is the Old Lady, the other the Old Man. The two Old Ones come from the sea with offerings of shrimp and traverse the town of San Pedro leaning on feathered canes, their bodies twisted by age. Before altars improvised in the streets, they stop and dance while the cantor sings and a musician beats a turtle shell. The naughty Old Lady waggles her hips and offers herself, and pretends to run away; the Old Man follows her and catches her from behind, embraces her and hoists her shoulder high. She kicks her legs in the air, dying of laughter, and pretends to defend herself with blows from her cane, happily clutching the body of the Old Man, who keeps grabbing at her, staggering and laughing as everyone applauds.

When Jesus saw the Old Ones making love, he raised his head and laughed for the first time. He laughs now every time the Tepehuas perform this impious dance for him.

In remote times, the Tepehuas, who have rescued Jesus from his sadness, were born from balls of cotton, there on the slopes of the Sierra of Veracruz. Instead of "it's dawning," they say, "God is here."

(359)

1781: Chincheros

Pumacahua

In the center gleams the Virgin of Montserrat. Mateo García Pumacahua is on his knees giving thanks. His wife and a group of relatives and captains appear in procession behind him. Pumacahua wears Spanish dress, vest and coat, shoes with buckles. Beyond him, the battle is fought, little soldiers and guns that look like toys: Pumacahua the puma beats the dragon Túpac Amaru. *Veni, vidi, vici* is written above.

After several months a nameless artist has finished his work. Over the door of the church of the town of Chincheros appear the images that will perpetuate the glory and the faith of chief Pumacahua in the war against Túpac Amaru.

Pumacahua, also a descendant of the Incas, has received a medal from the king of Spain and a plenary indulgence from the bishop of Cuzco.

(137 and 183)

1781: La Paz

Túpac Catari

He spoke only Aymara, the language of his people. He proclaimed himself viceroy of these lands that are not yet called Bolivia, and named his wife vicereine. He set up his court on the heights dominating the city of La Paz, hidden in a hollow, and laid siege to it.

He walked with a limp and an extraordinary brilliance lit up his eyes, deeply sunk in his young and already furrowed face. He dressed in black velvet, gave orders with a cane and fought with a spear. He beheaded priests suspected of celebrating denunciatory Masses and cut off the arms of spies and traitors.

Julián Apaza had been a sacristan and a baker before becoming Túpac Catari. Together with his wife, Bartolina Sisa, he organized an army of forty thousand Indians which kept in check troops sent by the viceroy from Buenos Aires.

Despite the defeats and massacres he suffered there was no way to catch him. Traveling at night he eluded every attempt at encirclement, until the Spaniards offered the governorship of Achacachi, on the banks of Lake Titicaca, to his best friend Tomás Inca Lipe, known as *the good*.

(183)

1782: La Paz

Rebel Women

Spanish cities of the New World, born as offerings to God and the king, have an enormous heart of beaten earth. In each city's main plaza are the gallows and the seat of government, the cathedral and the jail, the courthouse and the market. People stroll around the gallows and the fountain, to and fro in the main plaza, fortified plaza, garrison plaza, pass cavalier and beggar, silver-spurred horseman and barefoot slave, devout ladies taking their souls to Mass, and Indians delivering chicha in potbellied clay jugs.

Today there is a show in the main plaza of La Paz. Two women, leaders of the native rebellion, will be sacrificed. Bartolina Sisa, wife of Túpac Catari, emerges from the jail with rope around neck, tied to the tail of a horse. Gregoria Apaza, sister of Túpac Catari, is brought out on a donkey. Each of them carries a cross of sticks, like a scepter, in the right hand, and has a crown of thorns fastened on her head. Before them, prisoners sweep the ground clear with branches. Bartolina and Gregoria make several turns around the plaza, suffering in silence the stones and laughter of those who mock them as Indian queens, until the hour of the gallows strikes. Their heads and hands, the sentence reads, will be paraded through the towns of the region.

The sun, the old sun, also attends the ceremony.

(183 and 288)

1782: Guaduas

With Glassy Eyes,

from a wooden cage, the head of José Antonio Galán gazes at the town of Charalá. In Charalá, where he was born, they are exhibiting his right foot. A hand of his is nailed up in the plaza of Socorro.

The cream of colonial society has repented of the sin of insolence, these rich Creoles who prefer to keep paying tribute and obedience to the Spanish monarch, thus avoiding the *contagious plague* that Galán, like Túpac Amaru, like Túpac Catari, incarnated and spread in their days of fury. Galán, chief captain of the commoners' insurrection, has been betrayed and hunted down by those who were his comrades. In a hut he fell, after a long pursuit, together with his last twelve men.

Don Antonio Caballero y Góngora, the pompous archbishop, sharpened the sword that beheaded Galán. While throwing on the fire the treaty of peace, so promising, so deceiving, the Most Illustrious One added infamies against *the spiteful plebeian*. Galán has been quartered not merely as a rebel, but also as *a man of most obscure birth and lover of his own daughter*.

Now the archbishop has two thrones. Besides the apostolic one, he has acquired the viceregal throne of Bogotá.

(13 and 185)

1782: Sicuani

This Accursed Name

Diego Cristóbal, first cousin of Túpac Amaru and continuer of his war in Peru, has signed a peace treaty. The colonial authorities have promised pardon and a general amnesty.

Stretched out on the ground, Diego Cristóbal swears fidelity to the king. Multitudes of Indians come down from the mountains and surrender their arms. The marshal stages a banquet of merry toasts and the bishop a Mass of thanksgiving. From Lima, the viceroy orders all houses to be illuminated for three nights.

Within a year and a half, in Cuzco, in the Plaza of Happiness, the executioner will tear to pieces the flesh of this cousin of Túpac Amaru, with red-hot pincers, before hanging him from the gallows. His mother will also be hanged and quartered. The judge, Francisco Díaz de Medina, had passed sentence to the effect that *it is not fitting either for the King or for the State that any seed or race of this or any Túpac Amaru should remain, considering the great clamor and impression that this accursed name has aroused in the natives*.

(183)

1783: Panama City

For Love of Death

Ever since dawn the ground has been steaming, pleading for a drink, and the living seek shade and fan themselves. If the heat shrivels the living, what will it not do to the dead, who have no one to fan them?

The important dead lie in the churches. So much does custom require in the dry tableland of Castile, and so it has to be also in this fiery furnace of Panama. The faithful stand on memorial stones, or kneel on them, and from below death whispers to them: *Soon I'll come for you*. More than the panic of dying or the memory of irreparable loss though, it is the stink of putrefaction that brings tears to the eyes.

Sebastián López Ruiz, sage researcher into nature, writes a report showing that, here, this custom from over there is the enemy of hygiene and fatal for public health, and that it would be healthier to bury the gentry of Panama in some distant cemetery. The reply, when it comes, says in effect that the dead are well placed in the churches; and that what has been and is, will continue to be.

(323)

1783: Madrid
The Human Hand Vindicated

To the four winds trumpets proclaim that the king of Spain has decided to redeem the human hand. From here on, the gentleman who does manual work will not lose his noble condition. The king says that industriousness dishonors neither him who performs it, nor his family, and that no artisanship is unworthy of Spaniards.

Charles III wants to bring his reign up to date. His minister Campomanes dreams of promoting industry, popular education, and agrarian reform. From its great imperial feat in America, Spain gets the honors and other European monarchies get the benefits. How long will the silver of the colonies go on paying for merchandise that Spain does not produce? What is the point of the Spanish monopoly if the products leaving the port of Cadiz are English, French, Dutch, or German?

Knightly gentlemen, who in Spain are as abundant as monks, have hands that serve either to die for Spain or to kill her. Even if they are penniless, they don't lower themselves to produce anything except glory. A long time ago those hands forgot how to work, as a hen's wings have forgotten how to fly.

(175)

1785: Mexico City
Lawyer Villarroel Against the Pulque Saloon

Every pulque saloon is an office where adulteries, concubinages, rapes, pickpocketings, robberies, homicides, brawls, knifings, and other crimes are hatched . . . They are theaters in which men and women are transformed into the most abominable furies from hell, their mouths spewing the most refined obscenities, the vilest words, and most dissolute, infamous, offensive, and provocative things that the greatest of libertines could hardly utter if they were not perturbed by the fumes of the most fetid and disgusting of drinks . . . These are the effects of the negligence, the omissions and the tolerance of judges, who are not horrified at the sight of men and women lying in the streets as if they were dogs, exposed to being run over by a coachman as drunk as themselves, as often happens, dispatching them to eternity in such an unhappy situation as the one in which they find themselves.

(352)

The Pulque Saloon

When the viceroy expelled pulque from Mexico City, the outcast found shelter in the suburbs.

Liquor of the green plants . . . In taverns on the outskirts, the barman never stops coming and going between the big vats and the eager mugs, *you stun me, you kill me, you make me walk on all fours,* while a newborn child cries disconsolately in one corner and an old man sleeps off the effects in another.

Horses, donkeys, and fighting cocks, tethered to iron rings, grow old waiting outside. Inside, the bright-colored vats bear defiant names: "Don't stretch me out," "The stuff for the strong," "The brave one" . . . Inside, law does not exist, nor the time of day. Dice roll on the earth floor and flowery gambling cards are flung down on a barrel-top. Some fool sings to the sound of a merry harp, others pair off to kick up dust in a dance, a monk chats with a soldier and the soldier promises to get tough with a muleteer, *I am plenty tough, I'm too tough,* and the potbellied barman chimes in: *What about another?*

(153 and 266)

Pulque

Perhaps pulque brings their old gods back to the Indians. They offer it to them, sprinkling it on the ground or in the fire or raising a mug to the stars. Perhaps the gods are always thirsty for the pulque they sucked from the four hundred teats of mother Mayahuel.

Perhaps, too, the Indians drink to fortify themselves and to get even; certainly they drink to forget and to be forgotten.

According to the bishops, pulque is to blame for laziness and poverty and brings idolatry and rebellion. *Barbarous vice of a barbarous people,* says one of the king's officers. Under the effect of the maguey's heavy wine, he says, *the child denies the father and the vassal his lord.*

(153 and 331)

The Maguey

Armed with green swords, the maguey stands up to drought and hail, the icy nights and furious suns of the deserts of Mexico.

Pulque comes from the maguey, *the tree that gives suck,* and from the maguey come forage for animals, beams and tiles for roofing, fencing posts and fuel for fires. Its fleshy leaves provide rope, pouches, matting, soap, and paper, the paper of the ancient codices; and its thorns make good pins and needles.

The maguey only flowers when it is going to die. It opens and flowers as if saying farewell. A lofty stalk, perhaps a mast, perhaps a penis, shoots from the heart of the maguey toward the clouds in a burst of yellow flowers. Then the great stalk falls and with it falls the maguey, torn out by the root.

It is unusual to find a flowering maguey in the arid Mezquital valley. Hardly has it begun to shoot up when the Indian castrates it and turns the wound downward, and thus the maguey yields up its pulque, which quenches thirst, feeds, and consoles.

(32 and 153)

The Mug

The Mexican potter has a long history. Three thousand years before Hernán Cortés, his hands were converting clay into receptacles or human figures which fire hardened against time. Much later on, the Aztecs explained that a good potter *gives being to clay and makes things live*.

This ancient tradition still flourishes in a daily multiplication of bottles, jars, pots, and, above all, drinking mugs: the ivorylike mugs of Tonalá, the tough mugs of Metepec, the bulging shiny ones of Oaxaca, the humble little ones of Chilililco; the reddish mugs of Toluca, dripping black tears . . . The mug of cooked clay presides over fiestas and kitchens and accompanies prisoner and beggar. It receives the pulque, scorned by the crystal glass, and it is the gift of lovers:

When I die, old lady, take my clay if you can
And fashion a mug with this refrain:
If you thirst for me, drink;
And if it stops at the brink,
That will be kisses from your old man.

(18, 153, and 294)

1785: Mexico City
Fiction in the Colonial Era

The viceroy of Mexico, Matías de Gálvez, signs a new edict in favor of Indian workers. The Indians are to receive fair wages, good food, and medical attention; and they will have two rest hours at noon, and be able to change employers whenever they like.

(146)

1785: Guanajuato
The Wind Blows Where It Wants

An abyss of light opens in the clear air and between the black walls of the sierra shines the desert. In the desert, a glitter of domes and towers, rise Mexico's mining towns. Guanajuato, as densely populated as the viceroy's capital, is the most distinguished. Its owners go to Mass in sedan chairs followed by swarms of beggars through a labyrinth of lanes and alleys, Kiss Lane, Slide Lane, Four Winds Lane; and between the cobblestones polished by the feet of time grow grasses and phantoms.

In Guanajuato church bells organize life; and chance governs it. Some mysterious slippery-fingered joker deals the cards. They say that here one treads on gold and silver wherever one goes, but everything depends on the veins that snake underground and offer and deny themselves at their whim. Yesterday, a fortunate gentleman celebrated his stroke of luck, and toasted everybody in the best wine, and paid for flute and guitar serenades, and bought fine Cambray lace and velvet trousers and silk lamé jackets and camisoles from Holland; and today the thread of silver that made him knight for a day disappears without trace.

The life of the Indians, on the other hand, does not hang on chance. Breathing mercury in the alloy factories leaves them forever with the shakes and toothless, and their chests burst from breathing murderous dust and pestilent vapors in the mines. Sometimes exploding dust blows them to bits, and sometimes they slip into the void when they go down carrying stones or when they come up carrying on their backs the foremen who call Indians their "little horses."

(6, 261, and 349)

1785: Guanajuato
Silver Portrait

Using the language of fluttering fans, ladies chat in the leafy gardens. Somebody pees against the wall of a church and on one side of the plaza two beggars, sitting in the sun, pick at each other's lice. Beneath a stone archway a distinguished doctor in a huge cloak talks of the Rights of Man, and a monk moves down the lane muttering eternal condemnations against the drunks, whores, and rowdies who cross in front of him. Not far from the city, *collectors* hunt Indians with lassos.

Guanajuato has long since dethroned Potosí. The world queen of silver is hungry for labor. The workers, *free wage earners*, don't see a coin in all their lives, but are prisoners of debt. Their children will inherit the debts and also the fear of pain and prison and hunger, and of the old gods and the new.

(261 and 349)

1785: Lisbon
The Colonial Function

The Portuguese crown orders Brazil's textile workshops closed down; in the future they must only produce rustic clothing for slaves. In the name of the queen, Minister Melo e Castro issues the orders. The minister observes that *in most of the captaincies of Brazil have been set up, and are spreading ever more wildly, various factories and manufactories of cloth of differing qualities, including even gold and silver braid*. These, he says, are *pernicious transgressions*. If they continue, *the result will be that all the utilities and wealth of these most important colonies will end up as the patrimony of their inhabitants*. Brazil being such a fertile land, so abundant in fruits, *said inhabitants will become totally independent of their dominant me-tropolis: consequently it is indispensably necessary to abolish said factories and manufactories.*

(205)

1785: Versailles
The Potato Becomes a Great Lady

Two and a half centuries ago the Spanish conquistadors brought her from Peru. Since she came so highly recommended by the Indians, Europe destined her for hogs, jailbirds, and the dying. The potato has been jeered and castigated whenever she has tried to escape from pigsties, prisons, and hospitals. In several places she was banned; and in Besançon she was accused of causing leprosy.

Antoine Parmentier got to know the potato in jail. Parmentier was in a Prussian prison and they didn't provide anything else to eat. At first he thought her stupid, but later he came to love her and discovered her charm and savoriness.

Free again in Paris, Parmentier organizes a banquet. D'Alembert, Lavoisier, American ambassador Benjamin Franklin, and other celebrities attend. Parmentier offers them an all-potato menu: potato bread, potato soup, potato puree, salads of potatoes enlivened with dressings to taste, fried potatoes, potato buns and pastries. For dessert, potato tart. To drink, potato brandy. Parmentier makes a speech in her defense. He extolls her nutritive virtues, proclaims her necessary for the palate and for the blood, and says the potato could conquer hunger in Europe, being invulnerable to hailstorms and easily cultivated. The guests, abrim with potatoes, applaud him with emotion and conviction.

Then Parmentier convinces the king. Louis XVI orders potatoes planted in the Sablons estates near Paris, and has them surrounded by a permanent guard of soldiers. Thus, he excites curiosity and desire for the forbidden fruit.

The definitive consecration takes place at Versailles. Queen Marie Antoinette, decked out like a garden with potato flowers, bestows the royal kiss on the cheek of Antoine Parmentier. King Louis, who has still not lost his head, embraces Parmentier. All the nobility of France attends the apotheosis of the potato, in this kingdom where the art of good cuisine is the only religion without atheists.

(156 and 250)

The Potato Was Born of
Love and Punishment,
As They Tell It in the Andes

The Inca, they say, condemned two lovers who violated the sacred laws. Let them be buried alive and together, he decided.

She had been a virgin consecrated to the Sun god. She had fled from the temple to give herself to a peasant serf.

Alive and together, the Inca decided. They were buried in a deep pit, tied together, face up; and not a complaint was heard as the dirt covered them.

Night fell and the stars moved in unaccustomed courses. Shortly afterward, gold disappeared from the riverbeds, and the fields of the kingdom became sterile, nothing but dust and stones. Only the soil that covered the lovers was immune to the drought.

The high priests counseled the Inca to disinter the lovers, burn them and scatter their ashes to the wind. So let it be, decided the Inca.

But they could not find them. They dug wide and deep and found nothing but a root. That root multiplied and from then on the potato was the staff of the Andean people.

(248)

1790: Paris

Humboldt

At age twenty, Alexander von Humboldt discovers the ocean and revolution.

At Dunkirk the ocean struck him dumb, and in Calais the moon blossoming from the waves drew a shout of wonder. Astonishment at the sea, revelation of the revolution: in Paris, a year after July Fourteenth, Humboldt lets himself go in the sweet whirlwind of streets in fiesta, merges into the people who dance and sing to their newborn liberty.

He has lived in search of answers and found questions. Without let-up he has inquired of books, of the heavens, and of the earth, pursuing the enigmas of the soul and the mysteries of the cosmos and the secrets of beetles and stones, always in love with the world and with men and women who fill him with dizziness and panic. *Alexander will never be happy*, says his brother Wilhelm, his mother's favorite child.

At twenty, fever of living, fever of going places, Humboldt swears eternal fealty to the banners of the French revolution and swears he will cross the ocean, like Balboa and Robinson Crusoe, to the lands where it is always noon.

(30 and 46)

1790: Petit Goâve

The Missing Magic

The heft of the purse can at times achieve more than the color of the skin. In Haiti, poor mulattos are blacks, and free blacks who have accumulated enough cash are mulattos. Rich mulattos pay immense fortunes to become white, although few obtain the magic document that permits the offspring of master and slave to become a doctor, to style himself Monsieur, to wear a sword, or to touch a white woman without losing an arm.

From a gallows hangs the mulatto who claimed the rights of a citizen, recently proclaimed in Paris, and high on a pike through the town of Petit Goâve rides the head of another mulatto who wanted to be a deputy.

(115)

1791: Bois Caiman

The Conspirators of Haiti

The old slave woman, intimate of the gods, buries her machete in the throat of a black wild boar. The earth of Haiti drinks the blood. Under the protection of the gods of war and of fire, two hundred blacks sing and dance the oath of freedom. In the prohibited voodoo ceremony aglow with lightning bolts, two hundred slaves decide to turn this land of punishment into a fatherland.

Haiti is based on the Creole language. Like the drum, Creole is the common speech of those torn out of Africa into various Antillean islands. It blossomed inside the plantations, when the condemned needed to recognize one another and resist. It came from African languages, with African melody, and fed on the sayings of Normans and Bretons. It picked up words from Caribbean Indians and from

English pirates and also from the Spanish colonists of eastern Haiti. Thanks to Creole, when Haitians talk they feel that they touch each other.

Creole gathers words and voodoo gathers gods. Those gods are not masters but lovers, very fond of dancing, who convert each body they penetrate into music and light, pure light of undulating and sacred movement.

(115 and 265)

Haitian Love Song

I burn like firewood.
My legs shake like sugarcanes.
No dish tempts my mouth.
The strongest drink becomes water.
When I think of you,
my eyes brim up
and my reason falls vanquished
by my pain.
Isn't it very true, my beauty,
that soon you will be back?
Oh, come back to me, my ever faithful!
Believing is less sweet than feeling!
Don't delay too much.
It hurts a lot.
Come and free from his cage
the hungry bird.

(265)

1792: Rio de Janeiro

The Conspirators of Brazil

Barely half a century ago the mines of Brazil were expected to last as long as the world, but the gold and the diamonds steadily grow less, and the tributes that must be paid to the queen of Portugal and her court of parasites weigh ever more heavily.

Since that time, many voracious bureaucrats have been sent in from Portugal, and not a single mining technician. From there they have stopped the cotton looms producing anything but clothing for slaves, and from there they have banned both the exploitation of iron, which lies at arm's reach, and the production of gunpowder.

To break with Europe, *which sucks us like a sponge*, a handful of gentlemen entered a conspiracy. Three years ago, owners of mines and haciendas, monks, poets, doctors, veteran smugglers, organized a rising which aimed to convert this colony into an independent republic, in which blacks and native-born mulattos would be free and everyone would wear Brazilian clothes.

Before the first musket shot rang out, informers went to work. The governor jailed the Ouro Prêto conspirators. Under torture, they confessed; and they accused each other in enthusiastic detail. Basílio de Britto Malheiro pleaded innocent explaining that anyone fated to be born in Brazil copies the bad habits of blacks, mulattos, Indians, and other ridiculous folk. Cláudio Manuel da Costa, most illustrious of the prisoners, hanged himself in his cell, or was hanged, for not confessing, or for confessing too much.

There was one who remained silent. Lieutenant Joaquim Jose da Silva Xavier, known as *Sacamuelas*, the tooth-puller, only opened his mouth to say:

"I am the only one responsible."

(205 and 209)

1792: Rio de Janeiro

Tooth-Puller

They look like cadavers in the candlelight. Bound by enormous chains to the bars of the windows, the accused have been listening to the judge for eighteen hours, without missing a word.

The judge took six months to formulate the sentence. Far into the night, they find out: six are condemned. These six will be hanged, beheaded, and quartered.

Then the judge falls silent while the men who wanted independence for Brazil exchange reproaches and apologies, insults and tears, stifled cries of repentance or protest.

Early in the morning comes the queen's pardon. Five of the guilty six will not die but be exiled. But one, the only one who betrayed nobody and was betrayed by all, will walk to the gallows at dawn. For him the drums will beat and the mournful voice of the town crier will resound through the streets announcing the sacrifice.

Tooth-puller is far from white. He entered the army as a lieutenant and lieutenant he always remained, pulling teeth to round out his pay. He wanted Brazilians to be Brazilians. The birds that disappear behind the mountains as the sun rises know it well.

(205)

1794: Paris
"The remedy for man is man,"

say the black sages, and the gods always knew it. The slaves of Haiti are no longer slaves.

For five years the French revolution turned a deaf ear. Marat and Robespierre protested in vain. Slavery continued in the colonies. Despite the Declaration of the Rights of Man, the men who were the property of other men on the far plantations of the Antilles were born neither free nor equal. After all, the sale of blacks from Guinea was the chief business of the revolutionary merchants of Nantes, Bordeaux, and Marseilles; and French refineries lived on Antillean sugar.

Harassed by the black insurrection headed by Toussaint L'Ouverture, the Paris government finally decrees the liquidation of slavery.

(71)

1794: Mountains of Haiti
Toussaint

He came on the scene two years ago. In Paris they call him the *Black Spartacus*.

Toussaint L'Ouverture has the body of a tadpole and lips that occupy almost all of his face. He was a coachman on a plantation. An old black man taught him to read and write, to cure sick horses, and to talk to men; but he learned on his own how to look not only with his eyes, and he knows how to see flight in every bird that sleeps.

(71)

1795: Santo Domingo
The Island Burned

Scared by the freeing of the slaves in Haiti, the king of Spain cedes the territory of Santo Domingo to France. A stroke of the pen wipes out the frontier that cut the island in half, dividing the poorest of

Spanish colonies from the richest of French colonies. Don Manuel Godoy, the leading light at court, says in Madrid that the rebellion in Haiti has turned the whole island into an *accursed land for whites*.

This had been Spain's first colony in America. Here the empire had had its first tribunal, its first cathedral, its first university; from here the conquering hosts had sailed for Cuba and Puerto Rico. Such a birth presaged a glorious destiny, but two centuries ago Governor Antonio de Osorio turned this colony into smoke.

Day and night Osorio labored at roasting the sinful land, going from palm to palm burning houses and fortresses and boats, mills and pigsties and corrals and fields, spraying it all with salt. With his own hands, he strangled those who resisted. In the crackle of flames sounded the trumpets of the Last Judgement. After a year and a half of continuous burning, the arsonist stood up on the island he had destroyed and received from the king of Spain two thousand ducats for his work of redemption by fire.

Governor Osorio, verteran of the Flanders wars, had purified this ground. He had begun by burning the northern cities, because it was on that coast that the English and Dutch pirates landed bringing Bibles *of the sect of Luther* and spreading the heretical custom of eating meat on Good Friday. He had started in the north; and then he just couldn't stop.

(216)

1795: Quito

Espejo

He passed through history cutting and creating.

He wrote the sharpest words against the colonial regime and its methods of education, *an education for slaves*, and he disemboweled the pompous style of the Quito rhetoricians. He nailed up his diatribes on the doors of churches and at busy street corners, so that they would multiply from mouth to mouth, because *writing anonymously might very well remove the disguise from the false wise men and cause them to appear clothed in their true and natural ignorance*.

He wanted an America governed by those born there. He urged that the cry of independence should ring out simultaneously in all the viceroyalities and tribunals, and that the colonies should unite, to become fatherlands under democratic, republican governments.

He was the son of an Indian. At birth he received the name of Chusig, which means barn owl. To become a physician he decided to call himself Francisco Javier Eugenio de Santa Cruz y Espejo, a name suggesting ancient lineage; and only thus could he practice and spread his discoveries against smallpox and other pestilences.

He founded, edited, and wrote from cover to cover *First Fruits of Culture*, Quito's first journal. He was director of the public library. They never paid him his salary.

Charged with crimes against the king and against God, Espejo was shut up in a filthy cell. There he died, from confinement, and with his last breath asked forgiveness of his creditors.

The city of Quito does not list in its register of principal citizens the death of this precursor of Hispanic American independence, who was the most brilliant of its sons.

(17 and 249)

Espejo Mocks the Oratory of These Times

I bid farewell to the volatile breezes of inspiration; I lose the pulsing oscillations of life, when I hear these fulgurous incomprehensibilities of rhetorical concepts. What delicious satisfaction to hear the melodious swans of oratory, trilling with gutteral sonority, chirping dirges in their sweet syllables! What savory intervals of glorious contentment the soul perceives in the harmonious echoes of their oracular descriptions!

(17)

1795: Montego Bay

Instruments of War

The prestige of Cuban dogs is well merited. With them the French have hunted down many fugitive blacks in the mountains of Haiti, and a few Cuban dogs were enough to defeat the Miskito Indians, who had wiped out three Spanish regiments on the coasts of Nicaragua.

The English landowners of Jamaica send Colonel William Dawes Quarrell to Cuba to get dogs. The Assembly says the security of the island and the lives of the inhabitants demand it. Dogs are instruments of war. Don't the Asians use elephants in their battles? The most civilized and polished nations of Europe, so reason the English planters, pursue enemy infantry on horses. Why not use dogs then to track down the hideouts of runaway slaves, since blacks are more savage than dogs anyway?

Colonel Quarrell gets what he wants in Cuba, thanks to the good offices of Doña María Ignacia de Contreras y Justíz, marchioness of San Felipe and Santiago, countess of Castile, and owner and mistress of the Bejucal. Men and dogs embark in the schooner *Mercury*.

Mists of dusk in Montego Bay. The beasts arrive in Jamaica. In a flash the streets empty out, doors are shut tight. Forty Cuban rangers fall into line to the light of torches. Each leads three enormous dogs, tied to his belt by straining chains.

(86 and 240)

1795: Havana

Did the Gallilean Rebel Imagine He Would Be a Slave Overseer?

On Cuba's sugar plantations, the slaves do not suffer from neglect. The master redeems them by labor and shortens their stay in this vale of tears; and the monks save them from hell. The Church receives five percent of sugar production for teaching the slaves that God made them slaves, that the body is enslaved but the soul is free, that the pure soul is like white sugar, cleansed of brown taint in purgatory, and that Jesus Christ is the great overseer who watches, awards merits, punishes, and recompenses.

At times Jesus Christ is not only the overseer, but the master in person. The count of Casa Bayona washes the feet of twelve blacks, on Holy Thursday night, sits them down at his table and shares his supper with them. The slaves express their gratitude by setting fire to his sugar mill, and twelve heads end up on a row of lances beside the cane fields.

(222)

1796: Ouro Prêto

El Aleijadinho

El Aleijadinho, *the Little Cripple*, creator of abundances, sculpts with his stump. This sculptor of the loftiest beauties in Brazil's mining region is repugnantly ugly. One of the slaves he bought tried to kill himself to escape from serving such a horrendous master. His sickness, leprosy or syphilis or some mysterious curse, is devouring him bite by bite. For each bit of flesh that it tears from him, he gives the world new marvels of wood or stone.

In Congonhas do Campo they are awaiting him. Can he make it? Will he have the strength left to carve the twelve prophets and raise them against the sky of bluest blue? Will those who prophesied the love and anger of God dance their tormented dance of wounded animals?

No one believes he has life enough left for so much. Slaves carry him through the streets of Ouro Prêto, always hidden beneath his hood, and tie the chisel to what remains of his hand. Only they see the ravages of his face and body. Only they draw close to this monstrosity. Antonio Francisco Lisboa, El Aleijadinho, is falling to pieces; and no urchin dreams of hitting him with a spitball.

(29 and 118)

1796: Mariana
Ataíde

Manuel da Costa Ataíde puts gold and colors on the figures that El Aleijadinho carves in wood. And he is a painter famous in his own right. In churches, Ataíde creates heavens of this earth. Using the pigments of flowers and plants, he paints the Virgin with the face of María do Carmo, a woman born here, brown madonna from whom spring the sun and the stars; and he paints little angel musicians and singers with very fleshy eyelids and lips, nappy hair and startled or mischievous eyes. The mulatto angels are his children and the Virgin his children's mother.

In the San Francisco church in Mariana, African features mark the patron saint of Assisi who turned wolves into lambs. Next to him live white saints with real hair and the faces of madwomen.

(123)

1796: São Salvador de Bahia
Night and Snow

The mulatta lover offers a sexual spree, the white wife social prestige. To achieve a white wife, the mulatto has to whiten himself. If he has plenty of money, he buys some document that erases the stigma of the slave grandmother and permits him to wear sword and hat, leather buskins and silk parasol. He also has a portrait painted which his grandchildren can display without a blush in the living room. Artists have arrived in Brazil who know how to give a European appearance to any tropical model. Oval gold frames surround the head of the patriarch, a man with pink skin and straight hair and a grave and watchful expression.

(65 and 119)

1796: Caracas

White Skin For Sale

The Spanish crown no longer considers Indian lineage vile; black blood, on the other hand, *darkens births* for many generations. Rich mulattos can buy certificates of whiteness for five hundred silver coins.

To remove the stain that greatly afflicts him, the king pronounces Diego Mejías Bejarano, mulatto of Caracas, to be *white so that his sad and inferior condition should not be an impediment to his use, treatment, alternatives and mode of dress vis-à-vis other subjects*.

In Caracas, only whites can attend Mass in the cathedral or kneel on carpets in any church. The master race are known as *Mantuans* because the mantilla is the privilege of white ladies. No mulatto may be a priest or a doctor.

Mejías Bejarano has paid up the five hundred coins, but the local authorities decline to obey. An uncle of Simón Bolívar and the other *Mantuans* of the town council declare that the royal warrant *is frightening for the inhabitants and creoles of America*. The town council asks the king: *How is it possible for the white inhabitants and natives of this province to admit at their side a mulatto descended from their own slaves, or from the slaves of their fathers?*

(174 and 225)

1796: San Mateo

Simón Rodríguez

A mouse's ears, bourbon nose, mouth like a mailbox. A red tassel straggles from the cap that covers his premature baldness. The spectacles, wedged above the eyebrows, rarely help the blue, avid, darting eyes. Simón Carreño, Rodríguez by chosen name, wanders about preaching strange doctrines.

This reader of Rousseau claims that schools should be opened to the people, to those of mixed blood; that girls and boys should share the same classrooms, and that it would be more useful for the country to raise masons, blacksmiths, and carpenters than gentlemen and monks.

Simón the teacher and Simón the pupil. Simón Rodríguez is twenty-five years old and Simón Bolívar, the richest orphan in Venezuela, inheritor of mansions and plantations, owner of a thousand black slaves, is thirteen.

Far from Caracas, the teacher initiates the boy into the secrets of the universe and speaks to him of liberty, equality, fraternity; he reveals to him the hard life of the slaves who work for him, and tells him that the forget-me-not is also called *myosotis palustris*. He shows him how the foal is born of the belly of the mare, and cacao and coffee complete their cycles. Bolívar becomes a swimmer, a hiker, and a horseman; he learns to sow, to build a chair, and to name the stars in the sky of Aragua. Master and pupil cross Venezuela, camping wherever they may be, and together get to know the land that made them. By the light of a lantern they read and discuss *Robinson Crusoe* and Plutarch's *Lives*.

(64, 116, and 298)

1797: La Guaira

The Compass and the Square

The flight of his teacher interrupts Bolívar's education. Simón Rodríguez, suspected of plotting against the king, changes his name to Simón Robinson. From the port of La Guaira he sails to Jamaica and exile.

The plotters wanted an independent and republican America, without native tribute or black slavery, free from king and pope, where people of all races would be brothers and sisters in reason and in Jesus Christ.

Creole Masons, of the lodge founded by Francisco de Miranda in London, headed up the movement. Also accused are three Spanish Masons, exiled in Caracas. Frenchmen, schooled in revolutions and guillotines, are said to be in the conspiracy as well. Raids bring to light more banned books than dangerous weapons.

In the main plaza of Caracas, "Spain" is drawn and quartered: José María de España, chief of the plot.

(191 and 298)

1799: *London*
Miranda

It is thirty years since Francisco de Miranda left Venezuela. In Spain he was a victorious warrior. He became a Mason in Cadiz and left on a tour of Europe seeking arms and money for the independence of America. On a magic carpet he has journeyed from court to court, with no baggage but a flute, the false title of count, and many letters of introduction. He has dined with kings and he has slept with queens. In France, the revolution made him a general. The people of Paris acclaimed him as a hero, but Robespierre condemned him as a traitor; and to save his head, Miranda crossed the Channel to London with a false passport, a wig, and sunglasses.

The head of the English government, William Pitt, receives him in his office. He sends for General Abercromby, and the three talk while crawling on hands and knees over huge maps spread on the floor.

MIRANDA (in English): It should be clear that all this is to be done for the independence and freedom of those provinces, without which . . . (*gazing at the ceiling, he switched to Spanish*) . . . it would be an infamy.

ABERCROMBY (*nodding his head*): Independence and freedom.

MIRANDA: I need four thousand men and six warships. (*Points a finger at the map.*) We should start by attacking Caracas and . . .

PITT: Don't be offended, but I'll speak frankly to you. I prefer the oppressive government of Spain to the abominable system of France.

MIRANDA (*shuts his eyes and whispers in Spanish*): The enemy of my enemy is my friend. The enemy of my enemy is my friend. The enemy . . .

PITT: I wouldn't want to push the Americans into the calamities of such a revolution.

MIRANDA: I understand and share your concern, Your Excellency. Precisely for that I ask for the alliance, so that together we may fight against the monstrous principles of French liberty. (*Returns to the map.*) Caracas will fall without any difficulty . . .

ABERCROMBY: And if the colored people take up arms? And if they get control, as in Haiti?

MIRANDA: In my country the flag of liberty is in the hands of illustrious citizens of such civilized customs as Plato would have wanted for his republic. (*Slides his hand to the province of Santa Fe. The three fasten their eyes on the port of Cartagena.*)

ABERCROMBY: It looks difficult.

MIRANDA: It looks invulnerable. But I know a spot where the defense is extremely weak. On the right flank of the rampart . . .

(150 and 191)

Miranda Dreams of Catherine of Russia

Sometimes, very late at night, Miranda returns to Saint Petersburg and conjures up Catherine the Great in her intimate Winter Palace chambers. The endless train of the empress's gown, which thousands of pages hold up in the air, is a tunnel of embroidered silk through which Miranda rushes until he sinks into a sea of lace. Seeking the body that burns and waits, Miranda loosens golden fasteners and ropes of pearls and makes his way among rustling materials. Beyond the ample puffed skirt he is scratched by the wires of the crinoline, but manages to penetrate this armor and arrives at the first petticoat, tearing it off with one pull. Beneath it he finds another, and another and another, many petticoats of pearly smoothness, onion skins which his fingers peel with less and less spirit, and when with a great effort he breaks through the last petticoat the corset appears, invulnerable bastion defended by an army of belts and hooks and little laces and buttons, while the august lady, flesh that never tires, groans and beseeches.

1799: Cumaná

Two Wise Men on a Mule

The New World is too big for the eyes of the two Europeans who have just landed at Cumaná. The port sparkles on the river, set aflame by the sun, houses of white timber or bamboo beside the stone fort, and beyond, green sea, green land, the glowing bay. All truly new, never used, never seen: the plumage of the flamingos, the beaks of the pelicans, the sixty-foot coconut trees and the immense velvety flowers, tree trunks padded with lianas and foliage, the eternal siesta of the crocodiles, the skyblue, yellow, red crabs . . . There are Indians sleeping nude on the warm sand, and mulattas dressed in embroidered muslin, their bare feet caressing the places they tread. Here there is no tree that does not offer forbidden fruit from the center of the lost garden.

Alexander von Humboldt and Aimé Bonpland rent a house facing the main plaza, with a good flat on which to stand the telescope. Looking upward from this roof they see an eclipse of the sun and a shower of meteors, the angry sky spitting fire through a whole night, and looking down they see how the buyers of slaves open the mouths of blacks newly arrived at the Cumaná market. In this house they experience the first earthquake of their lives; and from it they go out to explore the region. They classify ferns and rare birds and look for Francisco Loyano, who suckled his son for five months and had tits and pure, sweet milk as long as his woman was sick.

Later Humboldt and Bonpland set out for the southern highlands. They carry their instruments: sextant, compass, thermometer, hygrometer, magnetometer. They also bring paper for drying flowers, bistouries for bird, fish, and crab autopsies; and ink and pen to sketch all the wonders. They go on muleback, weighed down with equipment, the German with the black top hat and blue eyes and the Frenchman with the insatiable magnifying glass.

Perplexed, the forests and mountains of America open up to these two lunatics.

(30 and 46)

1799: Montevideo

Father of the Poor

Francisco Antonio Maciel has founded the first meat-salting plant on this bank of the River Plata. His, too, is the soap and tallow candle factory. The lamplighter who patrols Montevideo's streets at nightfall, torch in hand and ladder on shoulder, lights Maciel's candles.

When not touring his fields, Maciel is at the salting plant checking the strips of jerky he will sell to Cuba or Brazil, or at the docks inspecting the hides he exports. He often accompanies his brigantines, which bear the names of saints, beyond the bay. Montevideans call him *Father of the Poor*, because he always has time, though it seems a miracle, to succor the sick left in the hands of God. Anywhere and at any hour the pious Maciel will stretch out a plate asking alms for the charity hospital he founded. Nor does he forget to visit blacks who spend Eastertide in the barracks at the mouth of the Miguelete River. He personally fixes the minimum price of each slave that his ships bring from Rio de Janeiro or Havana. Those with a complete set of teeth go for two hundred pesos; those who know the arts of masonry and carpentry, for four hundred.

Maciel is the most important of the Montevidean businessmen specializing in the exchange of cow meat for people meat.

(195 and 251)

1799: Guanajuato
Life, Passion, and Business
of the Ruling Class

All through the century that is dying, the owners of the Guanajuato and Zacatecas mines have been buying titles of high nobility. Ten mine owners have become counts and six marquises. While they planted family trees and tried on wigs, a new labor code was transforming their workers into debt-slaves. During the eighteenth century Guanajuato has multiplied eightfold its production of silver and gold.

Meanwhile, the magic wand of money has also touched seven Mexico City merchants, farm laborers from the mountains of northern Spain, and made them marquises and counts.

Some mine owners and merchants, anxious for aristocratic prestige, buy lands as well as titles. Throughout Mexico, innumerable haciendas advance, devouring the traditional lands of Indian communities.

Others prefer to go in for usury. The moneylender José Antonio del Mazo, for example, risks little and wins much. *Friend Mazo*, writes Francisco Alonso Terán, *is one of those who do the most business in Guanajuato. If God gives him long life, he will contain the whole city in his belly.*

(49 and 223)

1799: Royal City of Chiapas
The Tamemes

Don Augustín de las Quentas Zayas, governor of Chiapas, plans a new road from the River Tulijá to Comitán, on the way to Guatemala. Twelve hundred Tamemes will transport the necessary materials.

The Tamemes, two-legged mules, are Indians capable of carrying up to a hundred and seventy-five pounds. With ropes around their foreheads, they tote enormous bundles on their backs—even people seated in chairs—and thus cross high mountains and skirt precipices with one foot in life and the other out.

(146 and 321)

1799: Madrid
Fernando Túpac Amaru

On the street, someone plucks lamentations from a guitar. Inside, Fernando Túpac Amaru shakes with fever and dies dreaming that he is drooling snow.

The son of Peru's great chieftain does not reach his thirtieth year. Poor as a rat, he ends in Madrid his brief life of exile and prison.

Twenty years ago, violent rain swept the main plaza of Cuzco, and since then it has not stopped raining in the world.

The doctor says Fernando has died of melancholy.

(344)

1800: Apure River
To the Orinoco

America flames and spins, burned and dizzied by its suns. Giant trees embrace over the rivers and in their shade glows the canoe of the sages.

The canoe progresses pursued by birds and by hungry hordes of gnats and mosquitos. Slapping continuously, Humboldt and Bonpland defend themselves against the onslaughts of the lancers, which penetrate clothing and skin and reach to the bone, while the German studies the anatomy of the manatee, the fat fish with hands, or the electricity of the eel or the teeth of the piraña, and the Frenchman collects and classifies plants or measures a crocodile or calculates its age. Together they draw maps, register the temperature of the water and the pressure of the air, analyze the mica in the sand and the conches of snails and the passage of Orion's belt across the sky. They want America to tell them all it knows and here not a leaf or pebble is dumb.

They camp in a small cove, unloading the troublesome instruments. They light a fire to ward off mosquitos, and to cook. Suddenly, the dog barks as if to warn of an approaching jaguar, and runs to hide beneath Bonpland's legs. The toucan that Humboldt carries on his shoulder picks nervously at his straw hat. The undergrowth creaks and from among the trees appears a naked man, copper skin, Indian face, African hair:

"Welcome to my lands, gentlemen."

And he bows to them: "Don Ignacio, at your service."

Don Ignacio makes a face at the improvised fire. The sages are roasting a capybara rat. "That's Indian food," he says disdainfully, and invites them to sup in his house in splendid venison freshly hunted with an arrow.

Don Ignacio's house consists of three nets slung between trees not far from the river. There he presents them to his wife, Doña Isabela, and his daughter, Doña Manuela, not as naked as he is. He offers the travelers cigars. While the venison is browning, he riddles them with questions. Don Ignacio is hungry to know the news of the court of Madrid and the latest on those endless wars that are so wounding Europe.

(338)

1800: Esmeralda del Orinoco
Master of Poison

They sail on down river.

At the foot of a rocky mountain, at the remote Christian mission of Esmeralda, they meet the master of poison. His laboratory is the cleanest and neatest hut in the village. The old Indian, surrounded by smoking cauldrons and clay jugs, pours a yellowish juice into banana leaf cones and palm leaf funnels: the horrifying curare falls drop by drop, and bubbles. The arrow anointed with this curare will enter and kill better than the fang of a snake.

"Better than anything," says the old man, as he chews some liana and tree bark into a paste. "Better than anything you people make."

And Humboldt thinks: *He has the same pedantic tone and the same starchy manner as our pharmacists.*

"You people have invented black powder," the old man continues, as very slowly, with meticulous hand, he pours water onto the paste.

"I know it," he says after a pause, "that powder isn't worth a damn. It's noisy. It's unreliable. Powder can't kill silently and it kills even when you miss your aim."

He revives the fire under the kettles and pots. From within the smoke he asks, "Know how to make soap?"

"He knows," says Bonpland.

The old man looks at Humboldt with respect. "After curare," he says, "soap is the big thing."

(338)

Curare

Guam, the child-god of the Tukan Indians, managed to reach the kingdom of poison. There he caught the daughter of Curare and made love to her. She had spiders, scorpions, and snakes hidden between her legs. Each time he entered that body, Guam died; and on reviving he saw colors that were not of this world.

She took him to her father's house. Old Curare, who ate people, licked himself. But Guam turned himself into a flea, and in that form entered the old man's mouth, slithered down to his liver and took a bite. Curare covered his mouth, nose, ears, eyes, his navel, asshole and his penis, so that the flea would have no way to escape; but Guam tickled him inside and got out with the sneeze.

He flew back to his country, and in his bird's beak carried a little piece of Curare's liver.

So the Tukan Indians got poison, as the men of much time, the guardians of memory, tell it.

(164)

1800: Uruana

Forever Earth

Opposite the island of Uruana, Humboldt meets the Indians who eat earth.

Every year the Orinoco rises, *the Father of rivers*, flooding its banks for two or three months. While the flood lasts, the Otomacos eat soft clay, slightly hardened by fire, and on that they live. It is pure earth, Humboldt confirms, not mixed with corn flour or turtle oil or crocodile fat.

So these *wandering Indians* travel through life toward death, clay wandering toward clay, erect clay eating the earth that will eat them.

(338)

1801: Lake Guatavita
The Goddess at the Bottom of the Waters

On the maps of America, El Dorado still occupies a good part of Guyana. The lake of gold takes flight when its hunters approach, and curses and kills them; but on the maps it is a tranquil blot of blue joined to the upper Orinoco.

Humboldt and Bonpland decipher the mystery of the elusive lake. In the glittering mica on a mountain which the Indians call Golden Mountain, they discover part of the hallucination; and another in a little lake which in the rainy season invades the vast plain neighboring the source waters of the Orinoco and then, when the rains cease, disappears.

In Guyana lies the phantom lake, that most tempting of America's deliriums. Far away, on the plateau of Bogotá, is the true El Dorado. After covering many leagues by canoe and mule, Humboldt and Bonpland discover it in the sacred Lake Guatavita. This mirror of waters faithfully reflects even the tiniest leaf in the woods surrounding it: at its bottom lie the treasures of the Muisca Indians.

To this sanctuary came princes, their naked bodies gleaming with gold dust, and at the center of the lake dropped their goldsmiths' finest works, then plunged in themselves. If they came up without a single speck of gold on the skin, the goddess Furatena had accepted their offerings. In those times the goddess Furatena, snake goddess, governed the world from the depths.

(326 and 338)

1801: Bogotá
Mutis

The old monk talks as he peels oranges and an unending shower of gold spirals down into a pan between his feet.

To see him, to listen to him, Humboldt and Bonpland have detoured from their southward route and have gone upriver for forty days. José Celestino Mutis, patriarch of America's botanists, is put to sleep by speeches but enjoys intimate chats as much as anyone.

The three men, sages ever astonished by the beauty and mystery of the universe, exchange plants, ideas, doubts, discoveries. Mutis is excited by talk of Lake Guatavita, the salt mines of Zipaquirá, and the Tequendama waterfall. He praises the map of the Magdalena River which Humboldt has just drawn, and discreetly suggests some changes with the sureness of one who has traveled much and knows much, and knows very deep inside himself that something of him will remain in the world.

And he shows everything and tells everything. While he eats and offers oranges, Mutis speaks of the letters that Linnaeus wrote him, and of how much those letters taught him, and of the problems he had with the Inquisition. And he recalls and shares his discoveries about the curative powers of quinine bark, and the influence of the moon on the barometer, and the cycles of flowers, which sleep as we do and stretch and wake up little by little, unfurling their petals.

(148)

1802: The Caribbean Sea

Napoleon Restores Slavery

Squadrons of wild ducks escort the French army. The fish take flight. Through a turquoise sea, bristling with coral, the ships head for the blue mountains of Haiti. Soon the land of victorious slaves will appear on the horizon. General Leclerc stands tall at the head of the fleet. Like a ship's figurehead, his shadow is first to part the waves. Astern, other islands disappear, castles of rock, splendors of deepest green, sentinels of the new world found three centuries ago by people who were not looking for it.

"Which has been the most prosperous regime for the colonies?"

"The previous one."

"Well, then, put it back," Napoleon decided.

No man, born red, black, or white can be his neighbor's property, Toussaint L'Ouverture had said. Now the French fleet returns slavery to the Caribbean. More than fifty ships, more than twenty thousand soldiers, come from France to bring back the past with guns.

In the cabin of the flagship, a female slave fans Pauline Bonaparte and another gently scratches her head.

(71)

1802: Pointe-à-Pitre

They Were Indignant

On the island of Guadeloupe, as in all French colonies, free blacks become slaves again. Black citizens reappear in their owners' inventories and wills as saleable goods; once more they form part of the tool inventories of plantàtions, the equipment of ships, and the arsenal of the army. The colonial government summons whites who have left the island and guarantees them the return of their property. Blacks unclaimed by their owners are sold off for the public treasury.

The hunt becomes a butchery. The authorities of Guadeloupe pay forty-four francs for each rebel head. The hanged rot in perpetuity on top of Constantine Hill. In Pointe-à-Pitre's Place Victoria, the bonfire of blacks never goes out and the flames rise higher than the houses.

Three whites protest. For their dignity, for their indignation, they are condemned. Millet de La Girardière, a several-times-decorated French army officer, is sentenced to death in an iron cage, exposed to the public, sitting naked on a spiny leaf. The other two, Barse and Barbet, will have their bones broken before being burned alive.

(180)

1802: Chimborazo Volcano

On the Roofs of the World

They climb over clouds, amid abysses of snow, clinging to the rough body of Chimborazo, tearing their hands against the naked rock.

They have left the mules half-way up. Humboldt carries on his shoulder a bag full of stones that speak of the origin of the Andean cordillera, born of an unusual vomiting from the earth's incandescent belly. At seventeen thousand feet Bonpland has caught a butterfly, and higher up an incredible fly, and they have continued climbing, despite the bitter cold and vertigo and slippings and the blood that spurts from their eyes and gums and parted lips. Mist envelops them as they climb blindly up the volcano, until a shaft of light breaks through and strips bare the summit, that high white tower, before the astounded travelers. Is it real, could it be? Never has any man climbed so close to the sky, and it is said that on the roofs of the world appear horses flying to the clouds and colored stars at noon. Is it a hallucination, this cathedral of snow rearing up between north and south skies? Are not their bruised eyes deceiving them?

Humboldt feels an abundance of light more intense than any delirium: we are made of light, Humboldt feels, of light ourselves, and of light the earth and time, and he feels a tremendous urge to tell it right away to brother Goethe, over there at his home in Weimar.

(338)

1803: Fort Dauphin
The Island Burned Again

Toussaint L'Ouverture, chief of the free blacks, died a prisoner in a castle in France. When the jailer opened the padlock at dawn and slid back the bolt, he found Toussaint frozen in his chair.

But life in Haiti moved on, and without Toussaint the black army has beaten Napoleon Bonaparte. Twenty thousand French soldiers have been slaughtered or died of fevers. Vomiting black blood, dead blood, General Leclerc has collapsed. The land he sought to enslave proves his shroud.

Haiti has lost half its population. Shots are still heard, and hammers nailing down coffins, and funeral drums, in the vast ash-heap carpeted with corpses that the vultures spurn. This island, burned two centuries ago by an exterminating angel, has been newly eaten by the fire of men at war.

Over the smoking earth those who were slaves proclaim independence. France will not forgive the humiliation.

On the coast, palms, bent over against the wind, form ranks of spears.

(71)

1804: Mexico City
Spain's Richest Colony

Theology professors still earn five times more than their colleagues in surgery or astronomy, but Humboldt finds in Mexico City an astonishing nursery of young scientists. This is the heritage of some Jesuit priests, friends of experimental physics, the new chemistry, and certain theories of Descartes, who despite the Inquisition taught and contaminated here; and it is also the work of the viceroy Revillagigedo, a man open to the winds of time, defier of dogmas, who a few years ago governed these lands with anguished concern about the lack of machines and laboratories and modern books to read.

Humboldt discovers and praises the School of Mining and its learned professors, while Mexico produces more silver than all the rest of the world, a river of silver flowing to Europe through the port of Veracruz. At the same time, Humboldt warns that cultivated land is little and badly worked, and that the colonial monopoly of commerce and the poverty of the people block the development of manufacturing. *Mexico is the land of inequality,* he notes. *The monstrous inequality of rights and fortunes* hits one in the face. Counts and marquesses paint newly purchased coats-of-arms on their carriages, and the people live in a misery that is the enemy of all industry. The Indians suffer atrocious penury. As in all of America, here too, *more or less white skin decides what class a man occupies in society.*

(163 and 217)

1804: Madrid

The Attorney General of the Council of the Indies advises against overdoing the sale of whiteness certificates,

to the end that persons of color should not seek to generalize these favors believing that these make them equal to whites with no difference but the accident of color, and believing themselves able to obtain all destinies and employments and to form links with any legitimate and mixture-free family . . . consequences which it is fitting to avoid in a monarchy, where the classification of classes contributes to better order, security, and good government . . .

Colored or brown persons stemming from infected mixtures constitute a very inferior species which, due to its vitiated nature, its arrogance, and inclination for freedom, has been and is little attached to our government and nation . . .

(174)

1804: Catamarca

Ambrosio's Sin

Bound to a post in the main plaza of Catamarca, Ambrosio Millicay receives twenty-five strokes of the lash.

The mulatto Ambrosio, who belongs to the commander Nieva y Castillo, was denounced to the authorities for having committed the crime of learning to read and write. They flayed his back with lashes *as a lesson to those pen-pushing Indians and mulattos who wish to ape Spaniards.*

Prone on the paving stones, Ambrosio groans and raves and dreams of vengeance. *"Pardon me,"* he pleads in his dream, and plunges in the knife.

(272)

1804: Paris

Napoleon

The solemn chords of the organ invoke the sixty kings who have ruled France, and perhaps too the angels, while the pope offers the crown to Napoleon Bonaparte.

Napoleon wreathes his own brow with the laurel of the Caesars. Then he descends, slowly, majestic in ermine and purple, and places on Josephine the diadem that consecrates her as the first empress in France's history. In a gold and crystal coach they have reached the throne of this nation, the small foreigner, great warrior, sprouted from the harsh mountains of Corsica, and his wife Josephine, born in Martinique, an Antillean whose embrace they say will burn you to a crisp. Napoleon, the artillery lieutenant who hated Frenchmen, becomes Napoleon I.

The founder of the dynasty that is inaugurated today has rehearsed this coronation ceremony a thousand times. Each personage in the retinue, each actor, has dressed as he prescribed, has placed himself where he wanted, has moved the way he ordered.

"Oh, José! If our father could see us . . ."

The voracious relatives, princes and princesses of France's new nobility, have done their duty. True, the mother, Laeticia, has refused to come, and is in the palace murmuring grudges, but Napoleon will order David, the official artist, to give Laeticia a prominent place in the painting which will tell posterity of these ceremonials.

The guests overflow the cathedral of Notre Dame. Among them, a young Venezuelan cranes his neck to miss no detail. At twenty, a hallucinated Simón Bolívar attends the birth of the Napoleonic monarchy: *I am no more than a diamond on the handle of Bonaparte's sword . . .*

During these days, in a gilded salon in Paris, Bolívar has met Alexander von Humboldt. The adventurer-sage, newly arrived from America, has said to him, *"I think your country is ripe for independence, but I don't see the man who can . . ."*

(20 and 116)

1804: Seville

Fray Servando

For wanting the independence of Mexico, and for believing that the pagan god Quetzalcoatl was the apostle Saint Thomas in person, Fray Servando has been sentenced to exile in Spain.

From prison to prison, from escape to escape, the Mexican heretic has been a guest of the most varied Spanish dungeons. But this artist of the file, the tunnel, and the high jump has managed to travel far on the old continent.

Globetrotter, globe breaker: a bird with agile wings and beak of steel, Fray Servando defends himself against Europe's fascination by cursing all he sees. *I am a Mexican*, he repeats at every step, and thinks Frenchwomen have faces like snub-nosed, big-mouthed frogs; that in France men are like women and women like children; that the Italian language is made for lying; and that Italy is the homeland of the superlative and the bogus, although it has one worthwhile city, Florence, because it is something like a Mexican city. Against Spain, the impertinent friar recites a whole rosary of insults: he says the Spaniards imitate the French like monkeys; that the Court is a brothel and the Escorial no more than a pile of stones; that the Basques drive nails with their foreheads, and the Aragonese likewise, except with the point upward; that the Catalans don't move a step without a lantern and won't admit any relative to their homes who doesn't bring food; and that the Madrileños are dwarfed stringers of rosaries and inheritors of prisons, condemned to a climate of eight months' winter and four months' hell.

Now, in the Seville jail, Fray Servando is pulling lice from his chest by the fistful while an army of bedbugs makes waves in his blanket and the fleas mock his slaps and the rats his lunges with a stick. They all want to lunch off Fray Servando and he pleads for a truce. He needs a moment of peace to round out the details of his next escape, which he already has nearly complete.

(318 and 346)

1806: Island of Trinidad
Adventures, Misadventures

After many years of futile waiting, Francisco de Miranda leaves London. The English have paid him a fairly good salary, given him a few promises and some benevolent smiles, but not a bullet for his liberating expedition. Miranda escapes from the chessboard of British diplomacy and tries his luck in the United States.

In New York he gets a ship. Two hundred volunteers accompany him. He lands on the Venezuelan coasts of the Gulf of Coro, after thirty-six years of exile. He has promised his recruits a glorious welcome, flowers and music, honors and treasure, but he meets silence. No one responds to the proclamations that announce freedom. Miranda occupies a couple of towns, covers them with flags and words, and quits Venezuela before the five thousand soldiers from Caracas can wipe him out.

On the island of Trinidad he receives outrageous news. The English have seized the port of Buenos Aires and plan the conquest of Montevideo, Valparaíso, and Veracruz. From London, the War Minister has given clear instructions: *The novelty will consist, simply and solely, of substituting the dominion of His Britannic Majesty for the dominion of the Spanish king.*

Miranda will return to London, to his house in Grafton Street, and loudly voice his protest. There they raise his annual pension from three hundred to seven hundred pounds sterling.

(150)

1808: Rio de Janeiro

Judas-Burning Is Banned

By will of the Portuguese prince, recently arrived in Brazil, the traditional burning of Judases during the Holy Week is to be banned in the colony. To avenge Christ and avenge themselves the people would throw on the fire, one night in the year, the marshal and the archbishop, the rich merchant, the big landlord and the chief of police; the naked ones have enjoyed seeing how the rag dolls, sumptuously adorned and filled with firecrackers, twist in pain and explode amid the flames.

From now on, those in power will not suffer even in Holy Week. The royal family, who have just come from Lisbon, demand silence and respect. An English ship has rescued the Portuguese prince with all his court and jewelry, and brought them to these remote lands.

This efficacious maneuver removes the Portuguese dynasty from the dangerous onslaught of Napoleon Bonaparte, who has invaded Spain and Portugal, and it affords England a useful center of operations in America. The English have taken a tremendous beating on the River Plata. Expelled from Buenos Aires and Montevideo, they now launch their next penetration through Rio de Janeiro, through the most helplessly unconditional of their allies.

(65 and 171)

1809: Chuquisaca

The Cry

of "America" explodes in Chuquisaca. While Spain seethes, up in arms against the French invaders, America rebels. The Creoles repudiate the throne that Joseph Bonaparte, brother of Napoleon, occupies in Madrid.

Chuquisaca is first. The rebellion of America's Salamanca announces that Spain will lose her dominion over the Indies.

Chuquisaca, formerly La Plata and Charcas, and the Sucre to be, lies at the foot of two mountains in love. From its patios and gardens rises the aroma of citrus blossoms, and through its streets pass more knightly gentlemen than commoners. Nothing is so abundant here as cloaks and clerical tonsures. Very Chuquisacan are doctors, stiff as their gilt-handled canes, and friars who go about sprinkling houses with hyssop.

Here, the world seemed immutable and secure. Astoundingly, the shrill cry of liberty has come from this mouth accustomed to falsetto Latin. La Paz and Quito and Buenos Aires will immediately echo it. To the north, in Mexico . . .

(5)

1810: Atotonilco

The Virgin of Guadalupe
Versus the Virgin of Remedios

Making its way through curtains of dust, the multitude crosses the town of Atotonilco.

"Long live America and death to the bad government!"

Father Miguel Hidalgo hauls from the church the image of the Virgin of Guadalupe and ties it to a spear. The raised standard glows over the crowd.

"Long live Our Lady of Guadalupe! Death to the Spanish dogs!"

Fervor of revolution, passion of religion. The bells have rung out from the church of Dolores, the priest Hidalgo calls for struggle, and the Mexican Virgin of Guadalupe declares war on the Spanish Virgin of Remedios. Indian Virgin defies white Virgin; the one who chose a poor Indian on the hill of Tepeyac marches against the one who saved Hernán Cortés in the flight from Tenochtitlán. Our Lady of Remedios will dress up as a general; and by order of the viceroy the firing squad will riddle with bullets the standard of the Virgin of Guadalupe.

Mother, queen, and goddess of the Mexicans, the Virgin of Guadalupe was called Tonantzin by the Aztecs before the archangel Gabriel painted her image in the Tepeyac sanctuary. Year after year the people stream to Tepeyac in procession, *Ave Virgin and Pregnant, Ave Damsel with Child,* go on their knees up to the rock where she appeared, to the crack from which roses bloomed, *Ave Possessed of God, Ave Most Beloved of God,* drink water from its springs, *Ave that Maketh God a Nest,* and beseech love and miracles, protection, counsel, *Ave Maria, Ave Ave.*

Now the Virgin of Guadalupe advances, killing for the independence of Mexico.

(178)

1810: Guanajuato

El Pípila

Hidalgo's troops storm out of the mountain scrub, and fall upon Guanajuato with volleys of stones. The mining town joins the insurgent avalanche.

Despite the havoc wrought by the king's fusillades, the multitude flood the streets, a surge that sweeps the soldiers aside and beats up against that bastion of Spanish power, the Corn Exchange. There, beneath the vaulted ceilings of its thirty halls, lie eight thousand bushels of corn and an incalculable fortune in silver, gold bars, and jewels. The lords of the colony, scared out of their wits, have locked themselves in with all of their treasure.

In vain, the dandies beg for mercy. Throat-cuttings, looting, a vast drunken spree follows, and the Indians strip the dead to see if they have tails.

El Pípila, a miner, is the hero of the day. They say he hoisted an enormous stone slab onto his back, scuttled like a turtle through the rain of bullets, and with a lighted torch and plenty of pitch set fire to the Corn Exchange door. They say that El Pípila's name is Juan José Martínez and they say he has other names too, all the names of the Indians who are or have ever been in the mines of Guanajuato.

(197)

1810: Guadalajara

Hidalgo

Everybody knew, in the town of Dolores, that the priest Hidalgo had the bad habit of reading as he walked through the streets, the great wings of his hat between the sun and the pages, and that it was a sheer miracle that neither horses nor the Inquisition ever hit him, because more dangerous than reading was what he read. At a slow pace the priest moved through the cloud of dust in the streets of Dolores, always with some French book covering his face, one of those books that talk of the social contract and the rights of man and the freedoms of citizens; and if he didn't greet people it was because of his thirst for erudition, not rudeness.

The priest Hidalgo rebelled along with the twenty Indians who made bowls and pots with him, and at the end of a week there were fifty thousand of them. Then the Inquisition went to work on him.

The Holy Office of Mexico has pronounced him *a heretic, apostate of religion, denier of the virginity of Mary, materialist, libertine, advocate of fornication, seditious, schismatic, and sectarian of French liberty.*

The Virgin of Guadalupe invades Guadalajara at the head of an insurgent army. Miguel Hidalgo has the portrait of King Ferdinand removed from the walls and replies to the Inquisition with a decree abolishing slavery, confiscating the goods of Europeans, ending the tributes paid by Indians, and recovering farmlands from those who have usurped them.

(127, 203, and 321)

1810: Pie de la Cuesta

Morelos

He is a country priest, like Hidalgo. Like Hidalgo, he was born in the Tarascan country, in the mountains of Michoacán where Bishop Vasco de Quiroga had created, two and a half centuries earlier, his communist utopia—lands of redemption later laid waste by plagues and by the forced labor of thousands of Indians dragged to the mines of Guanajuato.

"With violence I go to the hot lands of the south."

José María Morelos, shepherd and muleteer, parish priest of Carácuaro, joins the revolution. He takes the road with twenty-five spearmen and a few shotguns. Behind the white silk kerchief that binds his head, the troop keeps growing.

In search of Atoyac Indians hidden in the palm groves, Morelos crosses the little town of Pie de la Cuesta.

"Who goes there?"

"Holy God," say the Indians.

Morelos talks to them. From now on, to the cry of *"Who goes there?"* people will answer, *"America."*

(332 and 348)

1811: Buenos Aires

Moreno

Great fortunes in a few hands, thought Mariano Moreno, are stagnant waters that do not bathe the earth. *So as not to escape from tyrants without destroying tyranny,* parasitical capital amassed in colonial business would have to be expropriated. Why seek in Europe, at the price of extortionate interest, money that is more than abundant at home? From abroad should be brought machines and seeds, instead of Stoddard pianos and Chinese vases. The State, thought Moreno, should become a great entrepreneur of a newly independent nation. The revolution, he thought, should be terrible and astute, implacable with enemies and vigilant towards onlookers.

Fleetingly he held power, or thought he did.

"Thanks be to God," breathed the merchants of Buenos Aires. Mariano Moreno, *the demon of hell,* has died on the high seas. His friends French and Beruti go into exile. Castelli is sentenced to prison.

Cornelio Saavedra orders copies of Rousseau's *Social Contract,* which Moreno had published and circulated, rounded up; and he warns that no Robespierre has any place on the River Plata.

(2 and 267)

1811: Buenos Aires

Castelli

There were two of them: a pen and a voice. A Robespierre who wrote, Mariano Moreno, and another who spoke. *They are all perverse,* said a Spanish commandant, *but Castelli and Moreno are very perverse indeed.* Juan José Castelli, the great orator, is in jail in Buenos Aires.

Usurped by conservatives, the revolution sacrifices the revolutionaries. The charges pile up: Castelli is a womanizer, a drunk, a cardsharp, and a profaner of churches. The prisoner, agitator of Indians, seeker of justice for the poor, spokesman for the American cause, cannot defend himself. Cancer has attacked his mouth. His tongue has to be amputated.

The revolution falls dumb in Buenos Aires.

(84)

1811: Bogotá

Nariño

We have changed masters, writes Antonio Nariño in Colombia.

La Bagatela, the newspaper founded, directed, and edited by him from cover to cover, deprives puppets of heads and big shots of pedestals. Nariño proclaims that the patriotic uprising of the Colom-

bians is turning into a masked ball and demands that independence
be declared once and for all. He also demands, voice crying in the
desert, that the right of the poor to vote be recognized and that the
will of the naked plebeian is worth as much as that of the gentleman
sheathed in velvet.

We have changed masters, he writes. Some months ago the people invaded the main square of Bogotá, the men took the viceroy
prisoner and the women threw the vicereine into the whores' prison.
The ghost of José Antonio Galán, the commoners' captain, charged
at the head of the infuriated multitude. Then the doctors and bishops
and merchants and masters of lands and slaves were badly scared.
Swearing to avoid at any price *the errors of the libertines of France*,
they helped the viceregal couple to escape secretly.

We have changed masters. Colombia is governed by gentlemen
in very starched shirts and cassocks with many buttons. *Even in
Heaven there are hierarchies*, preaches the Canon of the Cathedral,
and not even the fingers of the hand are equal. The ladies cross
themselves, lowering a thicket of curls, flowers, and ribbons beneath
the black mantilla. The Junta of Notables issues its first decrees.
Among other patriotic measures, it resolves to despoil the despoiled
Indians of all that remains to them. Under the pretext of freeing them
from tribute, the Junta seizes the Indians' communal lands to force
them to serve in the big haciendas which feature a pillory in the
middle of the patio.

(185 and 235)

The World Upside Down,
Verses for Guitar Accompanied by Singer

*When you paint the world upside down
You see it in all its error:
The dog flees the fox in terror,
Thief chases judge in his gown.
The feet look down on the head,
The mouth drags along in the mire,
Water is put out by fire,
Letters are taught by the blind,
The carter is pulling the wagon,
The oxen are riding behind.*

On the banks of a man sits a river,
Sharpening his horse in the shade
And watering his blunted blade.

(179)

1811: Chilapa
Potbelly

In Mexico, military order is vanquishing popular tumult. Hidalgo has been executed in Chihuahua. It is said that he renounced his ideas, after four months of chains and torture. Independence now has only the forces that follow Morelos to rely on.

Ignacio López Rayón sends Morelos an urgent message of warning: *I have it from good sources that the viceroy has paid an assassin to kill you. I cannot tell you any more about this man, except that he is very potbellied . . .*

At dawn, in a burst of hooves, the messenger reaches the camp at Chilapa.

At noon, the assassin comes to offer his services to the national cause. Arms crossed, Morelos gets a broadside of patriotic speeches. Without saying a word he sits the assassin down on his right and invites him to share his dinner. He watches the assassin eating, as the man stares at his plate.

In the evening they sup together. The assassin eats and talks and chokes. Morelos, courteous statue, seeks out his eyes.

"I have a bad presentiment," he says suddenly and waits for the eyes to tense, the chair to creak, and then offers relief: "My rheumatism again. Rain."

His somber expression cuts short a laugh.

He lights a cigar. Studies the smoke.

The assassin dares not get up. He stammers thanks. Morelos faces him closely. "I shall be curious," he says.

He notices the assassin giving a start and counts the beads of sweat on his forehead. He draws out the question: "Are you sleepy?"

And without a pause: "Would you do me the honor of sleeping beside me?"

They stretch out, separated by a candle fluttering in its death agonies, yet undecided whether to die or not. Morelos turns his back. He breathes deeply, perhaps snores. Before dawn he hears a horse's hooves fading into the distance.

At midmorning, he asks his assistant for paper and pen.

A letter to Ignacio López Rayón: *Thanks for the tip. In this camp there is no one more potbellied than I.*

(348)

1811: East Bank Ranges
"Nobody is more than anybody,"

say the mounted cowboys. The land cannot have an owner, because the air doesn't have one. They know no better roof than the stars, nor any glory that compares with the freedom to wander aimlessly on friend horse across the prairie that rolls like the sea.

Having herds to drive in the open country is to have almost everything. The gauchos eat only meat, because the verdure is grass and grass is for cows. The roast is topped off with tobacco and rum, and with guitars that sing of events and miracles.

The gauchos, *loose men* whom the estates use and discard, join forces with José Artigas. The ranges east of the Uruguay River take fire.

(227 and 278)

1811: Banks of the Uruguay River
Exodus

Buenos Aires makes a deal with the viceroy and withdraws the troops that were besieging Montevideo. José Artigas refuses to observe the armistice, which restores his land to the Spaniards, and vows to carry on the war *even if it be with teeth, with nails.*

The leader emigrates northward to organize an army of independence. A dispersed people unites and is born in his tracks, a roving host that joins wild cowboys with peons and laborers, patriots of the estancias. To the north march women who heal wounds or take up a spear and monks who all along the march baptize newborn soldiers. The formerly well-sheltered opt for the rigors of outdoor life, those who lived quietly choose danger. Marching northward are masters of letters and the knife, loquacious doctors and worried bandits in debt for some death. Tooth-pullers and miracle workers, deserters from ships and forts, fugitive slaves. All are marching. Indians burn their huts and join up, bringing along only arrows and bolas.

Northward goes the long caravan of carts, horses, people on foot. As they go, the land that will be called Uruguay is stripped of those who want a fatherland. The land itself goes with its children, goes in them, and nothing is left behind. Not even an ash, not even silence.

(277)

1812: Cochabamba
Women

From Cochabamba, many men have fled. Not one woman. On the hillside, a great clamor. Cochabamba's plebeian women, at bay, fight from the center of a circle of fire.

Surrounded by five thousand Spaniards, they resist with battered tin guns and a few arquebuses; and they fight to the last yell, whose echoes will resound throughout the long war for independence. Whenever his army weakens, General Manuel Belgrano will shout those words which never fail to restore courage and spark anger. The general will ask his vacillating soldiers: *Are the women of Cochabamba present?*

(5)

1812: Caracas
Bolívar

An earthquake demolishes Caracas, La Guaira, San Felipe, Barquisimeto, and Mérida. They are the Venezuelan cities which have proclaimed independence. In Caracas, center of the Creole insurrection, ten thousand lie dead beneath the ruins. Nothing is heard but supplications and curses as people seek bodies among the stones.

Can God be Spanish? The earthquake has swallowed the gallows erected by the patriots and has not left standing one of the churches which had sung the Te Deum in honor of the nascent republic. In the ruined Mercedes church the column bearing Spain's imperial coat of arms still stands. Coro, Maracaibo, Valencia and Angostura, cities loyal to the king, have not suffered a scratch.

In Caracas, the air burns. From the ruins rises a dense dust which the eye cannot penetrate. A monk harangues the people, proclaiming that God will no longer tolerate such effrontery.

"*Vengeance!*"

The multitude presses around him in what was the San Jacinto convent. Perched on the ruins of the altar, the monk demands punishment for those who brought on God's wrath.

"*Vengeance!*" roars the scourge of Christ, and his accusing finger points at a patriot officer who, his arms crossed, contemplates the scene. The crowd turns against the officer—short, bony, in a brilliant uniform—and advances to crush him.

Simón Bolívar neither implores nor retreats: he attacks. Sword in hand he plunges through the frenzy, mounts the altar and with one blow topples the apocalyptic monk.

The people, silent, disperse.

(116)

1813: Chilpancingo

Independence Is Revolution or a Lie

In three military campaigns Morelos has won a good part of Mexico. The Congress of the future republic, a wandering Congress, travels behind its leader. The deputies sleep on the ground and eat soldiers' rations.

By the light of a thick tallow candle Morelos draws up the essentials of the national Constitution. He proposes a free, independent, and Catholic America; substitutes an income tax for Indian tributes and increases the wages of the poor; confiscates the goods of the enemy; establishes freedom of commerce, but with tariff barriers; suppresses slavery and torture and liquidates the caste system, which bases social differences on the color of skin, *so that only vice and virtue distinguish one American from another*.

The rich Creoles go from shock to shock as Morelos's troops march along expropriating fortunes and dividing up haciendas. A war against Spain or a rising of the serfs? This is not the sort of independence they were hoping for. They will make another.

(348)

1814: San Mateo

Boves

In Venezuela the word *independence* still does not mean much more than *freedom of commerce* for rich Creoles.

Blacks and browns look to the chief of the Spaniards, a Hercules with red beard and green eyes, as their leader. Slaves run away to find José Tomás Rodríguez Boves, *Papa* Boves. Ten thousand prairie horsemen set fire to plantations and cut masters' throats in the name of God and the king. Boves's flag, a skull on black ground, promises pillage and revenge, war to the death against the cacao oligarchy who want independence from Spain. On the plains of San Mateo, Boves rides his horses into the mansion of the Bolívar family and carves his name with a knife on the door of the main vestibule.

The spear does not repent; the bullet does not repent. Before killing with lead, Boves shoots salvos of gunpowder, for the pleasure of seeing the expressions on his victims' faces. Among his bravest soldiers he divides up the young ladies of the best families. He enjoys bullfighting elegant patriots, after sticking banderillas in their necks. He cuts heads off as if it were a joke.

Before long now, a spear will pierce him. He will be buried with bound feet.

(160)

1815: San Cristóbal Ecatepec
The Lake Comes for Him

On the thorny ridge of Tezmalaca the Spaniards catch José María Morelos. After so many mistakes and defeats, they hunt him down in the brambles, his clothing in shreds, without weapons or spurs.

They chain him. They insult him. Lieutenant-Colonel Eugenio Villasana asks, "What would you do if you were the winner, and I the defeated?"

"*Give you two hours to confess,*" says the priest Morelos, "*and shoot you.*"

They take him to the secret cells of the Inquisition.

They humiliate him on his knees. They shoot him in the back.

The viceroy says that the rebel died repentant. The Mexican people say that the lake heard the firing squad's blast and overflowed to carry off the body.

(178 and 332)

1815: Paris
Navigators of Seas and Libraries

Julien Mellet, writer and traveler, relates his adventures in South America to the European public. Among other things he describes *a very lively and lascivious dance* much done in Quillota, in Chile, and which was brought *by the blacks from Guinea.* Pretending to look the other way, Mellet copies a description of a dance of Montevideo's blacks, as published by the traveler Anthony Helms eight years previously in London. Helms had stolen his text line by line from the book that Dom Pernetty published in Paris in 1770. Pernetty, for his part, had portrayed at first hand the dance of the Montevideo slaves with words astonishingly similar to those that Father Jean Baptiste Labat had devoted to the blacks of Haiti, in a book published half a century earlier in The Hague.

From the Caribbean to the Chilean city of Quillota, passing through Montevideo, and from The Hague to Paris, passing through London, those passages of Father Labat's have traveled much further than their author. Without passport or disguise.

(19)

1815: Mérida, Yucatán
Ferdinand VII

The starched gentlemen of Yucatán cross the Plaza de Armas in Mérida, whitened by dust and sun, and enter the cathedral in very solemn procession. From the shade of its portico, the Indian tamale and necklace vendors don't understand why the bells ring so merrily, or know whose is that crowned head that the gentlemen carry on a banner.

The colonial aristocracy is celebrating the news from Madrid. It has been belatedly learned that the French were driven out and Ferdinand VII reigns in Spain. Messengers report that the cry being heard around the monarch is *"Long live chains!"* As court jesters tinkle their little bells, King Ferdinand orders the guerrillas who brought him to the throne jailed or shot, revives the Inquisition, and restores the privileges of the clergy and nobility.

(339)

1815: Curuzú-Cuatiá

The Hides Cycle on the River Plata

On the tip of a spear, the sharp-edged half-moon reaches for the fleeing animal's legs. Just one slash: the horseman strikes with sure aim, and the calf limps and gasps and falls. The horseman dismounts. He cuts the throat and begins to skin.

He does not always kill that way. Easier to drive the maverick cattle with yells into the corrals and knife them there, thousands and thousands of wild cattle or horses stampeded to their death; easier yet to surprise the animals in the hills by night, while they sleep.

The gaucho pulls off the hide and stakes it out in the sun. Of the remainder, what the mouth doesn't want is left for the crows.

The Robertson brothers, John and William, Scottish merchants, go around these lands with sacks that look like sausages, stuffed with gold coins. From an estancia in Curuzú-Cuatiá they send ten thousand hides to the town of Goya, in sixty carts.

The enormous wooden wheels creak as they turn, and goads urge the oxen on. The carts cut through the countryside. They climb hills, cross swamps and swollen rivers. At nightfall the encircled carts form a hearth. While the gauchos smoke and drink maté, the air thickens with the aroma of meat browning on the embers. After the roast, yarns are exchanged and guitars heard.

From the town of Goya, the hides will travel on to the port of Buenos Aires and cross the ocean to the tanneries of Liverpool. The price will have multiplied many times when the hides return to the River Plata, converted into boots, shoes, and whips of British manufacture.

(283)

1815: Buenos Aires

The Bluebloods Seek a King in Europe

The goose-quill pen writes: *José Artigas, traitor to his country*.

In vain they have offered him gold and glory. Shopkeepers expert in yard-measures and precise balances, the patricians of Buenos Aires calculate the price of Artigas dead or alive. They are ready to pay six thousand duros for the head of the leader of the rebel camps.

To exorcise these lands of the gaucho devil, Carlos de Alvear offers them to the English: *These provinces,* Alvear writes to Lord Castlereagh, *want to belong to Great Britain without any conditions.* And he implores Lord Strangford: *The British Nation cannot abandon to their fate the inhabitants of the River Plata in the very act of throwing themselves into its generous arms . . .*

Manuel de Sarratea journeys to London in search of a monarch to crown in Buenos Aires. The interior, republican and federal, threatens the privileges of the port, and panic prevails over any oath of allegiance. In Madrid, Manuel Belgrano and Bernardino Rivadavia, who had been ardent republicans, offer the throne to the Infante Francisco de Paula, brother of Ferdinand VII. The port city's emissaries promise hereditary power embracing all the River Plata region, Chile, and even Peru. The new independent kingdom would have a blue and white flag; freedom and property would be sacred and the court would be formed by distinguished Creoles promoted into dukes, counts, and marquesses.

Nobody accepts.

(2 and 278)

1815: Purification Camp

Artigas

Here, where the river gets mad and boils up in eddies and whirlpools, on a purple tableland surrounded by hollows and canyons, General Artigas governs. These thousand hearths of poor Creoles, these huts of mud and straw and leather windows, are the capital of the confederation of peoples of the River Plata interior. In front of the government shack, horses await the messengers who gallop back and forth bringing advice and taking decrees. No trimmings or medals adorn the uniform of the leader of the south.

Artigas, son of the prairie, had been a smuggler and a hunter of smugglers. He knew the meanderings of every river, the secrets of every hill, the savor of the grass of each field; and even more deeply, the diffident souls of the cowboys who only have their lives to give and give them fighting in a hallucinating whirlwind of spears.

The banners of Artigas fly over the region watered by the Uruguay and Paraná rivers, which extends to the sierras of Córdoba. Sharing this immense space are the provinces that refuse to be a colony of Buenos Aires after winning their liberation from Spain.

The port of Buenos Aires lives with its back to the land that it despises and fears. Glued to their lookout windows, the merchants await ships that bring novelties of dress, speech, and thought, but no king.

Against the avalanche of European merchandise, Artigas wants to build dikes to defend *our arts and factories*—with free passage only for machines, books, and medicines; and he diverts to the port of Montevideo the provincial trade over which Buenos Aires had long assumed a monopoly. The Artiguista federal league wants no king, but assemblies and congresses of citizens; and to top off the scandal, the leader decrees agrarian reform.

(277 and 278)

1816: East Bank Ranges

Agrarian Reform

In Buenos Aires they are crying bloody murder. East of the Uruguay River, Artigas expropriates the lands of the Belgrano and Mitre families, of the family of San Martín's father-in-law, of Bernardino Rivadavia, of Azcuénaga and Almagro and Díaz Vélez. In Montevideo they call the agrarian reform a *criminal project*. Artigas has jailed Lucas Obes, Juan María Pérez and other artists of the minuet and legerdemain.

For the owners of land, devourers of acreage eaten by grace of king, fraud, or plunder, the gaucho is cannon fodder or estancia serf—and anyone denying it should be put in the stocks or up against a wall.

Artigas wants every gaucho to own a piece of land. Poor folk invade the estancias. In the eastern ranges devastated by war, huts and tilled plots and corrals begin to sprout. The trampled peasantry starts to trample. The men who put their lives on the line in the war of independence refuse to accept further abandonment. For the Montevideo town council, Encarnación Benítez, Artigas's soldier who gallops about dividing land and cattle at the head of *a troop of villains*, is an *outlaw, pervert, vagrant, and agitator*. In the shade of his spear poor people find refuge; but this brown man, illiterate, courageous, perhaps fierce, will never be a statue, nor will any avenue or street or byroad ever bear his name.

(335)

1816: Chicote Hill

The Art of War

On Chicote Hill the royalist infantry have surrounded a handful of patriots of Upper Peru.

"I don't give myself up to the enemy!" yells the soldier Pedro Loayza, and throws himself over the precipice.

"We'll die for the fatherland!" proclaims commandant Eusebio Lira, as he too runs for the precipice.

"We'll die if we're idiots," drum major José Santos Vargas says abruptly, cutting him off.

"Let's set fire to the dry grass," proposes sergeant Julián Reinaga.

The tall grass blazes up and the wind fans the flames toward the enemy ranks. The fire thrusts forward in waves. Confused and terrified, the besiegers flee, throwing rifles and cartridge belts to the winds and imploring the Almighty for pity.

(347)

1816: Tarabuco

Juana Azurduy,

well versed in catechisms, born to be a nun in the Chuquisaca convent, is a lieutenant colonel in the guerrilla armies of independence. Of her four children the only survivor is the one who was born in the heat of battle, amid the thunder of horses and guns. The head of her husband is stuck high up on a Spanish pike.

Juana rides in the mountains in front of her men. Her sky-blue shawl flutters in the wind. One fist clutches the reins; the other severs necks with a sword.

Everything she eats is turned into bravery. The Indians do not call her Juana. They call her Pachamama; they call her Mother Earth.

(126)

1816: Port-au-Prince

Pétion

Haiti lies in ruins, blockaded by the French and isolated by everyone else. No country has recognized the independence of the slaves who defeated Napoleon.

The island is divided in two.

In the north, Henri Christophe has proclaimed himself emperor. In the castle of Sans-Souci, the new black nobility dance the minuet— the Duke of Marmalade, the Count of Lemonade—while black lackeys in snowy wigs bow and scrape, and black hussars parade their plumed bonnets through gardens copied from Versailles.

To the south, Alexandre Pétion presides over the republic. Distributing lands among the former slaves, Pétion aims to create a nation of peasants, very poor but free and armed, on the ashes of plantations destroyed by the war.

On Haiti's southern coast Simón Bolívar lands, in search of refuge and aid. He comes from Jamaica, where he has sold everything down to his watch. No one believes in his cause. His brilliant military campaigns have been no more than a mirage. Francisco Miranda is dying in chains in the Cadiz arsenal, and the Spaniards have reconquered Venezuela and Colombia, which prefer the past or still do not believe in the future promised by the patriots.

Pétion receives Bolívar as soon as he arrives, on New Year's Day. He gives him seven ships, two hundred and fifty men, muskets, powder, provisions, and money. He makes only one condition. Pétion, born a slave, son of a black woman and a Frenchman, demands of Bolívar the freedom of slaves in the lands he is going to liberate.

Bolívar shakes his hand. The war will change its course. Perhaps America will too.

(115, 116, and 202)

1816: Mexico City

El Periquillo Sarniento

The first Latin American novel is born in a printery on Zuleta Street. In three volumes, José Joaquín Fernández de Lizardi relates the misfortunes of *El Periquillo Sarniento*; readers devour and celebrate it. The viceroy bans the fourth volume when it is about to appear, but there is no way to jail the character.

El Periquillo, that American offspring of the Spanish picaresque, has won the streets of Mexico. He goes everywhere, stripping customs naked. He jumps from the cardsharp's table to the notary's office, and from the barber's chair to the prison floor. Many do not enjoy his adventures. The priest drowns him in edifying sermons. Lizardi, enlightened moralist, turns every game into a moral.

(9, 111, and 303)

1817: Santiago de Chile
The Devil at Work

Elegant youths smoke cigarettes in gold holders so as not to stain their fingers, but Santiago de Chile is bounded on all four sides by garbage. To the north, the houses look out on the Mapocho River garbage dump. To the south, trash piles up in the ravine. The sun rises on mountains of rubbish on Santa Lucía hill and its last rays light up the dumps in the San Miguel and San Pablo suburbs.

From one of these dumps sprouted the visitor who crossed the city last night, a sulphurous salvo that made the little tallow candles quiver in the street lamps, and that curiously or threateningly nosed around the Compañía temple until the night watchman's voice intoned eleven o'clock:

"Hail Mary full of gra-a-ace!"

The Devil fled hell-for-leather.

The shoe he lost is touring Santiago, house to house. A monk carries it, covered by a napkin, on a silver tray. Pious ladies cross themselves.

(256)

1817: Santiago de Chile
Manuel Rodríguez

Whoever talks of American emancipation signs his own death warrant. Whoever gets a letter from Mendoza marches to the gallows or the firing squad. The Vigilance Tribunal gives free rein to informers in Santiago de Chile.

Between Mendoza and Santiago, patriots are reorganizing the army ground to pieces by the Spaniards. Winds of resistance come and go, crossing the splendor of the cordillera's snow, without leaving a trace.

The messenger passes an order at the cockfights in Santiago, and another at a smart soiree, and at the same time picks up a report between two horseraces in the suburbs. The messenger announces himself at a big house—three taps of the doorknocker—and at the same time emerges in the mountains on the back of a mule, and gallops over prairies on horseback. The guerrilla makes an assault on Melipilla, but he is also crossing the town of San Fernando. Striking in Rancagua, the guerrilla dismounts in Pomaire and drinks a glass of wine.

The Spanish governor has put a price on the head of Manuel Rodríguez, the messenger, the guerrilla. But his head travels hidden beneath the monk's hood, the muleteer's sombrero, the street peddler's basket, or the fine gentleman's plush topper. No one can catch him because he flies without moving and goes out inward and comes in outward.

(106)

1817: Montevideo
Images for an Epic

An enormous army comes from Rio de Janeiro, by land and sea, with the mission of wiping out José Artigas, of obliterating even the shadow of a memory of his contagious example. With fire and sword, the Brazilians invade, announcing that they will clear the bandits off these plains. General Lecor promises to restore the damaged rights of property and heredity.

Lecor enters Montevideo beneath a canopy. Father Larrañaga and Francisco Javier de Viana offer the keys of the city to the redeemers of the great estates. Ladies throw flowers and little blue bows in the path of this phenomenal parade of braid, decorations, and plumes. Bored tolling for funerals, the cathedral bells ring out. Censers swing to and fro, and so do businessmen; their bowings and scrapings never end.

(195, 278, and 335)

1817: Quito

Manuela Sáenz

Quito was born between volcanoes, high, far from the sea; and between the cathedral and the palace, in the central plaza, was born Manuela. She arrived in Quito on a satin bed, on sheets from Brussels, daughter of a secret love affair of Don Simón Sáenz, killer of the Creoles who rose in rebellion here.

At fifteen, Manuela wore men's clothes, smoked, and broke in horses. She did not ride side-saddle like the ladies, but with open legs, and scorning harness. Her best friend was her black slave Jonatás, who meowed like a cat, sang like a bird, and when she walked undulated like a snake. Manuela was sixteen when they shut her up in one of this prayerful and sinful city's many convents, where monks help old nuns to die a good death and young ones to live a good life. In the Santa Catalina convent Manuela learned to embroider, to play the clavichord, to feign virtue, and to faint, rolling back her eyes. At seventeen, crazy about uniforms, she eloped with Fausto D'Elhuyar, an officer of the king.

At twenty, she sparkles. All the men want to be the oyster of this pearl. They marry her to James Thorne, a respectable English doctor. The party lasts a whole week.

(295)

1818: Colonia Camp

The War of the Underdogs

By now, Artigas's army is nothing but naked people. Those who own no more property than a horse, as well as the blacks and the Indians, know that in this war everyone's destiny is at stake. From fields and rivers groups of mounted rebels attack the well-armed Brazilians with spear and knife; and like birds they vanish in a flash.

While bugles call out slaughter in this invaded land, the Buenos Aires government spreads propaganda directed toward *those who have goods to lose*. A leaflet signed by "The Friend of Order" calls Artigas a *malevolent genie, apostle of the lie, ravenous wolf, scourge of his country, new Attila, disgrace of the century and affront to the human race.*

Someone brings the leaflets to the camp. Artigas does not take his eyes off the fire: *"My people don't know how to read,"* he says.

(277)

1818: Corrientes

Andresito

"Their rights come first," Artigas has said of the Indians; and they have suffered much death for being loyal to him.

Andrés Guacurarí, Andresito, Guaraní Indian, adopted son of Artigas, is the chief. He invaded Corrientes, a flood of men, a couple of months ago, arrows against rifles, and pulverized the allies of Buenos Aires.

Naked save for mud from the march and a rag or two, Andresito's Indians entered the city. They brought along a few Indian children whom the Corrientes people had held as slaves. They met with silence and closed shutters. The commander of the garrison buried his fortune in his garden and the notary died of fright.

The Indians had not eaten for some time, but they took nothing and asked for nothing. As soon as they arrived they put on a theater show in homage to the principal families. Huge wings of silver paper spread on cane frames turned the Indians into guardian angels. For no one, because no one came, they staged "The Temptation of Saint Ignatius," an old pantomime of the Jesuit period.

"So they don't want to come to Indian parties?" Andresito lit a big cigar, smoke emerging from his ears and eyes.

At dawn, drums beat to arms. At spear point Corrientes's most respectable gentlemen are forced to cut the grass on the plaza and to sweep the streets till they are transparent. All day long the gentlemen are kept at this noble task and that night, in the theater, they deafen the Indians with applause.

Andresito governs Corrientes until Artigas sends for him.

The Indians are moving off down the road. They wear those enormous silver wings. Toward the horizon ride the angels. The sun makes them shine and gives them the shadows of eagles in flight.

(283)

1818: Paraná River

The Patriot Pirates

Andresito's forces move down to Santa Fe, skirting the river. On the Paraná a flotilla of patriot pirates accompanies the Indians.

Canoes, launches, and a few well-armed brigantines make life impossible for the merchant ships of Brazil. Artigas's tricolor sails on the rivers and the sea, everywhere, fighting. The pirates strip enemy ships in sudden boardings and take the fruits of their raids to the far Antilles.

Pedro Campbell is the admiral of this squadron of ships and small boats. He arrived here with the English invaders years ago, deserted, and took to galloping over the prairies. The Irish gaucho with hooped earrings and a fierce expression peering from beneath a mop of red hair soon becomes famous. When Artigas makes him chief of the pirates Campbell has already been slashed in Creole duels and credited with deaths but no treachery. Everyone knows that his silver knife is a snake that never bites in the back.

(277 and 283)

1818: San Fernando de Apure

War to the Death

At the head of an army pulverized by defeats rides Bolívar. A pilgrim's hood shades his face; in the shadow, gleam eyes that devour as they look, and a melancholy smile.

Bolívar rides the horse of the late Rafael López. The saddle bears the silver initials of the dead man, a Spanish officer who took a shot at Bolívar while the patriot chief slept in a hammock.

The northern offensive has failed.

In San Fernando de Apure Bolívar reviews what remains of his forces.

"He's crazy," think or murmur his barefoot, exhausted, injured soldiers as he announces that they will soon carry this sacred war, war to the death, into Colombia and Peru and to the peak of Potosí.

(53 and 116)

1819: Angostura

Abecedarium: The Constituent Assembly

Beneath the awning, on a ship sailing the Orinoco, Bolívar dictates to his secretaries his projected Constitution. He listens, corrects, and dictates it again in camp, while smoke from the fire defends him against mosquitos. Other ships bring deputies from Caracas, Barcelona, Cumaná, Barinas, Guyana, and Margarita Island. Suddenly, the winds of war have changed, perhaps in homage to Bolívar's obstinacy, and in a flash half of Venezuela has fallen into the patriots' hands.

The delegates to the congress disembark at the port of Angostura, town of little houses drawn by a child. On a toy press is printed here, week after week, *El Correo del Orinoco*. From the jungle this organ of republican thought spreads the articles of Creole doctors and announcements of the arrival of beer, penknives, harnesses, and volunteer soldiers from London.

Three salvos salute Bolívar and his general staff. The birds take off, but a macaw swaggers indifferently with tough-guy strides.

The deputies mount the stone stairway.

Francisco Antonio Zea, major of Angostura, opens the session. His speech compares this patriot township with Memphis, Thebes, Alexandria, and Rome. The congress confirms Bolívar as head of the army and president with full powers. The cabinet is named.

Afterwards Bolívar takes the rostrum. *Ignorant people*, he warns, *confuse reality with imagination and justice with vengeance* . . . He expounds his ideas on the need to create Grand Colombia and lays the foundation of his projected Constitution, drawn up on the basis of the Englishmen's Magna Carta.

(202)

1820: Boquerón Pass

Finale

The three great southern ports, Rio de Janeiro, Buenos Aires, and Montevideo, could not prevail against the rural hosts of José Artigas, chief of the interior. But death has had better luck and taken most of his people. In the bellies of birds of prey lie half the men of the eastern campaign. Andresito lies dying in jail. Lavalleja and Campbell and others are prisoners; and a few have succumbed to treachery. Fructuoso Rivera calls Artigas a *criminal* and accuses him of having put *property at the mercy of despotism and anarchy.* Francisco Ramírez of Entre Ríos proclaims that *Artigas is the cause and origin of all the evils of South America,* and Estanislao López in Santa Fe does a somersault as well.

Landowner chiefs make common cause with port merchants, as the leader of the revolution goes from disaster to disaster. The last of his Indians and blacks still follow him, as do a handful of ragged gauchos under the command of Andrés Latorre, last of his officers.

On the banks of the Paraná, Artigas chooses the best horseman. He gives him four thousand silver coins, all that remain, to take to the prisoners in Brazil.

Then he sticks his spear in the bank and crosses the river. Ruefully he marches off to Paraguay, into exile, this man who didn't want America's independence to be a trap for her poorest children.

(277)

You

Without turning your head, you bury yourself in exile. I see you, I am watching you: the Paraná slips by with the sluggishness of a lizard, and over there your flaming torn poncho fades into the distance at a horse's trot and is lost in the foliage.

You don't say goodbye to your land. She would not believe you. Or perhaps you still don't know that you're leaving for good.

The countryside turns gray. You are going, defeated, and your land is left breathless. The children to be born of her, the lovers who come to her, will they give her back her breath? Those who emerge from that land, those who enter it, will they prove themselves worthy of such deep sadness?

Your land. Our land of the south. You will be very necessary to her, Don José. Every time the greedy hurt her and humiliate her, every time that fools believe her dumb or sterile, she will miss you. Because you, Don José Artigas, general of plain folk, are the best word she has spoken.

1821: Camp Laurelty
Saint Balthazar, Black King, Greatest Sage

From nearby towns and distant regions, Paraguayans flock to see these strange beings with skin like night.

Blacks are not known in Paraguay. The slaves Artigas has freed, who have followed his tracks into exile, make a town in Laurelty. With them is Balthazar, the black king chosen to welcome God on earth. Invoking Saint Balthazar, they work the gardens, and for him resound drums and war chants brought from Africa to the River Plata plains. Artigas's companions, the "Artigas-cué," put on red silk capes and crowns of flowers when January Sixth comes around; and, dancing, they ask the sage-king that slavery may never return, and that he give them protection against bad spirits who soften heads, and hens that crow like cocks.

(66)

1821: Carabobo

Páez

At fifteen he was born killing. He killed to defend himself; had to flee to the mountains, and became a nomad horseman on the immense prairies of Venezuela. Horseman leader of horsemen: José Antonio Páez, Páez of the plains, flies at the head of the cowpoke artists of spear and lasso, who ride bareback and charge like an avalanche. He rides a white horse, because white horses ride better. When he is not on a campaign, he learns to read and to play the cello.

The half-naked plainsmen, who in the times of Boves had served Spain, defeat Spain at the battle of Carabobo. With machetes they fight their way through the impossible brushland of the west, its marshes and thickets, take the enemy by surprise, chew him up.

Bolívar names Páez commander-in-chief of the Venezuelan armed forces. The plainsman enters Caracas by his side wearing, like him, a garland of flowers.

In Venezuela, the die is cast.

(202)

1822: Guayaquil

San Martín

Appointment in Guayaquil. Between the Caribbean Sea and the Pacific Ocean, an avenue of triumphal arches. General Bolívar appears from the north. From the south comes José de San Martín, the general who crossed the Andes cordillera in search of freedom for Chile and Peru.

Bolívar talks and talks, offers and offers.

San Martín laconically cuts him short. *"I am weary."* Bolívar does not believe him; or perhaps is mistrustful because he still does not know that glory also tires one out.

San Martín has spent thirty years in battle, from Oran to Maipú. As a soldier he fought for Spain, as a hardened general for America. For America, and never against her: when the Buenos Aires government sent him to smash the federal hosts of Artigas, San Martín disobeyed and took his army into the mountains to continue his campaign for the independence of Chile. Buenos Aires, which does not forgive, now denies him bread and salt. In Lima they don't like him either. They call him *King José*.

Disappointment in Guayaquil. San Martín, great chess player, evades the game.

"I am weary of commanding," he says, but Bolívar hears other words: *You and I. Together, we don't fit.*

Later there is a banquet and ball. Bolívar dances in the center of the room, the ladies competing for him. The noise makes San Martín dizzy. After midnight, without saying goodbye, he leaves for the docks. The baggage is already aboard the brigantine.

He gives the order to sail. He walks the deck, with slow steps, accompanied by his dog and pursued by mosquitos. The ship heads away from the coast and San Martín turns to contemplate the land of America which fades and fades.

(53 and 54)

1822: Buenos Aires

Songbird

At the edge of the village of Morón, a common grave swallows the bones of a poet who until yesterday had a guitar and a name.

> *It's better to travel light,*
> *like an eagle and without sorrows . . .*

Bartolomé Hidalgo, troubadour of Artigas's camps, lived only for a moment, always in a whirlwind of songs and battles, and has died in exile. The dogs of hunger chewed up his lungs. Through the streets and squares of Buenos Aires wandered Hidalgo, hawking his couplets which sing to free men and strip enemies bare. They afforded him little food but much life. His unshrouded body ends up in the earth; the couplets, also naked, also plebeian, abide in the winds.

(125)

1822: Rio de Janeiro
Traffic Gone Mad

The *Diario do Rio de Janeiro* announces novelties just arrived from London: machines to repair streets or heal lungs or squeeze manioc; lathes and stills and steam cookers; eyeglasses, telescopes, razors, combs. Also padded saddles, silver stirrups, shiny harnesses and carriage lanterns.

Still seen in the streets are lone horsemen and a few old gilded palanquins from another age; but fashion dictates late-model English carriages that draw sparks from the cobblestones. The streets of Rio de Janeiro are dangerous. Speeding accidents multiply, and the power of the coachman grows.

White gloves, top hats: from high on their perches the coachmen let fall bullying glances on other black slaves, and enjoy sowing panic among pedestrians. They are famous drunkards and pimps and good guitar players; and they are indispensable in modern life. A carriage is worth a fortune when it is sold with a fast horse and a skillful black.

(119)

1822: Quito
Twelve Nymphs Stand Guard
in the Main Plaza

and each one holds up a crown. Bands and fireworks explode and the tapping of horses' hooves on the long stone street sounds like the onset of rain. At the head of his army Bolívar enters Quito: a skinny gladiator, all nerve, his golden sword longer than his body. From the balconies rain down flowers and little embroidered kerchiefs. The balconies are altars upon which the ladies of Quito permit the erectness of their almost bare breasts to be worshipped amid lace and mantillas. Manuela Sáenz stands out like a dazzling ship's figurehead. She drops a hand, and from the hand falls a crown of laurel. Bolívar raises his head and fastens his glance on her, a spear in slow motion.

That night, they dance. They waltz until they are giddy, and the world spins round and round to the rustle of that peerless woman's thousand petticoats and the sweep of her long black hair.

(202, 249, and 295)

1823: Lima

Swollen Hands from So Much Applauding

He rides from El Callao, between two files of soldiers, on a road of flowers. Lima receives General Bolívar with a hundred-gun salute, a hundred flags, a hundred speeches and hundred-cover banquets.

The Congress grants him full powers to throw out the Spaniards, who have retaken half of Peru. The Marquess of Torre Tagle presents him with a biography of Napoleon, a set of Toledo blades and bouquets of florid phrases: *Victory awaits you on the icy peaks of the Andes to crown you with her laurels and the nymphs of the Rimac are already chanting hymns to celebrate your triumphs!* The War Minister gives orders to the goddess Fortune: *Take thy majestic flight from the foothills of Chimborazo to the peaks of our Andes and there await immortal Bolívar to crown his brow with the laurels of Peru!*

The Rimac, *the river that talks*, is the only one that keeps quiet.

(53 and 202)

1824: Lima

In Spite of Everything

He rides from El Callao, between two files of soldiers, on a road of flowers. Lima receives the chief of the Spaniards, General Monet, hoisting and cheering the king's flag. The flag flutters and speeches flutter. The Marquess of Torre Tagle melts with gratitude and implores Spain to save Peru from the menace of the accursed Bolívar, *the Colombian monster*.

Lima prefers to continue sleeping, amid rippling heraldry, the slumber of a colonial arcadia. Viceroys, saints and cavaliers, crooks and coquettes exchange sighings and bowings amid the sandy wastes of America, beneath a sky that denies rain and sun but sends angels to defend the city walls. Inside them, one breathes the aroma of jasmine; outside, solitude and danger lie in wait. Inside, hand-kissings and processions and courtings: every officer imitates the king and every monk the pope. In the palaces, stucco imitates marble; in the seventy churches of gold and silver, ritual imitates faith.

Far from Lima, Bolívar lies sick in the coast town of Pativilca. *On all sides*, he writes between fevers, *I hear the sound of disaster . . . Everything is born into life and dies before my eyes, as if split by a bolt of lightning . . . Dust, ashes, nothing.* All Peru, save for a few valleys, has fallen back into the hands of Spain. The independent governments of Buenos Aires and Chile have abandoned the cause of the freedom of this land; and not even the Peruvians themselves seem very interested.

"And now, what do you plan to do?" someone asks this battered and lonely man.

"Triumph," says Bolívar.

(53, 202, and 302)

1824: Montevideo

City Chronicles from a Barber's Chair

No breeze tinkles the tin washbasin that hangs from a wire over a hole in the door to announce that here they shave beards, pull teeth, and apply suction cups.

Out of sheer habit, or to shake off the languors of summer, the Andalusian barber makes speeches or sings while he finishes covering a customer's face with foam. Between phrases and fandangos, the razor whispers. One of the barber's eyes watches the blade, which plows through the meringue; the other watches the Montevideans who plod along the dusty street. The tongue is sharper than the razor, and no one escapes its fleecing. The customer, prisoner as long as the shave lasts, dumb, immobile, listens to this chattering chronicle of customs and events and from time to time tries to follow, from the corner of an eye, the victims passing by.

A yoke of oxen hauling a dead woman to the cemetery. Behind the cart, a monk telling his beads. The sound of a bell bidding a routine farewell to the third-class deceased reaches into the shop. The razor pauses in the air. The barber crosses himself and from his mouth come words pronounced with a change of tone: "Poor little thing. She was never happy."

The corpse of Rosalía Villagrán is crossing the city occupied by Artigas's enemies. For a long time she had believed she was someone else, and believed she was living in another time and another world, and in the charity hospital she kissed the walls and talked to the pigeons. Rosalía Villagrán, Artigas's wife, has entered the gates of death without a cent to pay for her coffin.

(315)

1824: Plain of Junín
The Silent Battle

Bolívar reorganizes his army, magic of his stubborn courage, and triumphs on the Peruvian plain of Junín. The world's best horsemen charge with sword and spear and wreak havoc. Not a shot is heard in the whole battle.

The American army is a mix of gauchos from the River Plata shores; Chilean peasants and plainsmen from Grand Colombia, who fight with reins tied to their knees; Peruvian and Ecuadoran patriots, heroes of San Lorenzo and Maipú, Carabobo, and Pichincha. The men have spears from Guayaquil and ponchos from Cajamarca; the horses, saddles from Lambayeque and shoes from Trujillo. Also following Bolívar are Englishmen, Germans, Frenchmen, and even Spaniards won over by the New World, European veterans of distant wars on the Guadiana or the Rhine or the Seine.

As the sun dies, the lives of the wounded are snuffed out. Dying in Bolívar's tent is Lieutenant Colonel Sowersby, an Englishman who was with Napoleon at Borodino; and not far away a little dog howls beside the body of a Spanish officer. That dog kept running at the side of his friend's horse throughout the entire battle of Junín. Now General Miller tries to catch it or chase it off, but there is no way.

(202)

1825: La Paz
Bolivia

The imperial standard falls in surrender at the feet of Antonio José de Sucre, general at twenty-three, grand marshal at thirty, Bolívar's favorite officer. The thunderous battle of the Ayacucho pampa finishes off Spanish power not just in Peru but on the whole continent.

When the news reaches Lima, Bolívar leaps onto the dining room table and dances, stepping on plates and breaking glasses and bottles.

Later Bolívar and Sucre ride together beneath the triumphal arches of the city of La Paz. There, a country is born. Upper Peru, which had been absorbed into the viceroyalties of Lima and Buenos Aires, now calls itself the Bolívar Republic, and will be called Bolivia, so that its sons may perpetuate the name of their liberator.

José Mariano Ruyloba, a monk with a great gift for oratory, a mouth full of gold, has prepared a splendid welcoming speech; but fate decrees that Ruyloba shall die before Bolívar can hear it. The speech is composed in Greek.

(202)

1825: Potosí
Abecedarium: The Hero at the Peak

In Potosí, Bolívar climbs to the peak of the silver mountain. Bolívar speaks, History will speak: *This mountain whose bosom is the wonder and envy of the world* . . . The wind seizes the flags of the new fatherlands and the bells of all the churches. *I think nothing of this opulence when I compare it* . . . Bolívar's arms embrace a thousand leagues. The valleys multiply the salvos of the guns and the echo of the words . . . *with the glory of having brought to victory the standard of liberty from the burning and distant beaches* . . . History will speak of the great man up on the heights. It will say nothing of the thousand wrinkles lining the face of this man, still unworn by years but deeply furrowed by loves and sorrows. History will not be concerned with the galloping colts in his breast when, from the skies of Potosí, he embraces the land as if it were a woman. The land as if it were *that* woman: the one who sharpens his swords; and strips him and forgives him with a glance. The one who knows how to listen to him beneath the thunder of guns and the speeches and ovations, when he says: *You will be alone, Manuela. And I will be alone, in the middle of the world. There will be no more consolation than the glory of having conquered ourselves.*

(53, 202, and 238)

1825: Potosí

England Is Owed a Potosí

The Spanish colonies that are born to independent life walk bent over. From the first day they drag a heavy stone hung from the neck, a stone that grows and overwhelms. The *English debt*, born of Britain's support in arms and soldiers, is multiplied by the grace of usurers and merchants. The moneylenders and their intermediaries, versed in the arts of alchemy, turn any old cobblestone into a golden jewel; and British traders find in these lands their most lucrative markets. The new countries, fearful of Spanish reconquest, need official recognition by England; but England recognizes no one without first signing a Treaty of Friendship and Commerce which assures freedom of invasion for its industrial merchandise.

I abhor the debts more than the Spaniards, writes Bolívar to the Colombian general Santander, and tells him that to pay those debts he has sold the Potosí mines to the English for two and a half million pesos. Furthermore, he writes, *I have indicated to the government of Peru that it should sell to England all of its mines, all of its lands and properties and all the other holdings of the government, for its national debt, which is not less than twenty million*.

The Rich Mountain of Potosí, down in the world, now belongs to a London firm, the phantom Potosí, La Paz, and Peruvian Mining Association. As happens with other delusions born of speculative fevers, the name is longer than the capital: the firm claims a million pounds sterling, but actually has fifty thousand.

(40, 172, and 134)

The Curse of the Silver Mountain

Potosí, which has yielded so much silver, is yielding little. The mountain does not want to.

For more than two centuries, Potosí heard Indians groaning in her entrails. The Indians, condemned to the tunnels, implored her to exhaust her seams. And finally the mountain cursed greed.

Since then, mysterious mule caravans have been arriving by night, diving into the mountain and secretly carrying off loads of silver. No one can see them, no one can catch them; but somehow the mountain keeps emptying herself night by night.

When a mule breaks a leg because the ore makes too heavy a load, the dawn rises upon a beetle limping painfully down the road.

(247)

1826: Chuquisaca
Bolívar and the Indians

The laws in Spain's American colonies were never obeyed. Good or bad, the laws never existed in reality—neither the many royal warrants which protected the Indians (and which confessed their own impotence through repetition), nor the ordinances that banned the circulation of Jews and novels. This tradition does not keep eminent Creoles, generals, or doctors, from believing that the Constitution is an infallible potion for public happiness.

Simón Bolívar weaves constitutions with fervor. Now he presents to the Congress a constitutional project for the new republic bearing his name. According to the text, Bolivia will have a president-for-life and three legislative chambers—tribunes, senators, and censors—*which have some resemblance*, says Bolívar, *to the Areopagus of Athens and the censors of Rome.*

People who cannot read will not have the right to vote; and since almost all Bolivians speak Quechua or Aymara, know nothing of the Castilian language, and cannot read, only a handful of select males will have that right. As in Colombia and Peru, Bolívar has decreed in the new country the abolition of native tribute and of forced labor for Indians; and has arranged to divide communal lands into private plots. And, so that the Indians, the country's immense majority, may receive the European light of Civilization, Bolívar has brought to Chuquisaca his old teacher, Simón Rodríguez, with orders to establish schools.

(42 and 172)

1826: Chuquisaca
Cursed Be the Creative Imagination

Simón Rodríguez, Bolívar's teacher, has returned to America. For a quarter of a century Simón was on the other side of the sea. There, he was a friend of the socialists of Paris, London, and Geneva; he worked with the printers of Rome, the chemists of Vienna, and even taught elementary lessons in a small town on the Russian steppe.

After the long embrace of welcome, Bolívar names him director of education in the newly founded country. With a model school in Chuquisaca, Simón Rodríguez begins the task of uprooting the lies and fears hallowed by tradition. Pious ladies scream, learned doctors howl, dogs bark at the scandal. Horror: the madman Rodríguez proposes to mix children of high birth with mestizos who until last night slept in the streets. What is he thinking of? Does he want the orphans to take him to heaven? Or does he corrupt them so they'll accompany him to hell? In the classrooms, neither catechism nor sacristy Latin, nor rules of grammar are heard, only a racket of saws and hammers unbearable to the ears of monks and pettifoggers schooled in the repulsiveness of manual work. *A school for whores and thieves!* Those who believe the body is shameful and woman an adornment, cry to high heaven. In Don Simón's school, boys and girls sit jammed side by side; and to top it all, their studying is playing.

The prefect of Chuquisaca heads the campaign *against the satyr who has come to corrupt the morals of youth.* Soon, Marshal Sucre, president of Bolivia, demands Simón Rodríguez's resignation, because he has not presented his accounts with due meticulousness.

(296 and 298)

The Ideas of Simón Rodríguez: Teaching How to Think

The author is considered mad. Let him transmit his ravings to the fathers yet to be born.

Everyone must be educated without distinction of race or color. Let us not deceive ourselves: without popular education, there will be no true society.

Instruction is not education. Teach, and you will have people who know; educate, and you will have people who do.

To order recital from memory of what is not understood, is to make parrots. Do not in any case order a child to do anything that has no "why" at the foot of it. If you accustom the child always to see reason behind the orders he receives, he misses it when he does not see it, and asks for it, saying, "Why?" Teach the children to be inquisitive, so that, asking the reasons for what they are told to do, they learn to obey reason, not authority like limited people, nor custom like stupid people.

Boys and girls should study together in the schools. First, so that in this way men should learn from childhood to respect women; second, so that women should learn not to be afraid of men.

The boys should learn the three principal trades: masonry, carpentry, and smithery, because with earth, wood, and metal the most essential things are made. Instruction and a trade should be given to women, so that they will not prostitute themselves out of necessity, nor make marriage a speculation to assure subsistence.

He who knows nothing can be deceived by anyone. He who has nothing, anyone can buy.

(297)

1826: Buenos Aires

Rivadavia

On the crest of the River Plata ravines, above the muddy bank of the river, lies the port that usurps the wealth of the whole country.

In the Buenos Aires Coliseum the British consul occupies the box of the viceroy of Spain. The Creole patricians use words from France and gloves from England, and thus they slip into the life of independence.

From the Thames flows the torrent of merchandise manufactured, to Argentine specifications, in Yorkshire and Lancashire. In Birmingham they imitate to the last detail the traditional copper boiler that heats water for maté, and they produce exact replicas of the wooden stirrups, bolas, and lassos used in this country. Workshops and textile mills in the provinces have scarcely a chance of resisting the assault. A single ship brings twenty thousand pairs of boots at bargain prices and a Liverpool poncho costs five times less than one from Catamarca.

Argentine banknotes are printed in London and the National Bank, with a majority of British shareholders, monopolizes their emission. Through this bank operates the River Plate Mining Association, which pays Bernardino Rivadavia an annual salary of twelve hundred pounds.

From an armchair that will be sacred, Rivadavia multiplies the public debt and public libraries. Buenos Aires's illustrious jurist,

who goes about in a four-horse carriage, claims to be president of a
country he does not know and despises. Beyond the city walls of
Buenos Aires, that country hates him.

(55, 271, and 342)

1826: Panama

Lonely Countries

The infant said its first words. They were its last. Of those invited to
the baptism, only four reached Panama, and instead of a baptism
there was extreme unction. Grief, father's grief, shrinks the face of
Bolívar. The condolences sound hollow.

Bells ring out for the unity of Hispanic America.

Bolívar had called on the new countries to unite, under British
protection, in one fatherland. He did not invite the United States or
Haiti, because they are foreign to our American ways; but he wanted
Great Britain to integrate the Hispanic American league, to defend
it from the danger of Spanish reconquest.

London has no interest in the unity of its new dominions. The
Congress of Panama has given birth to nothing but edifying decla-
rations, because the old viceroyalties have birthed countries tied to
a new empire overseas, and divorced among themselves. The colonial
economy, mines and plantations producing for abroad, cities that
prefer the bazaar to the factory, opens the way not for a great nation
but for a great archipelago. The independent countries are disinte-
grating while Bolívar dreams of a unified fatherland. They have not
signed a single trade agreement among themselves, but are flooded
with European merchandise and almost all have bought the chief
British export product, the doctrine of free trade.

In London, Prime Minister George Canning exhibits his trophy
before the House of Commons.

(202 and 207)

1826: London

Canning

The pearl of the crown speaks. Plebeian George Canning, chief of
British diplomacy, consecrates his work before the House of Commons. Canning spreads out his arms, his falcon wings: *"I called the*

New World into existence," proclaims the architect of empire, *"to redress the balance of the Old."*

From a corner comes a mocking giggle. A long silence follows. Canning rears up in the darkness his sharp ghost's profile and then the greatest ovation ever heard in this chamber explodes.

England is the axis of the planet. Lord Castlereagh had done much for the imperial project until one evening, overwhelmed, he slit his throat with a razor. Hardly had Castlereagh's successor, Canning, come to power when he announced that the knightly era had been left behind. Military glories should give way to astute diplomacy. Smugglers had done more for England than generals; and the time had come for merchants and bankers to win the real battles for world domination.

The patience of the cat is more effective than the fury of the tiger.

(171 and 280)

1828: Bogotá

Here They Hate Her

Without lowering their voices they call her "outsider" and "Messalina," and in secret they give her worse names. They say that on her account Bolívar goes about loaded with shadows and riddled with wrinkles, and that he is burning up his talents in bed.

Manuela Sáenz has fought with a spear in Ayacucho. The mustachios she tore from an enemy were a talisman of the patriot army. When the troops in Lima mutinied against Bolívar, she disguised herself as a man and went through the barracks with a pistol and a bag of money. Here, in Bogotá, she strolls in the shade of the cherry trees, dressed as a captain and escorted by two black women in hussar uniforms. A few nights ago, at a party, she put against the wall a rag doll labeled *"Death to Francisco de Paula Santander, Traitor,"* and shot it.

Santander has grown in the shadow of Bolívar. During the war years it was Bolívar who named him vice president. Now, Santander would like to assassinate the *king without a crown* at some masked ball or in treacherous ambush.

The night watchman of Bogotá, lamp in hand, says the last word. He is answered by the church bells, which scare the Devil and call all to go home.

Shots ring out, guards fall. The assassins burst up the stairs. Thanks to Manuela, who lies to put them off, Bolívar manages to escape out the window.

(53, 202, and 295)

1828: Bogotá

From Manuela Sáenz's Letter to Her Husband James Thorne

No, no, not again, man, for God's sake! Why do you make me write, breaking my resolution? Look, what good are you doing, only giving me the pain of telling you a thousand times no? Mister, you are excellent, you are inimitable. I will never say anything else about you. But, my friend, leaving you for General Bolívar is something. Leaving another husband without your qualities would be nothing.

. . . I know very well that nothing can unite me to him under the auspices of what you call honor. Do you think me less honorable for having him as my lover and not my husband? Oh, I don't live by the social concerns invented for mutual torture!

Leave me alone, my dear Englishman. Let's do something else. In heaven we'll be married again, but on earth, no . . . There, everything will be English style, because a life of monotony is reserved for your nation (in love, I mean, because in other ways . . . who are cleverer in trade and navies?). They take love without pleasure, conversation without humor, and walks without vigor; they greet with bows and curtsies, get up and sit down with caution, joke without laughing. These are divine formalities; but I, wretched mortal, who laugh at myself, at you, and at these English solemnities, how badly I would do in heaven! . . .

(238)

1829: Corrientes

Bonpland

He discovered America in the course of nine thousand leagues and seventy thousand little plants. When he returned to Paris, he missed America. His nostalgia made it clear to him that he belonged to the same land as the roots and flowers he had collected. That land called him as Europe had never called him; and for it he crossed the ocean again.

He was a professor in Buenos Aires and a laborer in the maté fields of the upper Paraná. There, the soldiers of Gaspar Rodríguez de Francia, Supreme and Lifetime Dictator of Paraguay, came upon him. They beat him with sticks and took him upriver in a canoe.

For nine years he has been imprisoned in Paraguay. Dictator Francia, who rules by terror and mystery, is said to have said it was for spying. Kings, emperors, and presidents intercede for the freedom of the famous sage; but neither mediations nor missions, entreaties nor threats have any effect.

The dictator condemned him on a day of north wind, the wind that turns the soul sour. One day of south wind, he decides to free him. Since Bonpland doesn't want to leave, the dictator expels him.

Bonpland has not been shut up in a cell. He was working lands that yielded cotton, sugarcane, and oranges, and has created a rum distillery, a carpentry shop, and a hospital; he attended the deliveries of women and cows throughout the region and gave out infallible concoctions against rheumatism and fever. Paraguay loved its barefoot prisoner with the oversized shirt, seeker of rare plants, man of bad luck who gave so much good; and now he leaves because soldiers take him out by force.

No sooner does he cross the frontier into Argentine territory than someone steals his horses.

(255)

1829: Asunción, Paraguay

Francia the Supreme

There are no thieves in Paraguay, that is, none above ground, nor beggars. At the call of a drum, not of a bell, the children go to school. Although everyone can read, no print shop or library exists, nor is any book, newspaper, or bulletin received from outside, and the post office has disappeared for lack of use.

Penned in upriver by nature and neighbors, the country lives on guard, waiting for Argentina or Brazil to lash out. So that the Paraguayans should repent of their independence, Buenos Aires has cut off their outlet to the sea, and their ships rot at the wharves; but they persist in their poverty and dignity. Dignity, national solitude: high over the vast acreage, Gaspar Rodríguez de Francia commands and keeps watch. The dictator lives alone, and alone eats the bread and salt of his land in dishes previously sampled by dogs.

All Paraguayans are spies or spied upon. Very early in the morning, while sharpening his razor, Alejandro the barber gives El Supremo the first report of the day on rumors and conspiracies. After nightfall the dictator hunts stars with his telescope; and they too tell him what his enemies are plotting.

(82 and 281)

1829: Rio de Janeiro
The Snowball of External Debt

It has been seven years since Prince Pedro proclaimed himself emperor of Brazil. The country was born into independent life knocking at the doors of English bankers. King Juan, Pedro's father, had stripped the bank bare and taken with him to Lisbon the last grams of gold and silver. The first millions of pounds sterling soon arrived from London. The customs income was mortgaged as a guarantee, and native intermediaries got two percent of every loan.

Now Brazil owes double what it received and the debt rolls on, growing like a snowball. The creditors give the orders; and every Brazilian is born in debt.

In a solemn speech Emperor Pedro reveals that the public treasury is exhausted, *in a miserable state*, and that total ruin threatens the country. However, he announces salvation: the emperor has decided to take *measures which will destroy the cause of the existing calamity at one blow*. And he explains what those radical measures are: they consist of new loans that Brazil expects to receive from the houses of Rothschild and Wilson in London, with stiff but honorable interest.

Meanwhile, the newspapers report that a thousand fiestas are being prepared to celebrate the emperor's wedding to Princess Amelia. The advertisements in the papers offer black slaves for sale or hire, cheeses and pianos newly arrived from Europe, English jackets of fine woolens, and Bordeaux wines. The Hotel do Globo on Quitanda Street seeks a *white, foreign chef who is not a drunkard or a puffer of cigars*, and at 76 Duvidor Street they need *a lady who speaks French to look after a blind person*.

(186 and 275)

1830: Magdalena River

The Boat Goes Down to the Sea

Green land, black land. In the far distance mist shrouds the mountains. The Magdalena is carrying Simón Bolívar downstream.

"No."

In the streets of Lima, the same people who gave him a diamond-studded sword are burning his Constitution. Those who called him "Father of the Country" are burning his effigy in the streets of Bogotá. In Caracas, they officially dub him "enemy of Venezuela." Over in Paris, the defamatory articles about him get stronger; and the friends who know how to praise him do not know how to defend him.

"I cannot."

Was this the history of mankind? This labyrinth, this futile game of shadows? The Venezuelan people curse the wars that have taken half their sons to remote areas and given them nothing for it. Venezuela tears itself loose from Grand Colombia and Ecuador follows suit, while Bolívar lies beneath a dirty canvas in the boat that sails down the Magdalena to the sea.

"I can no more."

Blacks are still slaves in Venezuela, despite the laws. In Colombia and Peru, the laws passed to *civilize* Indians are applied to despoil them. The tribute, the colonial tax that Indians pay for being Indians, has been reimposed in Bolivia.

Was this, was this history? All grandeur ends up dwarfed. On the neck of every promise crawls betrayal. Great men become voracious landlords. The sons of America destroy each other. Sucre, the chosen inheritor, who had saved himself from poison and dagger, falls in the forests on the way to Quito, toppled by a bullet.

"I can no more. Let us go."

Crocodiles and timber interweave in the river. Bolívar, yellow-skinned, no light in his eyes, shivering, delirious, moves down the Magdalena toward the sea, toward death.

(53 and 202)

1830: Maracaibo

The Governor Proclaims:

. . . Bolívar, genius of evil, torch of anarchy, oppressor of his country, has ceased to exist.

(202)

1830: La Guaira

Divide et Impera

The North American consul in La Guaira, J. G. Williamson, prophet and protagonist of the disintegration of Grand Colombia, sent the State Department a well-informed report. A month ahead of the event, he announced the separation of Venezuela and the end of the customs duties that do not suit the United States.

Simón Bolívar dies on December Seventeenth. On another December Seventeenth, eleven years ago, he had founded Grand Colombia, a fusion of Colombia and Venezuela which later also embraced Ecuador and Panama. Grand Colombia has died with him.

The North American consul in Lima, William Tudor, has helped to weave the conspiracy against the American project of Bolívar, *the dangerous madman of Colombia*. Tudor was upset not only by Bolívar's fight against slavery, a bad example for the southern United States, but also and above all by *the excessive aggrandizement* of the America liberated from Spain. With all logic at his command, the consul has said that *England and the United States have common and potent reasons of State* against the development of a new power. The British Admiral Fleming, meanwhile, comes and goes between Valencia and Cartagena encouraging the division.

(207 and 280)

1830: Montevideo

Abecedarium: The Oath of the Constitution

The English government, Lord John Ponsonby had said, *will never consent that only two states, Brazil and Argentina, should be exclusive masters of the east coasts of South America.*

Through London's influence, and under its protection, Uruguay becomes an independent state. The most rebellious province of the River Plata, which has expelled the Brazilians from its soil, breaks off from the old trunk and takes on a life of its own. The port of Buenos Aires is free at last from the nightmare of this unfriendly prairie where Artigas rose in rebellion.

In the Mother church of Montevideo, Father Larrañaga offers a thanksgiving chant to God. Fervor illuminates the face of the priest, as in that other Te Deum he celebrated some years back, from the same pulpit, in homage to the invaders from Brazil.

The Constitution is sworn beneath the City Hall balconies. The ladies, who do not exist in the laws, accompany the juridical consecration of the new country as if it involved them. With one hand they clutch their gigantic hairdos, dangerous on windy days, and with the other hold open against their breasts fans painted with patriotic themes. High starched collars keep the gentlemen from turning their heads. The Magna Carta resounds through the plaza, clause after clause, over a sea of top hats. According to the Constitution of the new republic, there will be no citizenship for the men who offered their bodies against the bullets of Spain, Buenos Aires, and Brazil. Uruguay is not being made for poor gauchos, or Indians, or blacks, who still don't know that a law has freed them. Not permitted to vote or hold public office, says the Constitution, are servants, peons, rank-and-file soldiers, vagrants, drunkards, and illiterates.

At nightfall the Coliseum is packed. It is opening night for *The Happy Deceit; or, The Triumph of Innocence*, by Rossini, the first complete opera sung in this city.

(278)

1830: Montevideo
Fatherland or Grave

The first bard of the Uruguayan Parnassus, Francisco Acuña de Figueroa, began his career with an ode, in eight-line stanzas, to the military glory of Spain. When Artigas's gauchos took Montevideo, he fled to Rio de Janeiro. There, he dedicated his adulatory rhymes to the Portuguese prince and all of his court. Still shouldering his lyre, Don Francisco followed the Brazilian invaders back to Montevideo, and rhapsodized over the occupying troops. Years later, on the day following the ouster of the Brazilians, the muses breathed patriotic decasyllables into Don Francisco's ear, words of laurel to crown the brows of the heroes of independence; and now the reptilian poet writes the national anthem of the newborn country. We Uruguayans will be forever condemned to listen to his verses standing up.

(3)

1832: Santiago de Chile

National Industry

In Chile, too, gentlemen dance and dress in French styles, imitate Byron in knotting their ties, and, at table, obey the dictates of French chefs; à la English they take tea, and à la French they down their wine.

When Vicente Pérez Rosales set up his brandy factory, he bought the best stills in Paris and a great quantity of labels with gilded arabesques and fine lettering that said in English: *Old Champagne Cognac*. On the door of his office he had a big sign painted:

DIRECT

IMPORTATION

The taste would not be too-too, but it was nearly-nearly, and no one got stomach ulcers. The business went like a house on fire. The factory could not keep up with the demand, but Don Vicente came down with an attack of patriotism and decided he could not go on living in a state of treason.

"This good reputation belongs only to Chile."

He threw the European labels in the fire and had another sign put on his door, this time even larger:

NATIONAL

INDUSTRY

The bottles now wear a new dress: labels printed here, which say in Spanish: *Chilean Cognac*.

Not even one can be sold.

(256)

Street Cries in the Santiago
de Chile Market

"Carnations and basil for stocky little girls!"

"WA-A-FER COOKIES!"

"Pretty buttons, one penny the string!"

"Sulphur matche-e-es!"

"Belts, cinches, soft like a glove!"

"Charity, for the love of God!"

"Good beef!"

"A penny for a poor blind man?"

"BROO-OO-OMS! LAST CHANCE FOR BROOMS!"

"Baccy, chewing baccy?"

"M i r a c l e   m e d a l s,   s i n g l e
o r   b y   t h e   b o x!"

"Look at these brandy cakes!"

"Knives f'yer personal security!"

"SHA-A-ARP BLADES!"

"Who'll buy this rope?"

"Get this lovely bread!"

"L i t t l e   b e l l s,   o n l y   o n e
l e f t!"

"WATERMELONS, DEARIE!"

"Get this lovely bread, fresh from a woman's hands!"

"WA-A-ATERMELONS!"

"Get this lovely bread! It's piping hot!"

(288)

1833: Arequipa

Llamas

"*Happy creatures,*" says Flora Tristán.

Flora is travelling through Peru, her father's country, and in the mountains discovers *the only animal man has not been able to debase*.

The gentle llamas are more agile than mules and climb higher. They resist cold, exhaustion, and heavy loads. With no reward they give the mountain Indians transport, milk, meat, and the clean and brilliant wool that covers their bodies. But they never let themselves be tied up or mistreated, nor do they take orders. When they let up their queenly stride, the Indian implores them to get going again. If anyone hits them, insults them, or threatens them, llamas throw themselves on the ground, and, raising their long necks, they turn their eyes heavenward, the most beautiful eyes in Creation, and softly die.

"*Happy creatures,*" says Flora Tristán.

(337)

1833: San Vicente

Aquino

The head of Aquino lies in the executioner's basket.

May he rest in war. The chief of the Indians of El Salvador had raised three thousand spears against the robbers of lands. He got the better of the muskets, which the enemy fired with glowing cigars, and stripped Saint Joseph naked on the high altar of a church. Clad in the cloak of the father of Christ, he proclaimed that Indians would never again be slaves, nor soldiers, nor famished, nor drunk. But more troops arrived, and he had to seek refuge in the mountains.

His lieutenant, named Cascabel, turned him in.

"*Now I am a jaguar without claws or fangs,*" said Aquino, when they loaded him with shackles and chains; and he confessed to Fray Navarro that in all his life he had only been frightened by the anger or tears of his wife.

"*I am ready to play blindman's buff,*" he said, when they put on the blindfold.

(87)

1834: Paris

Tacuabé

On the headlands of the Quequay, General Rivera's cavalry have completed the civilizing operation with good marksmanship. Now, not an Indian remains alive in Uruguay.

The government donates the four last Charrúa Indians to the Natural Sciences Academy in Paris. They are sent over in the hold of a ship, as baggage, among other packages and valises.

The French public pay admission to see the savages, rare specimens of a vanished race. The scientists note their gestures, clothing, and anthropometric measurements. From the shape of their skulls, they deduce their small intelligence and violent character.

Before two months have passed, the Indians let themselves die. Academicians fight over the cadavers. Only the warrior Tacuabé survives, and escapes with his newly born daughter, reaching the city of Lyons—who knows how—disappearing there.

Tacuabé was the one who made music. He made it in the museum after the public left. He would rub a bow with a little saliva-moistened stick and draw sweet vibrations from its horsehair strings. Frenchmen who spied on him from behind the curtains said he produced very soft, muffled, almost inaudible sounds, as if he were talking in secret.

(19)

1834: Mexico City

Loving Is Giving

A calabash filled with vinegar mounts guard behind each door. On every altar a thousand candles pray. Doctors prescribe bloodlettings and chloride fumigations. Colored flags mark houses invaded by the plague. Lugubrious chants and cries indicate the passage of carts full of the dead through streets with nobody on them.

The governor issues a proclamation banning certain foods. According to him, stuffed chilis and fruits have brought cholera to Mexico.

On Holy Ghost Street, a coachman is cutting an enormous chirimoya. He stretches out from his perch to enjoy eating it bit by bit. Someone passing by leaves him with his mouth open.

"Barbarian! Don't you see you're committing suicide? Don't you know that that fruit takes you to the grave?"

The coachman hesitates. He contemplates the milky flesh, undecided whether to bite. Finally he gets up, walks a few steps and offers the chirimoya to his wife, who is sitting at the corner.

"You eat it, my love."

(266)

1835: Galapagos Islands

Darwin

Black hills rise from the sea and mist. On the rocks, as if taking siestas, move turtles as big as cows; and between the crannies slide iguanas, dragons without wings.

"The capital of hell," comments the captain of the *Beagle*.

"Even the trees feel bad," Charles Darwin confirms, as the anchor falls.

In these islands, the Galapagos, Darwin approaches the revelation of the *mystery of mysteries*. Here, he senses the keys to the never-ending transformation of life on earth. He discovers here how chaffinches have perfected their beaks; how the beak that breaks big hard seeds has taken on the form of a nutcracker, and the one that seeks nectar from cactuses that of a pincers. The same has occurred, Darwin discovers, with the shells and necks of turtles, according to whether they eat on ground level or prefer lofty fruits.

In the Galapagos is the origin of all my opinions, Darwin will write. *I go from surprise to surprise*, he writes now, in his travel journal.

When the *Beagle* sailed four years ago from an English port, Darwin still believed every word of the Sacred Writings. He thought God had made the world the way it is now, in six days, and had ended his work, as Archbishop Usher insists, at 9 A.M. on Saturday October 12 of the year 4004 before Christ.

(4 and 88)

1835: Columbia

Texas

Fifteen years ago, a wagon train creaked across the desert prairie of Texas, and the mournful voices of owls and coyotes bid them illcome. Mexico ceded lands to these three hundred families that came from Louisiana with their slaves and plows. Five years ago, there were already twenty thousand North American colonists in Texas, and they had many slaves purchased in Cuba or in the corrals where the gentry of Virginia and Kentucky fatten up little blacks. Now, the colonists hoist their own flag, the image of a bear, and decline to pay taxes to the government of Mexico or to obey Mexican law which has abolished slavery in all the national territory.

The vice president of the United States, John Calhoun, believes that God created blacks to cut wood, pick cotton, and carry water for the chosen people. Textile factories demand more cotton and cotton demands more land and more blacks. *There are powerful reasons*, said Calhoun last year, *for Texas to form part of the United States*. At that time President Jackson, who breathes frontiers with an athlete's lungs, had already sent his friend Sam Houston to Texas.

The rugged Houston forces his way in with his fists, makes himself an army general, and proclaims the independence of Texas. The new state, soon to be another star on the United States flag, has more land than France.

And war breaks out against Mexico.

(128 and 207)

1836: San Jacinto

The Free World Grows

Sam Houston offers land at four cents an acre. Battalions of North American volunteers pour in by every road and weapons arrive by the shipload from New York and New Orleans.

The comet that announced calamity in the skies over Mexico was no news to anybody. Mexico has lived in a perpetual state of calamity since the murderers of Hidalgo and Morelos declared independence in order to grab the country for themselves.

The war does not last long. Mexican General Santa Anna arrives calling for a bloodbath, and makes one at the Alamo, but at San Jacinto loses four hundred men in a quarter of an hour. Santa Anna gives up Texas in exchange for his own life and returns to Mexico City with his beaten army, his personal chef, his seven-thousand-dollar sword, his countless decorations and his wagonload of fighting cocks.

General Houston celebrates his victory by naming himself president of Texas.

Texas's constitution assures the master perpetual rights over his slaves, as legitimately acquired property. *Extend the area of liberty* had been the slogan of the victorious troops.

(128)

1836: *The Alamo*
Portraits of the Frontier Hero

At the outbreak of the Texas war, when fortune still smiles on the Mexican troops, Colonel Davy Crockett falls pierced by bayonets. He falls in the Alamo fort, together with his band of heroic outlaws, and the buzzards finish his story.

The United States, which fattens on the lands of Indians and Mexicans, has lost one of its frontier heroes. Davy Crockett had a rifle named Betsy which could kill five bears with a single bullet.

Crockett could well have been the son of Daniel Boone, the legendary pioneer of the previous century, a very macho and lonely killer, who hated civilization but earned a living by placing colonists on lands robbed from his Indian friends. And he could well have been the father of Natty Bumppo, a fictional character so famous that he now seems flesh and blood.

Since Fenimore Cooper published *The Last of the Mohicans*, Natty Bumppo, the crude and noble hunter, has incorporated himself into the daily life of the United States. Nature has taught him all he knows of morality and his energy comes from the mountains and the woods. He is ugly, only one tooth in his enormous mouth; but without expecting anything in return he protects beautiful white virgins, who, thanks to him, pass invincible through thicket and desire. Natty Bumppo praises silence with many words and tells no lie when he says that he doesn't fear death, or when he admires the Indians while ruefully killing them.

(149 and 218)

1836: Hartford
The Colt

Samuel Colt, engineer, registers in Hartford, Connecticut, the patent of the "revolving pistol" he has invented. It is a pistol with a revolving cylinder of five shots, which kills five times in twenty seconds.

From Texas comes the first order.

(305)

1837: Guatemala City
Morazán

A storm of cassocks explodes. Rafael Carrera is the lightning flash that instills fear, and all over Guatemala roll the thunderclaps: *"Long live religion! Death to the foreigners! Death to Morazán!"*

No candle stays unlit. Nuns pray so fast that in nine seconds they roll off nine novenas. Choirs intone salutations to Mary and curse Morazán with the same fervor.

Francisco Morazán, president of Central America, is the *heretical foreigner* who has unleashed these mystical furies. Morazán, born in Honduras, has not only unified the Central American provinces into one nation, he has also reduced counts and marquesses to the category of mere citizens, and has created public schools that teach things of this world and say nothing of Heaven. According to his laws, a cross is no longer necessary for a grave nor a priest for a wedding, and he makes no distinction between a child born in the conjugal bed and a child made, without previous contract, on the straw of a stable, the one having the same inheritance rights as the other. Gravest of all, Morazán has separated Church and State, decreed freedom to believe or not to believe, suppressed the tithes and first fruits of the Lord's officers and put their lands up for sale.

The monks blame Morazán for the plague that is devastating Guatemala. Cholera is killing people off, and from the pulpits rain fulminating accusations: Morazán has poisoned the water; the Antichrist has pacted with the Devil to sell him the souls of the dead.

The people of the mountains rise against the poisoner. Rafael Carrera, the hog farmer who leads the insurrection, is just over twenty and already has three bullets in his body. He goes about covered with scapularies and medals and with a green bough stuck in his hat.

(220 and 253)

1838: Buenos Aires

Rosas

Great tamer of ponies and people, Juan Manuel de Rosas is the boss of the River Plata ranges. Guitarist and dancer, he tells the stories that provoke the most fear or laughter around the campfire, but he is made of marble and even his children call him "master." He has the cook who ruins his chicken arrested; and he has himself whipped when he carelessly violates one of his own rules.

His estancias are the most prosperous; his meat-salting plants are the best organized. Rosas owns the best of the sea of grasslands that extend from the port of Buenos Aires to the Indian villages.

Rosas governs. He has decreed a customs law that protects Argentinian production of ponchos and mattresses, shoes, carriages, ships, wine and furniture, and he has closed the interior rivers to foreign merchants.

The *Revue des Deux Mondes* demands that France give a lesson in civilization and discipline *to the degenerate sons of the Spanish conquest.* The French squadron, under command of Admiral Leblanc, blockades Buenos Aires, the only Argentine port equipped for overseas commerce.

(166, 271, and 336)

1838: Buenos Aires

The Slaughterhouse

Esteban Echeverría writes the first story of River Plata literature. In *The Slaughterhouse*, the Rosas dictatorship is the harassment of a defenseless Buenos Aires doctor by a knife-wielding mob.

Born in the slums and hardened by street-fights, but polished in Paris, Echeverría despises "the rabble." A slaughterhouse in the south of the city offers a fantastic setting for the writer to describe dogs fighting over entrails with the black women eviscerators, and to tell of the "fuck-you's" bubbling up from vulgar throats as blood flows from the beasts' necks. The throat-cutter of the story wears a gaucho's poncho, has his face daubed with blood, buries his knife up to the handle in a steer's throat, and later corners the elegant black-tied gentleman who has refused him common courtesy.

(104)

More on Cannibalism in America

In his last cavalry charge, Colonel Juan Ramón Estomba hurls his horsemen against nobody. The war against Spain has ended, but much more atrocious is the war of Argentines against Argentines. Colonel Estomba raises his sword and howls: *Charge!* and in a whirlwind of war-cries and sword-thrusts the horses attack the empty horizon.

This torn country is mad with fury. The heroes of independence devour one another. Estanislao López receives the head of Pancho Ramírez, wrapped in a sheep's hide, puts it in an iron cage, and spends a whole night joyfully contemplating it. Gregorio Lamadrid loads the mother of Facundo Quiroga with chains and drags her through the streets, before Facundo falls in an ambush, a bullet in his eye. In a corral, on a carpet of cowshit, Juan Lavalle executes Manuel Dorrego; and ever since, the ghost of Dorrego has been following Lavalle, biting at his heels until one day he catches up to him and sews him with bullets to the nude body of his lover, so that Lavalle may have the pleasure of dying inside a woman.

(55, 103, 110)

1838: Tegucigalpa

Central America Breaks to Pieces

while Morazán fights in Guatemala against the multitude inflamed by the monks.

One after another, the feeble threads that had sewn this country together break. Costa Rica and Nicaragua nullify the federal pact and Honduras, too, declares itself independent. The city of Tegucigalpa celebrates with drums and cymbals and speeches the failure of its son who, ten years ago, launched from here his great unifying campaign. Provincial rancor, envy and greed, old poisons, prove more powerful than the passion of Morazán. The Federal Republic of Central America lies torn into four pieces, soon to be five, and then six. Poor pieces. For each other, they feel more hatred than pity.

(220)

1839: Copán

A Sacred City Is Sold for Fifty Dollars

and the buyer is John Lloyd Stephens, United States ambassador to Central America. It is the Maya city of Copán, in Honduras, invaded by jungle on the bank of a river.

In Copán the gods have turned to stone, and into stone also the men whom the gods chose or chastised. In Copán, more than a thousand years ago, lived the wise astronomers who discovered the secrets of the morning star and measured the solar year with a precision never equaled.

Time has mutilated, but not conquered, the temples of lovely friezes and carved stairs. The divinities still look out from the altars, playing hide-and-seek among the plumage of masks. Jaguar and snake still open their fangs on steles rising from the underbrush, and men and gods breathe from these stones, silent but never dumb.

(133)

1839: Havana

The Drum Talks Dangerously

The Captain General of Cuba decides to authorize drum dances on the plantations, provided that they are held on fiesta days and under the vigilance of foremen.

The foremen are to prevent the drums from transmitting voices of rebellion. Black drum, live drum, it does not sound alone. The drum converses with other drums, the macho drum calls, and talks dangerously to people and gods. When the drum calls, the gods appear and enter bodies and fly from them.

In very ancient times, the scorpion Akeké killed boredom by plunging his stinger into a human couple. Since then, the blacks come dancing out of the mother's belly, dancing, they say, love or pain or fury; and dancing they pierce the ferociousness of life.

(22, 222, and 241)

1839: Havana

Classified Ads

(276)

ECONOMIC SECTION
Sales of Animals

For sale, a Creole negro woman, young, healthy and without blemishes, very humble and faithful, good cook, with some knowledge of washing and ironing, and excellent for managing children, for the sum of 500 pesos. Further information at 150 Daoiz Street.　　　　　　　　　　　　　　　　　　　　　　　　3//11

For sale, a handsome horse of fine breeding, six spans and three inches . . .

DOMESTIC GOODS FOR HIRE.

Negro women for service in the home. Negroes as peons and for any work, and small negroes to play with children. Full information at 11 Daoiz Street.　　　Mar. 21

LEECHES superior quality just arrived from the peninsula, for sale . . .

1839: Valparaíso

The Illuminator

Up a hill, in the Rinconada barrio of the Chilean port of Valparaíso, in front of a plain house there is a sign:

> AMERICAN LIGHTS AND VIRTUES
> That is, tallow candles, patience,
> soap, resignation, strong glue,
> love of work

Inside, kitchen smoke and uproar of children. Here lives Simón Rodríguez. Bolívar's teacher has in his house a school and a small factory. He teaches the children the joy of creating. Making candles and soaps, he pays the bills.

(298)

1839: Veracruz

"For God's Sake, a Husband, Be He Old, One-Armed, or Crippled"

The Spanish ambassador treads Mexican soil for the first time. He finds in Veracruz no birds except vultures stalking corpses. Arm-in-arm with his wife, he goes out to stroll the sad streets, to learn the customs of the country.

In a church the ambassador finds a battered saint. Spinsters ask him for miracles by throwing stones at him. The young women throw stones hopefully, believing that the best marksmanship will give them the best husband; and for vengeance the dried-up ones, who no longer expect from Saint Anthony of Padua either husband or consolation, strike him, shrieking insults. They have poor Saint Anthony quite broken up, the face destroyed, stumps for arms, and his chest nothing but a big hole. At his feet, they leave him flowers.

(57)

1840: Mexico City

Masquerade

Mexico City's dressmakers and hairdressers have to keep running from house to house, from lady to lady. Who will be the most elegant at the great benefit ball for the poor? Which beauty will triumph?

Madame Calderón de la Barca, wife of the Spanish ambassador, tries on the Mexican national dress, typical costume of the valley of Puebla. Joy of the mirror that receives the image; white blouse with lace trimmings, red skirt, a sparkle of sequins on the embroidered petticoats. Madame Calderón twirls the multicolored sash a thousand turns around her waist, and combs her hair with a part down the middle, linking the tresses with a ring.

The whole city hears of it. The Council of Ministers meets to avert the danger. Three ministers—Foreign Relations, State, and War—present themselves at the ambassador's home and offer him an official warning. The most important ladies cannot believe it: swoonings, smelling salts, winds of fans. Such a worthy lady, so unworthily dressed! And in public! Friends advise, the diplomatic corps pressures. Careful now, avoid scandal, such clothes are for women of doubtful reputation.

Madame Calderón de la Barca abandons the national dress. She won't go to the ball as a Mexican. She will wear the dress of an Italian peasant woman of the Lazio. One of the dance's patronesses will appear decked out as the queen of Scotland. Other ladies will be French courtesans or Swiss, English, or Aragonese peasants, or will wrap themselves in the extravagant veils of Turkey.

The music will sail on a sea of pearls and diamonds. The dancing will be clumsy: not because of the feet but because of the shoes, so miniscule and torturing.

(57)

Mexican High Society:
Introduction to a Visit

"How are you? Are you well?"
"At your service. And you?"
"Nothing new, at your service."
"How did you pass the night?"
"At your service."
"How happy I am! And how are you, señora?"
"At your disposition. And you?"
"Many thanks. And your husband?"
"At your service, nothing new."
"Do please sit down."
"After you, señorita."
"No, señora, you first, please."
"Oh well, to oblige you, without ceremony. I am an enemy of
formalities and etiquette."

(57)

A Day of Street Cries in Mexico City

"Coal, sir?"

"Lard! Lard for a penny and a half!"

"Salt beef! Good salt beef!"

"Any old grease?"

"BUTTO-O-ONS! SHIRT BUTTO-O-ONS!"

"Crab apples for hot peppers! Fresh crab apples!"

"Bananas, oranges, pomegranates!"

"LITTLE MIRRO-O-ORS!"

"F a t   l i t t l e   b u n s   h o t
f r o m   t h e   o v e n!"

"Who wants Puebla mats, five-yard mats?"

"Honey cakes! Cheese and honey!"

"*Candies! Coconut candies! Merr-i-i-ingues!*"

"Last little lottery ticket, only one left for a halfpenny!"

"TORTIIIILLAS!"

"W   h   o   w   a   n   t   s   n   u   t   s?"

"CURD TORTILLAS!"

"Ducks, my love! Hot ducks!"

"*Tamales, little tamales!*"

Hot roasted chestnu-u-uts?"

(57)

Mexican High Society:
The Doctor Says Goodbye

By the bedside:
    "*Señora, I am at your service!*"
    "*Many thanks, señor.*"
At the foot of the bed:
    "*Consider me, señora, your most humble servant!*"
    "*Good morning, señor.*"
Pausing by the table:
    "*Señora, I kiss your feet!*"
    "*Señor, I kiss your hand!*"
Nearing the door:
    "*Señora, my poor house, and what it contains, and I myself,*
although useless, and all that I have, are yours!"
    "*Many thanks, doctor!*"
Turns his back to open the door, but turns again after opening it.
    "*Adieu, señora, your servant!*"
    "*Adieu, señor.*"
Finally leaves, but half opens the door and sticks his head in:
    "*Good morning, señora!*"

(57)

1840: Mexico City
A Nun Begins Convent Life

Thou hast chosen the good road
now no one can remove thee
chosen one

At sixteen she says goodbye to the world. She has passed in a carriage through streets she will never see again. Relatives and friends who will never see her again attend the ceremony in the Santa Teresa convent.

no one no one nothing
can remove thee

She will eat with the other brides of Christ, from a clay bowl, with a skull for a table centerpiece. She will do penance for sins she did not commit, mysterious sins that others enjoy and that she will redeem by tormenting her flesh with a belt of barbs and a crown of thorns. She will sleep forever alone, on a bed of mortification. She will wear cloth that sands her skin.

far from the battles of great Babylon
corruptions temptations dangers
far

She is covered with flowers and pearls and diamonds. They strip her of every adornment, they undress her.

never

To the sound of the organ, the bishop exhorts and blesses. The pastoral ring, an enormous amethyst, makes the sign of the cross over the kneeling girl's head. The nuns chant:

Ancilla Christi sum . . .

They dress her in black. The nuns, kneeling, press their faces against the floor, black wings unfurled around the circle of candles.
A curtain is drawn, like the lid on a coffin.

(57)

1842: San José, Costa Rica

Though Time Forget You, This Land Will Not

In Guatemala City, ladies and monks prepare Rafael Carrera, boss from the mountains, for a long dictatorship. They try on him the three-cornered hat, the dress coat and the ceremonial sword. They teach him to walk in patent leather boots, to write his name, and to tell time on a gold watch. Carrera, a hog breeder, will continue plying his trade by other means.

In San José, Costa Rica, Francisco Morazán prepares to die. He screws up his courage. For Morazán, lover of life, a man with so much life, it is hard to tear himself away. He spends the night with his eyes fixed on the ceiling of the cell, saying goodbye. The world has been great. The general puts off his farewell. He would have liked to govern more and fight less. He has spent many years making war, machete in hand, for the great Central American motherland, while she persisted in tearing herself to bits.

Before the military trumpet, comes the song of the trumpet bird. The song comes from high in the heavens and from deep in his childhood, as before, as always, at the end of the darkness. This time it announces the final dawn.

Morazán faces the firing squad. He uncovers his head and himself gives the order to load and aim. He corrects the aim, gives the order to fire.

The volley returns him to the earth.

(220)

1844: Mexico City

The Warrior Cocks

The Church, landlord and moneylender, possesses half of Mexico. The other half belongs to a handful of gentlemen and to Indians penned up in their communities. The proprietor of the presidency is General López de Santa Anna, who watches over public peace and the good health of his fighting cocks.

Santa Anna governs with a cock in his arms. Thus, he receives bishops and ambassadors, and to tend to a wounded cock he abandons cabinet meetings. He founds more cockfight arenas than hospitals and issues more cockfight rules than decrees on education. Cockfighting men form his personal court, along with cardsharps and widows of colonels who never were.

He is very fond of a piebald cock that pretends to be a female and flirts with the enemy, then after making a fool of him slashes him to death; but of them all he prefers the fierce Pedrito. He brought Pedrito from Veracruz with some soil too, so Pedrito could wallow in it without nostalgia. Santa Anna personally fixes the blade on the spur. He exchanges bets with muleteers and vagabonds, and chews feathers from the rival to give it bad luck. When he has no coins left, he throws medals into the cockpit.

"I'll give eight to five!"

"Eight to four if you like!"

A lightning flash pierces the whirl of feathers and Pedrito's spur tears out the eyes or opens the throat of any champion. Santa Anna dances on one leg and the killer raises his crest, beats his wings and sings.

(227 and 309)

1844: Mexico City

Santa Anna

frowns, stares off into space. He is thinking about some cock fallen in combat or about his own leg, which he lost, a venerated token of military glory.

Six years ago, during a small war against the king of France, a gun salvo tore off the leg. From his bed of pain, the mutilated president dictated to his secretaries a laconic fifteen-page message of farewell to the fatherland; but he came back to life and power, as was his habit.

An enormous cortege accompanied the leg from Veracruz to the capital. The leg arrived under a canopy, escorted by Santa Anna, who waved his white-plumed hat out of the carriage window; and behind, in full regalia, came bishops and ministers and ambassadors and an army of hussars, dragoons, and cuirassiers. The leg passed beneath a thousand rows of banners, and at its passing received prayers for the dead and speeches, odes, hymns, gun salutes, and the tolling of bells. On arriving at the cemetery, the president pronounced before the pantheon a final homage to that piece of himself death had taken by way of an advance.

Since then the missing leg hurts. Today, it hurts more than ever, hurts him excruciatingly, because the rebellious people have broken open the monument that guarded it and are dragging the leg through the streets of Mexico.

(227)

1845: Vuelta de Obligado
The Invasion of the Merchants

Three years ago, the British squadron humiliated the Celestial Empire. After the blockade of Canton and the rest of the coast, the English imposed opium consumption on the Chinese, in the name of Freedom of Commerce and Western Civilization.

After China, Argentina. The long years blockading the port of Buenos Aires have availed little or nothing. Juan Manuel de Rosas, who has his portrait worshipped and governs surrounded by buffoons dressed as kings, still refuses to open Argentina's rivers. English and French bankers and merchants have for years been demanding that this insolence be punished.

Many Argentines fall defending their land, but finally the guns of the warships of the world's most powerful countries smash the chains stretched across the Paraná River.

(271 and 336)

1847: Mexico City
The Conquest

"*Mexico sparkles before our eyes*": with these words President Adams had dazzled himself at the turn of the century.

At the first bite, Mexico lost Texas.

Now the United States has all Mexico on its plate.

General Santa Anna, master of retreat, flees to the south, leaving a trail of swords and corpses in the ditches. From defeat to defeat, he withdraws his army of bleeding, ill fed, never-paid soldiers, and beside them the ancient cannons hauled by mules, and behind them the caravan of women carrying children, rags, and tortillas in baskets. The army of General Santa Anna, with more officers than soldiers, is only good for killing poor compatriots.

In Chapultepec Castle, Mexican cadets, practically children, do not surrender. They resist the bombardment with an obstinacy not born of hope. Stones collapse over their bodies. Among the stones the victors plant the stars and stripes, which rises from the smoke over the huge valley.

The conquerors enter the capital. The city of Mexico: eight engineers, two thousand monks, two thousand five hundred lawyers, twenty thousand beggars.

The people, huddled together, growl. From the roofs, it rains stones.

(7, 127, 128, and 187)

1848: Villa of Guadalupe Hidalgo

The Conquistadors

In Washington, President Polk proclaims that his nation is now as big as all Europe. No one can halt the onslaught of this young voracious country. To the south and to the west, the United States grows, killing Indians, trampling on neighbors, or even paying. It bought Louisiana from Napoleon and now offers Spain a hundred million dollars for the island of Cuba.

But the right of conquest is more glorious and cheaper. The treaty with Mexico is signed in the Villa of Guadalupe Hidalgo. Mexico cedes to the United States, pistol at chest, half of its territory.

(128)

1848: Mexico City

The Irishmen

In the main plaza of Mexico City, the conquerors mete out punishment. They scourge the rebel Mexicans. They brand with hot irons the faces of the Irish deserters and then hang them from the gallows.

The Saint Patrick Irish battalion came in with the invaders, but fought alongside the invaded. From the north to Molino del Rey, the Irish made theirs the fate, ill fate, of the Mexicans. Many died defending the Churubusco monastery without ammunition. The prisoners, their faces burned, rock to and fro on the gallows.

(128)

1848: Ibiray
An Old Man in a White Poncho
in a House of Red Stone

He never liked cities. His heart's desire is a garden in Paraguay and his carriage, a wheelbarrow full of medicinal greens. A cane helps him to walk, and black Ansina, a minstrel of happy songs, helps him to work the ground and to receive without somber shadows the light of each day.

"José Artigas, at your service."

He offers maté and respect, but few words to the visitors that sometimes come from Uruguay.

"So my name is still heard over there."

He is past eighty years old, twenty-eight of them in exile, and he won't go back. The ideas he created and the people he loved are still beaten. Artigas well knows the weight of the world and of memory, and prefers to be silent. There is no plant to heal the wounds inside a man.

(277)

José Artigas, According to
Domingo Faustino Sarmiento

He was a highwayman, no more, no less. Thirty years of practice in murdering or robbing are indisputable qualifications for the the exercise of command over a horde of mutinous Indian peasant scum for a political revolution, and among them the fearsome name of Artigas is encrusted as bandit chief . . . Who obeyed him? The poor or savage Indians whom he led by right of being the most savage, the most cruel, the greatest enemy of whites . . . Uncouth, since he never frequented cities, foreign to all human tradition of free government; and although white, commanding natives even less educated than himself . . . Considering the antecedents and actions of Artigas, we feel a sort of revolt of reason, of the instincts of the man of white race, when someone tried to endow him with political thought and human sentiment.

(311)

1848: Buenos Aires
The Lovers (I)

Dramatis Personae:

Camila O'Gorman.   Born in Buenos Aires, in a house with three patios, twenty years ago. Educated in the odor of sanctity, to be successively virgin, wife, and mother in the strait and narrow path that leads to conjugal peace, the offices of the needle, evenings at the piano, and the rosary told with black mantilla on head. She has eloped with the parish priest of the Socorro Church. The idea was hers.

Ladislao Gutiérrez.   Minister of God. Age twenty-five. Nephew of the governor of Tucumán. He could not sleep after placing the Host on the tongue of that woman kneeling by the light of candles. Ended by dropping missal and cassock, setting loose a stampede of little angels and campanile pigeons.

Adolfo O'Gorman.   Begins each meal reciting the ten commandments, from the head of a long mahogany table. From a chaste woman, he has engendered a priest son, a policeman son, and a fugitive daughter. An exemplary father, he is the first to ask exemplary punishment for *the horrendous scandal* which shames his family. In a letter to Juan Manuel de Rosas, he pleads for a firm hand *against the most atrocious and unheard-of act in the country.*

Felipe Elortondo Y Palacio.   Secretary of the Curia. Also writes to Rosas asking the capture of the lovers and their inflexible punishment, to prevent similar crimes in the future. Explains in his letter that he had nothing to do with the appointment of the priest Gutiérrez, which was an affair of the bishop.

Juan Manuel De Rosas.   Orders the lovers hunted down. His messengers gallop from Buenos Aires. They carry a leaflet describing the fugitives. Camila: *white, black eyes, pleasant expression; tall, slim body, well distributed.* Ladislao: *dark, thin, full beard and curly hair.* Justice will be done, Rosas promises, *to satisfy religion and the laws and to prevent the consequent demoralization, libertinage, and disorder.* The whole country is on guard.

Also participating:

The Opposition Press.   From Montevideo, Valparaíso, and La Paz, Rosas's enemies invoke public morality. The daily newspaper *El Mercurio Chileno* tells its readers: *To such an extreme has come the horrible corruption of the customs under the alarming tyranny of the "River Plata Caligula," that impious and sacrilegious priests of Buenos Aires elope with the daughters of the best society, without the infamous satrap adopting any measure against these monstrous immoralities.*

The Horses.   They take the lovers to the north across open country, avoiding cities. Ladislao's had a golden hide and long legs. Camila's is grayish, fat, and bobtailed. They sleep, like their riders, outdoors. They do not tire.

Baggage.   His: a woolen poncho, some clothes, a couple of penknives and a pair of pistols, a pouch, a silk tie, and a glass inkpot. Hers: a silk shawl, several dresses, four linen petticoats, a fan, a pair of gloves, a comb, and a gold wedding ring, broken.

(166 and 219)

The Lovers (II)

They are two by an error that the night corrects.

1848: Holy Places
The Lovers (III)

In the summer they elope. They spend the autumn at the port of Goya, on the shores of the Paraná. There they go by other names. In the winter they are discovered, betrayed, and caught.

They are taken south in separate carts. The wheels leave scars on the road.

They are shut up in separate dungeons in the Holy Places prison.

If they beg pardon, they will be pardoned. Camila, pregnant, does not repent. Nor does Ladislao. Irons are fixed on their feet. A priest sprinkles the shackles with holy water.

They are shot in the patio, with their eyes blindfolded.

(219)

1848: Bacalar

Cecilio Chi

The ears of corn have spoken, warning of hunger. Huge sugar plantations are devouring the Maya communities' cornfields in the Yucatán region of Mexico. Men are purchased, as in Africa, and paid for with rum. *The Indians hear with their backs*, says the lash.

And war breaks out. Sick of contributing dead to other people's wars, the Mayas answer the call of the hollow trunk drum. They erupt from the brush, from the night, from nothing, machete in one hand, torch in the other: haciendas burn along with their owners and the sons of their owners, and the documents that make debt-slaves of Indians and sons of Indians burn too.

The Maya tornado whirls and destroys. Cecilio Chi fights with fifteen thousand Indians against guns that kill en masse, and so falls the proud city of Valladolid de Yucatán which thinks itself so noble, so Castilian; and Bacalar, and many other towns and garrisons, one after the other.

Cecilio Chi exterminates enemies invoking the old-time rebel Jacinto Canek and the even earlier prophet Chilam Balam. He proclaims that blood will flood the Mérida plaza up to the people's ankles. He offers firewater and fireworks to the patron saints of each town he occupies: If the saints refuse to change sides, and continue at the masters' service, Cecilio Chi cuts their throats with his machete and throws them on the fire.

(144 and 263)

1849: Shores of the Platte River

A Horseman Called Smallpox

Of every four Pawnee Indians, one has died this year of smallpox or cholera. The Kiowas, their eternal enemies, have saved themselves thanks to Old Uncle Saynday.

The old ruffian wandered these plains from heartache to heartache. *My world is finished*, he muttered over and over while vainly seeking deer and buffalo, and the Washita River offered him red mud instead of clear water. *Soon my Kiowa people will be surrounded like cows*.

Old Uncle Saynday was walking along buried in these sad thoughts when he saw over in the east, instead of the sun, a blackness, a great dark stain spreading across the prairie. As it drew closer, he saw that the stain was a horseman dressed in black, with a high black hat and a black horse. The horseman had ferocious scars on his face.

"My name is Smallpox," he introduced himself.

"I never heard . . ." said Saynday.

"I come from far away, the other side of the sea," the stranger explained. "I bring death."

He asked for the Kiowas. Old Uncle Saynday knew how to turn him around. He explained to him that the Kiowas weren't worth his trouble, a small and starveling people, and instead recommended the Pawnees, who are many, handsome and powerful, and showed him the rivers where they live.

(198)

1849: San Francisco

The Gold of California

From Valparaíso, Chileans stream in. They bring a pair of boots and a knife, a lamp and a shovel.

The entry to San Francisco Bay is now known as "the golden gate." Until yesterday, San Francisco was the Mexican town of Yerbas Buenas. In these lands, usurped from Mexico in the war of conquest, there are three-kilo nuggets of pure gold.

The bay has no room for so many ships. An anchor touches bottom, and adventurers scatter across the mountains. No one wastes time on hellos. The cardsharp buries his patent leather boots in the mud:

"Long live my loaded dice! Long live my jack!"

Simply landing on this soil turns the bum into a king and the beauty who had scorned him dies of remorse. Vicente Pérez Rosales, newly arrived, listens to the thoughts of his compatriots: "Now I have talent! Because in Chile, who's an ass once he has cash?" *Here losing time is losing money.* Endless thunder of hammers, a world on the boil, birth-pang screams. Out of nothing rise the awnings under which are offered tools and liquor and dried meat in exchange for leather bags filled with gold dust. Crows and men squawk, flocks of men from all lands, and night and day eddies the whirlwind of frock coats and seamen's caps, Oregon furs and Maule bonnets, French daggers, Chinese hats, Russian boots, and shiny bullets at the waists of cowboys.

Under her lace sunshade, a good-looking Chilean woman smiles as best she can, squeezed by her corset and by the multitude that sweeps her over the sea of mud paved with broken bottles. In this port she is Rosarito Améstica. She was born Rosarito Izquierdo more years ago than she'll tell, became Rosarito Villaseca in Talcahuano, Rosarito Toro in Talca, and Rosarito Montalva in Valparaíso.

From the stern of a ship, the auctioneer offers ladies to the crowd. He exhibits them and sings their praises, one by one, *look gentlemen what a waist what youth what beauty what* . . .

"Who'll give more?" says the auctioneer. "Who'll give more for this incomparable flower?"

(256)

1849: El Molino
They Were Here

Man calls and gold falls from the sands and rocks. Sparks of gold jump on the winds; gold comes docilely to the hand of man, from the bottom of California's rivers and ravines.

El Molino is one of many camps that have sprung up on these golden shores. One day the miners of El Molino notice columns of smoke rising from the distant cypress forests. At night they see a line of fires mocking the wind. Someone recognizes the signals: the telegraph of the Indians is calling for war against the intruders.

In a flash, the miners form a detail of a hundred and seventy rifles and attack by surprise. They bring in a hundred prisoners and shoot fifteen to teach them a lesson.

(256)

Ashes

Since he had the dream of the White Rabbit, the old man talked of nothing else, though he had trouble talking at all, and for a long time had been unable to stand. The years made his eyes watery and bent him irremediably. He lived in a basket, his face hidden behind his pointy knees, poised for the return to the belly of the earth. Stuck in the basket, he traveled on the back of some son or grandson and told his dream to everybody: *White Rabbit gonna devour us*, he babbled. *Gonna devour our seed, our grass, our living*. He said the

White Rabbit would come mounted on an animal bigger than a deer, an animal with round feet and hair on its neck.

The old man did not live to see the gold fever in these Californian lands. Before the miners arrived on horseback, he announced: *"Can't feed my children no more. Like old root, just ready for growing now. Speak no more."*

They burned him in his basket, on firewood that he had selected.

(229)

1849: Baltimore

Poe

At the door of a tavern in Baltimore the dying man lies face up, strangling in his vomit. Some pious hand drags him to the hospital, at dawn; and nothing more, nevermore.

Edgar Allan Poe, son of ragged itinerant comedians, vagabond poet, convicted and confessed guilty of disobedience and delirium, had been condemned by invisible tribunals and crushed by invisible pincers.

He got lost looking for himself. Not looking for gold in California; no, looking for himself.

(99 and 260)

1849: San Francisco

Levi's Pants

The flashes of violence and miracles do not blind Levi Strauss, who arrives from far-off Bavaria and realizes at one blink that here the beggar becomes a millionaire and the millionaire a beggar or corpse in a click of cards or triggers. In another blink he discovers that pants become tatters in these mines of California, and decides to provide a better fate for the strong cloths he has brought along. He won't sell awnings or tents. He will sell pants, tough pants for tough men in the tough work of digging up rivers and mines. So the seams won't burst, he reinforces them with copper riveting. Behind, under the waist, Levi stamps his name on a leather label.

Soon the cowboys of the whole West will claim as their own these pants of blue Nîmes twill which neither sun nor years wear out.

(113)

1850: San Francisco
The Road to Development

The Chilean Pérez Rosales is looking for luck in the mines of California. Learning that, a few miles from San Francisco, fabulous prices are paid for anything edible, he gets a few sacks of worm-eaten jerky and some jars of jam and buys a launch. Hardly has he pushed off from the pier when a customs agent points a rifle at his head: *"Hold it there."*

This launch cannot move on any United States river *because it was built abroad and its keel is not made of North American wood.*

The United States had defended its national market since the times of its first president. It supplies cotton to England, but customs barriers block English cloth and any product that could injure its own industry. The planters of the southern states want English clothing, which is much better and cheaper, and complain that the northern textile mills impose on them their ugly and costly cloth from baby's diaper to corpse's shroud.

(162 and 256)

1850: Buenos Aires
The Road to Underdevelopment: The Thought of Domingo Faustino Sarmiento

We are not industrialists or navigators and Europe will provide us for long centuries with its artifacts in exchange for our raw materials.
(310)

1850: River Plata
Buenos Aires and Montevideo at Mid-Century

From his seat in the French Academy to the River Plata docks, sails the poet Xavier Marmier.

The great European powers have reached an agreement with Rosas. The Buenos Aires blockade has been lifted. Marmier thinks he is on the Rue Vivienne as he strolls down Peru Street. In the shop windows he finds Lyons silks and the *Journal de Modes*, the novels of Dumas and Sandeau and the poems of de Musset; but in the shade of the City Hall's porticos saunter barefoot blacks in soldiers' uniforms, and the pavements ring with the trot of a gaucho's horse.

Someone explains to Marmier that no gaucho dispatches anybody without first kissing the blade of his knife and swearing by the Immaculate Virgin; and if the dead man was a friend, the killer mounts him on his steed and ties him to the saddle so that he may enter the cemetery on horseback.

Further on, in the suburban plazas, Marmier finds the carts, ships of the pampa, which bring hides and wheat from the interior and on the return trip take cloth and liquor which have arrived from Le Havre and Liverpool.

The poet crosses the river. For seven years Montevideo has been under siege from the rear, harassed by General Oribe's gaucho army, but the city survives, facing the river-ocean, thanks to French ships which pour merchandise and money onto the docks. One Montevideo newspaper is *Le Patriote Français* and the majority of the population is French. In this refuge of Rosas's enemies, Marmier notes, *the rich have gone poor and all have gone mad*. A suitor pays an ounce of gold to stick a camellia in his girl's hair and the mistress of the house offers the visitor a bouquet of honeysuckle held by a ring of silver, rubies, and emeralds. For the ladies of Montevideo, the war between vanguardists and conservatives seems more important than the war against the Uruguayan peasants, a real war that kills people. Vanguardists wear their hair very short; conservatives, luxuriantly rolled.

(196)

1850: Paris

Dumas

Alexandre Dumas rolls up his cuffs of fine batiste and with a stroke of the pen writes the epic pages of *Montevideo; or, The New Troy*.

The novelist, a man of fantasy and gluttony, has priced at five thousand francs this professional feat of the imagination. He calls Montevideo's humble hill a "mountain" and turns the war of foreign merchants against the gaucho cavalry into a Greek epic. The hosts of Giuseppe Garibaldi, which fight for Montevideo, fly not the flag of Uruguay but the classic pirate skull and crossbones on a black field;

but in the novel Dumas writes to order, only martyrs and titans take part in the defense of the almost French city.

(101)

1850: Montevideo
Lautréamont at Four

Isidoro Ducasse has been born in the port of Montevideo. A double wall of fortifications separates the countryside from the besieged city. Isidoro grows up dazed by cannon fire, with the daily spectacle of dying men hanging from their horses.

His shoes take him to the sea. Standing on the sand, face to the wind, he asks the sea where music goes after it leaves the violin, where the sun goes when night arrives, and where the dead go. Isidoro asks the sea where his mother went, that woman he cannot remember, nor should name, nor knows how to imagine. Someone has told him that the other dead people threw her out of the cemetery. The sea, which talks so much, does not answer; and the boy flees up the cliff and, weeping, embraces an enormous tree with all his strength, so it won't fall.

(181)

1850: Chan Santa Cruz
The Talking Cross

Three long years of Indian war in Yucatán. More than a hundred and fifty thousand dead, a hundred thousand fled. The population has been reduced by half.

One of the captains of the rebellion, the mestizo José María Barrera, leads the Indians to a cave deep in the jungle. There, a spring offers fresh water in the shade of a very tall mahogany tree. The tree has given birth to the little cross that talks.

Says the cross, in the Maya language: *"The time has come for Yucatán to rise. I am falling hour by hour, they are cutting me with machetes, stabbing me with knives, poking sticks into me. I go about Yucatán to redeem my beloved Indians . . ."*

The cross is the size of a finger. The Indians dress it. They put a huipil and skirt on it; they adorn it with colored threads. She will unite the dispersed.

(273)

1851: Latacunga

"I Wander at Random and Naked . . ."

Instead of thinking about Medes and Persians and Egyptians, let us think about Indians. It is more important for us to understand an Indian than Ovid. Start your school with Indians, Señor Rector.

Simón Rodríguez offers his advice to the college of the town of Latacunga, in Ecuador: that a chair be established in the Quechua language instead of in Latin, that physics be taught instead of theology; that the college build a pottery factory and a glass factory; that it offer degrees in masonry, carpentry, and smithery.

Along the Pacific shores and through the Andes, from town to town, Don Simón makes his pilgrimage. He never wanted to be a tree, but the wind. For a quarter of a century he has been raising dust on America's roads. Since Sucre ousted him from Chuquisaca, he has founded many schools and candle factories and published two books with his own hands, letter by letter, since no typographer can cope with so many brackets and synoptic charts. This old vagabond, bald and ugly and potbellied, tanned by the sun, carries on his back a trunk of manuscripts condemned by lack of money and readers. He carries no clothing. He has only what he wears.

Bolívar used to call him, *My teacher, my Socrates*. He said, *You have molded my heart for the great and the beautiful*. People clench their teeth to keep from laughing when mad Rodríguez launches into his perorations about the tragic destiny of these Hispanic-American lands.

"We are blind! Blind!"

Almost no one listens to him, no one believes him. They take him for a Jew, because he goes about sowing children wherever he passes, and does not baptize them with Saints' names, but calls them Corncob, Calabash, Carrot and other heresies. He has changed his surname three times and says he was born in Caracas, but also that he was born in Philadelphia and in Sanlúcar de Barrameda. It is rumored that one of his schools, in Concepción in Chile, was destroyed by an earthquake which God sent when he learned that Don Simón taught anatomy parading himself stark naked before the students.

Each day Don Simón grows more lonely. The most audacious, most lovable of America's thinkers, every day more lonely.

At eighty, he writes: *I wanted to make the earth a paradise for all. I made it a hell for myself.*

(298)

The Ideas of Simón Rodríguez:
"Either We Invent or We Are Lost"

Look at the way Europe invents, and look how America imitates!

Some see prosperity in having their ports full of foreign ships, and their homes turned into warehouses for foreign effects. Every day brings a shipment of ready-made clothing, even caps for the Indians. Soon we shall see little gilded packages, with the royal coat-of-arms, containing earth prepared "by a new process," for the lads accustomed to eating earth.

Women making their confessions in French! Missionarees absolveeng seens een Spaneesh!

America should not servilely imitate, but be original.

The wisdom of Europe and the prosperity of the United States are, in America, two enemies of freedom of thought. The new republics do not want to admit anything that does not carry a pass ... To form their institutions, the statesmen of those nations consulted no one but reason; and this they found on their own soil. Imitate originality, since you try to imitate everything!

Where shall we go in search of models? We are independent, but not free; masters of our soil, but not of ourselves.

Let us open up history; and for that which is not yet written, let each read it in his own memory.

(285)

1851: La Serena
The Precursors

Misery is not being able to think or store in the mind any memory except pain, says Francisco Bilbao, and adds that the exploitation of man by man leaves man no time to be man. Society is divided into those who *can* do everything and those who *do* do everything. To revive Chile, *giant buried under weeds*, an end must be put to a system that denies shelter to those who toil to build palaces, and dresses in rags those who weave the best clothing.

The precursors of socialism in Chile are not yet thirty years old. Francisco Bilbao and Santiago Arcos, tuxedoed young men cultivated in Paris, have betrayed their class. Searching for a *society of solidarity*, they have in the course of this year set off various military rebellions and popular uprisings throughout the country, against the wig-wearers and the monks, and private property.

On the last day of the year the last revolutionary bastion falls, in the city of La Serena. Many *reds* also fall—before firing squads. Bilbao, who on another occasion escaped disguised as a woman, this time has fled over the rooftops and gone into exile with cassock and missal.

(39)

1852: Santiago de Chile

"What has independence meant to the poor?" the Chilean Santiago Arcos asks himself in jail.

Since independence the government is and has been of the rich. The poor have been soldiers, national militias, have voted as their employer told them, have worked the land, have dug ditches, have worked the mines, have carried on their backs, have cultivated the country, have kept on earning a penny and a half, have been whipped and pilloried . . . The poor have enjoyed glorious independence as much as the horses that charged against the king's troops in Chacabuco and Maipú.

(306)

The People of Chile Sing to the Glory of Paradise

Saint Peter, the patron of me and of you,
sent an acolyte out for some sausage and wine
and a nice side of bacon and pigs' feet fine
to go in the pot for a succulent stew,
with a good heady punch, the way earth folks do;

and, not to be supercilious,
a basket of tortillas
so that little angels all
could out of heavenly boredom fall
and have themselves a genuine ball.
Saint Anthony, when the hour was tardy
swayed to his feet and said "Well, sirs,
damn all the devils in hell, sirs,
isn't this quite a party!
To no one's abuse
it's time to let loose
with an innocent ruse:
I'll go up to Saint Clara
and before she's aware-a'
her plump little bottom I'm going to goose."

(182)

1852: Mendoza

The Lines of the Hand

Even the little altar angels wear red sashes in Argentina. To refuse
challenges the fury of the dictator. Like many enemies of Rosas,
Doctor Federico Mayer Arnold has suffered exile and prison.

Not long ago this young Buenos Aires professor published a book
in Santiago de Chile. The book, adorned with French, English, and
Latin quotations, began this way: *Three cities have expelled me from
their bosoms and four jails have received me to theirs. I have, however, thrown my thoughts freely in the despot's face. Now again I
launch my ideas into the world, and await without fear what Fate
has in store for me.*

Two months later, on turning a corner, Doctor Federico Mayer
Arnold falls in a spray of blood. But not by order of the tyrant:
Federico's mother-in-law, Doña María, an ill-humored woman from
Mendoza, has paid the knife-wielding thugs. She has ordered them
to kill her son-in-law because he does not please her.

(14)

1853: La Cruz

The Treasure of the Jesuits

She knows. That's why the crow follows her, flies behind her every morning, on the way to Mass, and waits for her at the church door.

She has just had her hundredth birthday. She will tell the secret when she is ready to die. If not, Divine Providence would punish her.

"Three days hence," comes the promise.

And after three days, *"Next month."*

And after the month, *"Tomorrow we'll see."*

When people pester her, her eyes go blank and she pretends to be dazed, or explodes with laughter moving her little legs, as if being so old were something naughty.

The whole town of La Cruz knows that she knows. She was just a little girl when she helped the Jesuits bury the treasure in the Misiones woods, but she hasn't forgotten.

Once, taking advantage of her absence, the neighbors opened the old chest which she spent her days sitting on. Inside there was no bag full of gold pieces. In the chest they found only the dried navels of her eleven children.

Come the death throes, the whole town is at the foot of her bed. She opens and closes her fishlike mouth as if trying to say something.

She dies in the door of sanctity. The secret was the only one she had in her life and she goes without telling it.

(147)

1853: Paita

The Three

She no longer dresses as a captain, nor fires pistols, nor rides horseback. Her legs don't work and her whole body is distorted with fat; but she sits on her invalid's chair as if it were a throne and peels oranges and guavas with the most beautiful hands in the world.

Surrounded by clay pitchers, Manuela Sáenz reigns in the shaded portico of her house. Beyond, among mountains the color of death, extends the Bay of Paita. Exiled in this Peruvian port, Manuela lives by making sweets and fruit preserves. Ships stop to buy. Her goodies enjoy great fame on these coasts. Whalers sigh for a spoonful.

At nightfall Manuela amuses herself by throwing scraps to stray dogs, which she has baptized with the names of generals who were disloyal to Bolívar. As Santander, Páez, Córdoba, Lamar, and Santa Cruz fight over the bones, her moonface lights up, and, covering her toothless mouth with a fan, she bursts out laughing. She laughs with her whole body and her many flying laces.

Sometimes an old friend comes from the town of Amotape. The wandering Simón Rodríguez sits in a rocking chair, beside Manuela, and the two of them smoke and chat and are silent together. The persons Bolívar most loved, the teacher and the lover, change the subject if the hero's name filters into the conversation.

When Don Simón leaves, Manuela sends for the silver coffer. She opens it with the key hidden in her bosom and fondles the many letters Bolívar had written *to the one and only woman*, worn-out paper that still says: *I want to see you and see you again and touch you and feel you and taste you* . . . Then she asks for the mirror and very carefully brushes her hair, in case he might come and visit her in dreams.

(295, 298, and 343)

1854: Amotape

A Witness Describes Simón Rodríguez's Farewell to the World

As soon as he saw the Amotape priest enter, Don Simón sat up in bed, waved the priest to the only chair in the room and started making something like a speech on materialism. The priest sat there stupefied, and scarcely had the heart to pronounce a few words trying to interrupt him . . .

(298)

1855: New York

Whitman

For lack of a publisher, the poet pays out of his own pocket for the publication of *Leaves of Grass*.

Waldo Emerson, theologist of Democracy, gives the book his blessing, but the press attacks it as prosaic and obscene.

In Walt Whitman's grandiose elegy multitudes and machines roar. The poet embraces God and sinners, he embraces the Indians and the pioneers who wipe them out, he embraces slave and master, victim and executioner. All crime is redeemed in the ecstasy of the New World, America the muscular and the subjugator, with no debt to pay to the past, winds of progess that make man the comrade of man and unchain virility and beauty.

(358)

1855: New York

Melville

The bearded sailor is a writer without readers. Four years ago he published the story of a captain who pursues a white whale through the seas of the universe, bloodthirsty harpoon in pursuit of Evil, and no one paid it much attention.

In these times of euphoria, in these North American lands in full expansion, Herman Melville's voice sings out of tune. His books are mistrustful of Civilization, which attributes to the savage the role of Demon and forces him to play it—as Captain Ahab does with Moby Dick in the immensity of the ocean. His books reject the only and obligatory Truth that certain men, believing themselves chosen, impose on the others. His books have doubts about Vice and Virtue, shadows of the same nothingness, and teach that the sun is the only lamp worthy of confidence.

(211 and 328)

1855: Washington Territory

"You people will suffocate in your own waste," warns Indian Chief Seattle.

The earth is not the white man's brother, but his enemy, and when he has conquered it, he moves on. But all things are connected. Whatever befalls the earth befalls the sons of the earth . . .

The clatter of cities only seems to insult the ears . . .

The air is precious to the red man. For all things share the same breath—beasts, trees, man. Like a man dying for many days, he is numb to the stench . . .

It matters little where we pass the rest of our days; they are not many. A few more hours, a few more winters . . . The whites, too, shall pass—perhaps sooner than other tribes. Continue to contaminate your bed, and you will one night suffocate in your own waste . . .

(229)

The Far West

Is anyone really listening to old Chief Seattle? The Indians are condemned, like the buffalo and the moose. The one that does not die by the bullet dies of hunger or sorrow. From the reservation where he languishes, old Chief Seattle talks in solitude about usurpations and exterminations and says who knows what things about the memory of his people flowing in the sap of the trees.

The Colt barks. Like the sun, the white pioneers march westward. A diamond light from the mountains guides them. The promised land rejuvenates anyone sticking a plow in it to make it fertile. In a flash cities and streets spring up in the solitude so recently inhabited by cacti, Indians, and snakes. The climate, they say, is so very healthy that the only way to inaugurate cemeteries is to shoot someone down.

Adolescent capitalism, stampeding and gluttonous, transfigures what it touches. The forest exists for the ax to chop down and the desert for the train to cross; the river is worth bothering about if it contains gold, and the mountain if it shelters coal or iron. No one walks. All run, in a hurry, it's urgent, after the nomad shadow of wealth and power. Space exists for time to defeat, and time for progress to sacrifice on its altars.

(218)

1856: Granada

Walker

The son of Tennessee shoots from the hip and buries without epitaph. He has eyes of cinders. He neither laughs nor drinks. He eats as a duty. No woman has been seen with him since his deaf and dumb fiancée died; and God is his only friend worthy of trust. He calls himself the Predestined. He dresses in black. He hates anyone touching him.

William Walker, Southern gentleman, proclaims himself President of Nicaragua. Red carpets cover the main square of Granada. Trumpets flash in the sun. The band plays North American military marches as Walker kneels and takes the oath with one hand on the Bible. Twenty one salutes are fired. He makes his speech in English and then raises a glass of water and toasts the president of the United States, his compatriot and esteemed colleague. The North American ambassador, John Wheeler, compares Walker with Christopher Columbus.

Walker arrived in Nicaragua a year ago, at the head of the Phalanx of Immortals. *I will order the death of anyone who opposes the imperial march of my forces.* Like a knife into meat came the adventurers recruited on the wharves of San Francisco and New Orleans.

The new president of Nicaragua restores slavery, abolished in Central America over thirty years ago, and re-implants the slave trade, serfdom, and forced labor. He decrees that English is Nicaragua's official language and offers lands and hands to any white North Americans who care to come.

(154, 253, and 314)

1856: Granada

Stood

Five or none. Nicaragua wasn't much. William Walker wanted to conquer all of Central America.

The five pieces of Morazan's fatherland, united against the pirate, chop his force to bits. The people's war kills many North Americans; morbus cholera, which turns you wrinkled and gray and suddenly finishes you off, kills more.

The Messiah of slavery, roundly defeated, crosses Lake Nicaragua. Flocks of ducks and swarms of plague-infected flies pursue him. Before returning to the United States, Walker decides to punish the city of Granada. Nothing should remain alive there. Neither its people, nor its tile-roofed houses, nor its sandy streets lined with orange trees.

Flames rise to the sky.

At the foot of the ruined wharves a lance is stuck into the ground. A strip of leather hangs from the lance like a dejected flag. In red letters it says, in English: *Here stood Granada.*

(154 and 314)

Walker: "In Defense of Slavery"

The enemies of American civilization—for such are the enemies of slavery—seem to be more on the alert than its friends.

Something is due from the South to the memory of the brave dead who repose in the soil of Nicaragua. In defense of slavery these men left their homes, met with calmness and constancy the perils of a tropical climate, and finally yielded up their lives . . .

If there, then, be yet vigor in the South—and who can doubt that there is—for the further contest with the soldiers of anti-slavery, let her cast off the lethargy which enthrals her, and prepare anew for the conflict . . . The true field for the exertion of slavery is in tropical America; there it finds the natural seat of its empire and thither it can spread if it will but make the effort . . .

(356)

1858: Source of the Gila River

The Sacred Lands of the Apaches

Here, in the valley where the river is born, among the rocky heights of Arizona, is the tree that sheltered Geronimo thirty years ago. He had just sprouted from his mother's belly and was wrapped in a cloth. They hung the cloth from a branch. The wind rocked the baby while an old voice entreated the tree: "*Let him live and grow to see you give fruit many times.*"

This tree is at the center of the world. Standing in its shade, Geronimo will never confuse north with south, nor evil with good.

All around spreads the vast country of the Apaches. In these rugged lands they have lived ever since the first of them, Son of the Storm, donned the feathers of the eagle who defeated the enemies of light. Here, animals to hunt have never been lacking, nor herbs to cure the sick, nor rocky caves to lie in after death.

Some strange men have arrived on horseback, carrying long ropes and many stakes. Their skin looks as if it had been drained of blood, and they speak a language never before heard. They stick bright-colored signals into the ground and ask questions of a white medal which replies by moving a needle.

Geronimo does not know that these men have come to measure the Apaches' lands, to sell them.

(24 and 91)

1858: Kaskiyeh
Geronimo

The Apaches had gone unarmed to the market of Kaskiyeh in the southern lands betweeen Sonora and Casas Grandes to exchange buffalo and deerskins for food. Mexican soldiers demolished their camps and took their horses. Among the dead lie the mother and the wife of Geronimo, and his three children.

Geronimo says nothing while his comrades meet and sadly vote. They are surrounded, unarmed, and have no choice but to leave.

Sitting by the river, motionless, he watches his people march off behind Chief Mangas Colorado. Here the dead remain. Finally, Geronimo leaves as well, looking over his shoulder. He follows his people *at the right distance to hear the soft padding of the Apaches' feet in retreat.*

During the long trek to the north, he does not open his mouth. Upon arriving home, he burns his house of skins and his mother's house and all of his things and his wife's and his mother's things, and burns his children's toys. Then, his back to the fire, he raises his head and sings a war chant.

(24)

1858: San Borja
Let Death Die

His sore body is aching to mix itself with the American earth. Aimé Bonpland knew this was where he would end up and linger on, ever since that distant day when he landed with Humboldt on the Caribbean coast.

Bonpland dies of his death, in a mud and straw hut, serenely, knowing that the stars do not die; that ants and people will not stop being born; that there will be new cloverleaves, and new oranges or suns on the branches; and that foals, newly upright on their mosquito legs, will be stretching out their necks in search of a teat. The old man bids farewell to the world as a child does to the day at bedtime.

Afterwards, a drunk stabs the body; but this sinister imbecility of mankind is a detail of no importance.

1860: Chan Santa Cruz

The Ceremonial Center
of the Yucatán Rebels

"My father didn't put me among the rich. He didn't put me with the generals or with those who have money, or with those who claim to have it." The Mother of Crosses, she who sprouted from the mahogany tree beside the spring, had announced this in Yucatán. And when soldiers ax down the mahogany and burn the little cross dressed by the Indians, she has already had daughters. From cross to cross the word has survived: *"My father put me with the poor, because I am poor."*

Around the cross, around the crosses, has grown Chan Santa Cruz, the great sanctuary of Maya rebels in the Yucatán jungle.

The soldiers of Colonel Acereto's expedition go in without resistance. They find no Indians and are left open-mouthed. The Mayas have built an immense church of sturdy walls with a lofty dome, the House of God, the House of the Jaguar God, and in the tower hang the bells taken from Bacalar.

In the sacred city, empty of people, everything is scary. There is little water in the canteens, but Colonel Acereto forbids drinking from the wells. Six years ago other soldiers drank and vomited and died while from the thickets Indians asked them if the water was fresh.

From patience to impatience the soldiers pass the days. Meanwhile, Indians flock from a hundred villages and a thousand corn patches. They bring a rifle or a machete and a little sack of corn flour. They mass in the brush; and when Colonel Acereto decides to withdraw, they mop up his troop in one sweep.

The band, which has been captured intact, will teach music to the children and play polkas in the church, where the cross lives and talks, surrounded by Maya gods. There, in the church, the people celebrate communion with corn tortillas and honey, and once a year elect interpreters for the cross and warrior-chiefs, who wear a gold earring but work in the cornfields like anyone else.

(273 and 274)

1860: Havana

Poet in Crisis

At a cost of thirteen deaths per kilometer, Cuba has constructed the railway that takes sugar from the Güines cane fields to the port of Havana: dead Africans, Irishmen, Canary Islanders and Chinese from Macao, slaves or wretched day laborers brought by traffickers from afar—and the sugar boom demands more and more.

Ten years ago the first shipment of Maya slaves reached Cuba from Yucatán. A hundred and forty Indians, prisoners of war, were sold at twenty-five pesos a head; children, gratis. Later Mexican President Santa Anna granted a monopoly on the traffic to Colonel Manuel María Jiménez and the price rose to a hundred and sixty pesos per man, a hundred and twenty per woman and eighty per child. The Maya war has gone on and on, and with it more and more Cuban loans of money and rifles. The Yucatán government collects a tax on each slave sold, and thus pays with Indians for the war against the Indians.

The Spanish poet José Zorrilla has purchased in the port of Campeche a shipment of Indians to sell in Cuba. He was all set to embark when yellow fever killed his capitalist partner Cipriano de las Cagigas in Havana, and now the author of "Don Juan Tenorio" consoles himself writing verses on a coffee plantation.

(222 and 273)

1861: Havana

Sugar Hands

Soon the city of Havana will be staging its floral games. The intellectuals of the Literary Society propose a great central motif. They want the literary competition to be on the theme of asking Spain for sixty thousand new slaves. The poets will thus support the black importation project, which already enjoys the patronage of the newspaper *Diario de La Marina* and the legal blessing of the attorney general.

Hands are needed for sugar. Blacks smuggled in via the Mariel, Cojímar, and Batabanó beaches are scarce and expensive. Three sugar mill owners have drawn up the project, because *Cuba lies exhausted and desolate*, imploring the Spanish authorities *to hear her cries of woe and provide her with blacks*, meek and loyal slaves to whom *Cuba owes her economic prosperity*. It will be easy, they insist, to bring them from Africa. *They will run joyfully to the Spanish ships, when they see them arriving.*

(222 and 240)

Sugar Language

The window grills of Havana homes are adorned with iron spirals and the columns with plaster curlicues; the doorways with lacy woodwork; the stained-glass windows with peacock feathers. The talk of doctors and monks gleams with arabesques. Poets reach for unheard-of rhymes and prose writers for the most reverberant adjectives. Orators strive to make their points, their restless and fugitive points; a point peeks out from behind an adverb or a parenthesis and the orator throws more and more words at it; the speech stretches out trying to catch it, but the point keeps fleeing; and the chase continues ad infinitum.

Account books, on the other hand, speak the rough language of reality. In sugar mills throughout Cuba, they register the birth or purchase of every black slave as the acquisition of merchandise, calculating depreciation at three percent annually. A man's illness is equivalent to the faultiness of a valve and the end of a life is like the loss of a head of cattle: *The killed cattle are bulls. We lost the ceiba sow. The Negro Domingo Mondongo has died.*

(222)

1861: Bull Run
Grays Against Blues

Near the city of Washington the first battle of the Civil War is fought. A big audience has turned out, in carriages or on horseback, to see the show. The blood hardly begins to flow when horses bolt and the crowd stampedes, howling with panic. Soon the capital's streets are filled with the mutilated and dying.

Two opposing countries had previously shared the map, the flag, and the name of the United States. A Southern newspaper reported the election of Abraham Lincoln in its "News from Abroad" section. Within months the Southern states formed a separate nation and war broke out.

Lincoln, the new president, embodies the ideals of the North. He has proclaimed in his campaign that it is impossible to continue half slave and half free, and has promised farms instead of plantations and higher tariffs against the competition of European industry.

North and South: two spaces, two periods. In the North, factories that already produce more than fields; tireless inventors creating the electric telegraph, the sewing machine, and the reaper; new cities sprouting on all sides, a million inhabitants in New York and wharves too small for the ships filled with desperate Europeans seeking a new country. In the South, pride of ancestry and nostalgia, fields of tobacco, enormous cotton plantations: four million black slaves producing raw materials for Lancashire textile mills; gentlemen fighting duels over the tainted honor of a sister or the fair name of a family; ladies airing themselves in carriages through the flowering countryside and fainting on the verandahs of their palaces at dusk.

(70)

1862: Fredericksburg
The Pencil of War

His back against a wall, legs crossed on the ground, a young soldier looks without seeing. Several months' growth of beard flattens the open collar of his tunic. A soldier's hand strokes the head of a dog sleeping on his knees.

John Geyser, recruit from Pennsylvania, sketches himself and his comrades while the war kills. His pencil freezes them for an instant on the way to the ditch excavated by cannon fire. Soldiers load rifles, or clean them, or eat the ration of army biscuit and bacon, or stare with sad eyes. Sadly, they look without seeing, or perhaps see beyond what they look at.

(69)

1863: Mexico City
"The American Algeria"

is the new name for Mexico according to the Paris press. The army of Napoleon III attacks and conquers the capital and the chief cities.

In Rome, the pope jumps for joy. The government of Benito Juárez, dislodged by the invaders, was guilty of blasphemy against

God and his properties in Mexico. Juárez had stripped the Church naked, despoiling it of its sacred tithes, of its estates vast as the sky, and of the State's loving protection.

The Conservatives join the new conquistadors. Twenty thousand Mexican soldiers help the thirty thousand from France, who have just finished storming the Crimea, Algeria, and Senegal. Napoleon III takes over Mexico invoking the Latin spirit, Latin culture, and the Latin race, and in passing demands repayment of an immense and phantasmal loan.

Taking charge of the new colony is Maximilian of Austria, one of Europe's many unemployed princes, accompanied by his stunning wife.

(15)

1863: London

Marx

"Napoleon III will break his head on Mexico, if they don't hang him first," announces a wise and penurious prophet, who lives on what he can borrow in London.

While he corrects and polishes the drafts of a work that is going to change the world, Karl Marx does not miss a detail of what is happening in the world. In letters and articles he calls the third Napoleon an imperial Lazarillo de Tormes* and the invasion of Mexico an infamous enterprise. He also denounces England and Spain, who would like to share with France the territory of Mexico as war booty, and all the nation-thieving nations, accustomed to sending thousands and thousands of people to the slaughterhouse so that usurers and traders may extend the scope of their business.

Marx no longer believes that the imperial expansion of the most developed countries is a victory for progress over backwardness. Fifteen years ago, however, he did not disagree when Engels applauded the invasion of Mexico by the United States, believing that this would turn Mexican campesinos into proletarians and bring the bishops and feudal lords down from their pedestal.

(129 and 201)

---

* Anonymous Spanish picaresque novel of the sixteenth century.

1865: La Paz

Belzu

A flood of rebellious Indians has restored Belzu to power. Manuel Isidoro Belzu, "Grandpa Belzu," avenger of the poor, scourge of doctors, returns to La Paz riding a human wave.

When he was in power a few years back, the capital of Bolivia was wherever he happened to be on the haunch of his horse; and the masters of the country, who attempted more than forty military coups, never succeeded in overthrowing him. Foreign merchants hated him, because Belzu barred the door to them and protected the Cochabamba artisans against the invasion of British-made ponchos. The pettifoggers of Chuquisaca, in whose veins run ink or water, were terrified of him. Also conspiring against him were the masters of the mines, who could never dictate a decree to him.

Belzu, lean and handsome, has come back. He enters the palace on horseback, at a gentle pace, as if steering a ship.

(172)

From a Speech by Belzu
to the Bolivian People

The time has come to ask the aristocracy to give back their titles, and private property its privileges . . . Private property is the chief source of most of the offenses and crimes in Bolivia; it is the cause of the continuing struggle between Bolivians; it is the dominant principle of that selfishness eternally condemned by universal morality. No more property, no more proprietors, no more inheritances! Down with aristocrats! Let the lands be for all! Enough of exploitation of man by man!

(213)

1865: La Paz

Melgarejo

Mariano Melgarejo, Belzu's fiercest enemy, is a Hercules who can carry a horse on his shoulder. He was born in Tarata, highland of tall grass, of a father who loved and left. He was born on an Easter Sunday.

"God has chosen me to be born while He was reviving."

Before learning to walk, he knew how to gallop horses whose heads barely peeked out above the verdure; and before the maternal teat, he got to know the chicha that makes you roll or fly, the best chicha in Bolivia, milk of Tarata, corn chewed and expectorated by old women with the most villainous saliva. Before he could even sign his name, he was unstoppable in daredevil battle charges, body to body, his tunic in rags, lifting and splitting people with dagger, spear, or sword.

He has finished off many. Eternal rebel and troublemaker, he has killed in broad daylight and on moonless nights and twice has been condemned to death. Between sprees and free-for-alls, he has known exile and power. The night before last he slept on the throne and last night in mountain furrows. Yesterday he entered this city of La Paz at the head of his army, riding on an enormous cannon, his red poncho flaming like a flag; and today he crosses the plaza somber and alone.

(85)

1865: La Paz
The Shortest Coup d'État in History

It is Belzu's hour. Melgarejo, the vanquished, comes to surrender. Melgarejo crosses the plaza through the shouts.

"Long live Belzu!"

In the huge second-floor chamber, Belzu waits. Melgarejo enters the palace. Without looking up, his black beard flattened against his bull chest, he mounts the stairs. The crowd yells in the plaza.

"Long live Belzu! Grandpa Belzu!"

Melgarejo walks toward Belzu. The president rises, opens his arms.

"I forgive you."

Through the open windows thunder the voices.

"Grandpa Belzu!"

Melgarejo lets himself be embraced, and shoots. The shot rings out, and the body crashes to the floor.

The victor goes out on the balcony. He shows the body, offers it.

"Belzu is dead! Who's next?"

(85)

1865: Appomattox

General Lee Surrenders His Ruby Sword

The Northern soldiers, in the middle of a crushing advance, await the order for the final assault. At that moment, a cloud of dust rises from the enemy lines. It grows and grows. From the hungry, shattered army of the grays, a horseman breaks away. He carries a white rag tied to a stick.

In the final battles, the Southern soldiers had their names inscribed on their backs, so that they would be recognized among the dead. The South, devastated, has lost the war long ago, and continues only out of a stubborn sense of honor.

Now the beaten general, Robert E. Lee, proffers with gloved hand his sword embellished with rubies. The victorious general, Ulysses Grant, without sword or insignias, his tunic unbuttoned, smokes, or at least chews, a cigar.

The war has ended, slavery has ended. With slavery have fallen the walls that prevented the full development of United States industry and the expansion of its national market. Six hundred thousand young men have died in battle; among them, half of all the blacks who wore the blue of the Northern battalions.

(70)

1865: Washington

Lincoln

Abe comes from Kentucky. There, his father wielded the ax and pounded the hammer, and the cabin had walls and a roof and beds of dry leaves. Every day his ax cut wood for the fire, and one day it wrested from the forest the wood needed to bury Abe's mother under the snow. Abe was a small boy when that hammer knocked in those wooden nails for the mother who would never again make white bread on Saturdays, or flutter those ever-perplexed eyes; and the ax brought in wood to make a raft so that the father could take his children down river to Indiana.

He comes from Indiana. There Abe draws his first letters with a charcoal, and becomes the best railsplitter in the district.

He comes from Illinois. In Illinois, he loves a woman named Ann and marries another named Mary, who speaks French and has

started the crinoline fashion in the city of Springfield. Mary decides
that Abe will be president of the United States. While she is bearing
boy children, he writes speeches and a few poems in the sad island
of his mind, that magic island bathed in liquid light.

He comes from the Capitol in Washington. Leaning from the
window, he sees the slave market, a kind of stable where blacks are
penned up like horses.

He comes from the White House. He came to it promising agrarian reform and protection for industry, and proclaiming that anyone
depriving another of his freedom is not worthy of enjoying it himself.
He entered the White House swearing he would govern in such a
way as still to have a friend inside himself when he no longer had
friends. He governs in wartime and in wartime fulfills all his promises.
At dawn, he can be seen in slippers, standing at the White House
door, waiting for the newspaper.

He comes unhurriedly. Abraham Lincoln is never in a hurry.
He walks like a duck, setting his enormous feet down flat, and juts
out like a tower from the multitude that acclaim him. He enters the
theater and slowly mounts the stairs into the presidential box. In the
box, over flowers and flags, his bony, long-necked head cuts a profile
in the shadows, and in the shadows shine the sweetest eyes and most
melancholy smile in America.

He comes from victory and from dream. Today is Good Friday
and five days ago General Lee surrendered. Last night, Lincoln dreamed
of a sea of mystery and a strange ship that sailed toward misty shores.

Lincoln comes from his whole life, walking unhurriedly toward
this appointment in the box of the comedy theater in the city of
Washington.

Now comes toward him the bullet that splits open his head.

(81 and 188)

1865: Washington

Homage

How many blacks have been hanged for stealing a pair of pants or
looking into the eyes of a white woman? What were the names of the
slaves who set fire to New York over a century ago? How many whites
have followed in the footsteps of Elijah Lovejoy, whose printing press
was twice thrown in the river and who was assassinated in Illinois,
without anyone being sought or punished for it? The history of the

abolition of slavery in the United States has had infinite protagonists, black and white. Such as:

- John Russwurm and Samuel Cornish, who made the first newspaper for blacks; and Theodore Weld, who founded the first higher education center that admitted women and blacks.
- Daniel Payne, who managed to keep open for six years his school for blacks in Charleston; and Prudence Crandall, Quaker teacher in Connecticut, who for taking a black girl into her school lost her white students and was insulted, stoned, and jailed; and where her school had stood only cinders remained.
- Gabriel Prosser, who sought freedom for his brothers in Virginia and found a gallows for himself; and David Walker, for whose head the Georgia authorities paid ten thousand dollars, and who went about announcing that killing a man who is tearing out your life is like drinking water when you are thirsty, and kept on saying it until he disappeared or was disappeared.
- Nat Turner, who during a solar eclipse saw written in the sky the sign that the last should be first and went mad with murderous fury; and John Brown, hunter's beard, eyes aflame, who attacked a Virginia armory and from a railway roundhouse launched a battle against the marines and then refused to let his lawyer plead insanity and walked with dignity to the scaffold.
- William Lloyd Garrison, fanatical enemy of the robbers of men, who was paraded through the streets of Boston with a rope around his neck; and Henry Garnet, who preached in church that the resigned slave sins against God; and Henry Ward Beecher, the Brooklyn minister who said that in certain cases a rifle can be more useful than the Bible, so that arms sent to the slaves of the South came to be called "Beecher's Bibles."
- Harriet Beecher Stowe, whose *Uncle Tom's Cabin* won many whites to the cause; and Frances Harper, the poet who found the right words to curse power and money; and Solomon Northrup, Louisiana slave who could bear witness to cotton plantation life—from the sound of the horn before sunrise to the dead of night.
- Frederick Douglass, fugitive slave from Maryland, who in New York turned the Independence Day proclamation into an indictment and declared that freedom and equality sounded like a hollow parody.

- Harriet Tubman, illiterate peasant who organized the escape of more than three hundred slaves by the Pole Star Road to Canada.

(12 and 210)

1865: Buenos Aires

Triple Infamy

While in North America history wins a war, in South America a war begins which history will lose. Buenos Aires, Rio de Janeiro, and Montevideo, the three ports that wiped out José Artigas half a century ago, get set to devastate Paraguay.

Under the successive dictatorships of Gaspar Rodríguez de Francia, Carlos Antonio López and his son Francisco Solano, wielders of very absolute power, Paraguay has become a dangerous example, offering grave risk of contagion to its neighbors. In Paraguay landlords do not govern, nor do merchants speculate, nor do usurers asphyxiate. Blockaded from outside, the country has grown inward, and continues growing, without obeying the world market or foreign capital. While the others dangle from the noose of their debts, Paraguay owes no one a centavo and walks on its own legs.

The British ambassador in Buenos Aires, Edward Thornton, is high priest of this ferocious ceremony of exorcism. Argentina, Brazil, and Uruguay will exorcise the devil by sticking bayonets in these arrogant bellies.

(47, 60, and 83)

1865: Buenos Aires

The Alliance Woven of Spider-Spittle

Like a grotesque crown on a little tree, Chacho Peñaloza's head, stuck on the pike—a mane of hair held by a headband—adorns the center of a plaza. Chacho and his horse had been one single muscle. They caught him without his horse and treacherously beheaded him. *To keep the rabble quiet* they exhibited the head of the gaucho warrior of the Rioja prairie. Domingo Faustino Sarmiento congratulated the executioners.

The war against Paraguay prolongs another war which has continued for half a century: the war of Buenos Aires, the vampire port, against the provinces. The Uruguayan Venancio Flores has collaborated with Mitre and Sarmiento in exterminating rebel gauchos. As reward he gets the presidency of Uruguay. Brazilian ships and Argentine arms impose Flores on the government. The invasion of Uruguay opens up with a bombardment of the unprotected city of Paysandú. Paysandú resists for a month, until the chief of the defense, Leandro Gómez, is executed amid the flaming ruins.

Thus the double alliance has become triple. With English blessings and English credits the governments of Argentina, Brazil, and Uruguay undertake the redemption of Paraguay. They sign a treaty. They are making war, says the treaty, in the name of peace. Paraguay will have to pay the expenses of its own extermination and the victors will provide an appropriate government. In the name of respect for Paraguay's territorial integrity, the treaty guarantees Brazil one-third of its land area and assigns to Argentina all of Misiones and the vast Chaco. The war is also waged in the name of freedom. Brazil, which has two million slaves, promises freedom to Paraguay, which has none.

(47, 244, and 291)

1865: San José

Urquiza

He kisses a woman's hand, they say, and leaves her pregnant. He collects children and acreage. Of children, he has a hundred and fifty, without counting the doubtfuls, and of lands, who knows? He adores mirrors, Brazilian medals, French porcelain, and the clink of silver coins.

Justo José de Urquiza, venerable boss of the Argentine coast, the man who years ago defeated Juan Manuel de Rosas, has his doubts about the Paraguay war. He resolves them by selling thirty thousand horses from his estancias to the Brazilian army, at an excellent price, and contracting to supply bully beef to the allied armies. Freed of his doubts, he orders the death of anyone who refuses to kill Paraguayans.

(271 and 291)

1866: Curupaytí
Mitre

Splinters that once were ships drift in the waters. The Paraguayan navy is dead, but the allied fleet cannot press the invasion upriver. The guns of Curupaytí and Humaitá stop it, and between the two forts floats a line of demijohns, perhaps mines, stretched from shore to shore.

Under the command of Bartolomé Mitre, Argentine president and generalissimo of the Triple Alliance, soldiers storm the ramparts of Curupaytí with naked bayonets. The bugle looses successive waves of soldiers to the assault. Few reach the moat and none the palisade. The Paraguayans take target practice against an enemy who persists in showing himself in open country, in broad daylight. The roar of cannons, rumble of drums, is followed by the rattle of rifle fire. The Paraguayan fort spits tongues of fire; and when the smoke clears, slow-drifting mist, thousands of dead, shot down like rabbits, wallow in the swamps. At a prudent distance, telescope in hand, in black frock coat and chambergo hat, Bartolomé Mitre contemplates the results of his military genius.

Lying with admirable sincerity, he had promised the invading troops that in three months they would reach Asunción.

(61 and 272)

1866: Curupaytí
The Paintbrush of War

Cándido López, one Mitre's soldiers, will paint this disaster of Curupaytí and the earlier battles he has fought in, and also daily life in the camps. He will paint with the left hand, because at Curupaytí a grenade blew off his right one.

He will paint without imitating anyone and no one will imitate him. During the week, he will sell shoes in a Buenos Aires shop and on Sundays will make pictures that say: *"The war was like this."* The stupid left hand will become wise, by love of memory, but no artist will pay him the slightest attention, nor will any critic take him seriously, nor will anyone be interested in buying his remembrances of a rank-and-file soldier.

"I am a paintbrush chronicler."

The solitary Cándido López will paint multitudes. In his works, there will be no foregrounds of flashing swords and dashing steeds, nor dying heroes pronouncing last words with hands on bleeding breasts, nor allegories of Glory with bared breats. Through his child-like eyes will march innumerable tin soldiers and merry-go-round horses playing in ordered formation the horrendous game of war.

(100)

1867: Catamarca Plains

Felipe Varela

The mounted hillsmen of five Argentine provinces rise in rebellion. The shearing knife tied to a spear challenges the cannon of the line regiments, seeking a hand-to-hand fight; and out of the dust storm of these encounters the cry goes up: *Long live Paraguay!*

Down from the Andes comes Felipe Varela, arousing the peasantry of the Catamarca plains against Buenos Aires, the port that usurps Argentina and negates America. He denounces the bankruptcy of the nation, embroiled in enormous loans for the purpose of annihilating a sister nation. In their heads, his mountaineers carry into battle the watchword *American Union*, and in their hearts an old rage: *A provincial is a beggar without a country.*

A lanky gaucho, nothing but cheekbone and chin, born and raised on horseback, Varela is the harsh voice of the poor at the end of their tether. Provincial "volunteers" are being taken in shackles to the marshes of Paraguay, shut up in corrals, and shot when they rebel or desert.

(239)

1867: Plains of La Rioja

Torture

Colonel Pablo Irrazábal takes testimony from the rebel plainsmen of La Rioja. He takes testimony, that is, he puts them in the pillory, or makes them walk with flayed feet, or slits their throats little by little with a blunt knife.

The port of Buenos Aires uses various instruments of persuasion against the rebellious provinces. One of the most effective is called the "Colombian pillory." The prisoner is doubled up in the pillory and tied with moist leather strips between two rifles so that, when the strips dry out, the spine cracks and breaks in pieces.

(214)

1867: La Paz
On Diplomacy, the Science of International Relations

Mounted on Holofernes, his horse in war and fiesta, President Melgarejo arrives at the cathedral of La Paz. Seated under a canopy on a velvet chair, he hears the solemn Mass. He wears the uniform of a Chilean army general and on his breast gleams the grand ribbon of the Imperial Order of Brazil.

After so many comings and goings and killings, Melgarejo has learned not to trust even his own shirt. They say that sometimes he tears it off and riddles it with bullets.

"The commander commands, with his finger on the trigger."

There are two beings in the world, just two, at whom the iron general does not look askance: the horse Holofernes and the lovely Juana Sánchez. The Chilean ambassador raises his glass and joins Holofernes in a toast, when the black horse appears at the presidential table to drink beer among the ministers, bishops, and generals. The Brazilian ambassador covers the body of Juana Sánchez with such necklaces, diadems, and bracelets as Melgarejo's woman has not seen in her wildest dreams.

His breast covered with Brazilian decorations, Melgarejo cedes to Brazil sixty-five thousand square kilometers of Bolivian forest in Amazonia. Transformed into a general of the Chilean army, Melgarejo presents to Chile half of the Atacama coastal desert, very rich in nitrates. There, Chilean and British capitalists are exploiting the fertilizer most coveted by Europe's exhausted lands. With the amputation of the Atacama desert, Bolivia begins to lose its outlet to the sea.

(85, 107, and 172)

Inscriptions on a Rock in the Atacama Desert

Antonia, for you I die.
                    You know who.
THE CHAÑARCILLO JUDGE IS STEALING.
Pay me my three ounces, Ramón.
The Administrator is a lout.
Don T.P. says he isn't a mulatto.

(256)

1867: Bogotá

A Novel Called *María*

Ladies sway in their hammocks, ringlets fluttering behind their ivory necks, rocked by gentlemen dressed like the dead with faces like boiled chickens. A caravan of blacks, baskets on heads, passes silently in the distance, as if begging pardon for existing and being a nuisance. In the plantation garden, aroma of coffee, fragrance of gardenias, Jorge Isaacs moistens his pen with tears.

All Colombia sobs. Efraín didn't arrive in time. While he plowed the seas, his cousin María, victim of a hereditary and incurable disease, drew her last breath and went to Heaven a virgin. At the grave, Efraín presses to his breast the inheritance of his love. María has left him a kerchief (embroidered by herself and wetted by herself), some white lily petals, so like herself and as withered as herself, a ring slipped from the rigid hand which had been an elegant rose of Castile, and a lock of her long hair in the locket that her lily lips managed to kiss while death was freezing them.

(167 and 208)

1867: Querétaro

Maximilian

The army of Juárez and the thousand guerrilla bands of the Mexican people run the Frenchmen out. Maximilian, the emperor, topples into the mud crying *Long live Mexico*.

At the end, Napoleon III pulls out his army, the pope hates Maximilian, and the conservatives call him *Empoorer*. Napoleon had ordered him to administer the new French colony, but Maximilian did not obey. The pope expected to get his earthly properties back, and the conservatives thought he would exorcise Mexico of the liberal demon; but Maximilian, while making war on Juárez, issued laws quite like those of Juárez.

A black carriage arrives in Querétaro in the rain. President Juárez, conqueror of the intruders, goes up to the open and flowerless coffin, where lies the prince with the languid blue eyes, who liked to stroll down the Alameda dressed as a Mexican cowboy with broad-brimmed sombrero and sequins.

(94 and 143)

1867: Paris

To Be or to Copy, That Is the Question

To Paris's Universal Exhibition come oil-on-cloth paintings sent from Ecuador. All the paintings are exact copies of the most famous works of European artists. The catalog praises the Ecuadoran artists *who, if they have no great originality, at least have the merit of reproducing, with noteworthy faithfulness, masterworks of the Italian, Spanish, French, and Flemish schools.*

Meanwhile another art flourishes in the Indian markets and poor outskirts of Ecuador. It is the despised work of hands able to create beauty out of clay and wood and straw, bird-feathers, sea shells, bread crumbs. This art, as if begging pardon, is called artisanship. Academicians don't do it, only poor folk who eat flea hearts or mosquito tripe.

(37)

Song of the Poor in Ecuador

"Hungry, ducks?"
"Yes."
"Eat the pain in your guts.
Stab a mosquito,
suck blood from the cuts,
keep the tripe for a treat or
tomorrow's cold cuts."

(65)

1869: Mexico City
Juárez

The face of this Mexican Indian, who defeated the pope of Rome and the third Napoleon, has been carved out of Oaxaca stone. Without smile or speech, always in frock coat and high collar, always in black, Benito Juárez is a rock surrounded by a chorus of doctors who whirl around him discoursing and declaiming and reciting, learned pedants blessed with golden beaks and gilded plumes.

Mexico has more priests than teachers, and the Church owns half of everything, when Juárez comes to power and the liberals prescribe their civilizing potion for a country sick from ignorance and backwardness. The therapy of modernization calls for peace and order. It is necessary to do away with wars that kill more people than malaria or tuberculosis, but the plague of war harasses Juárez without mercy. First, the war against the French invaders; and since then, the war against the military hero-bosses who decline to retire, and against Indians who decline to lose their community lands.

Mexican liberals profess blind faith in universal suffrage and freedom of expression, although the vote is the privilege of few and few express themselves. They believe in salvation by education, although the few schools are all in the cities, because liberals, after all, get along better with muses than with Indians. As big estates get bigger, they dream about pioneer farmers fertilizing uncultivated lands, and they dream about magical rails, smoke of locomotives, smoking chimneys, ideas and people and capital that will bring progress from Europe.

Juárez himself, son of Zapotec Indians, is convinced that if Mexico copies North American laws, it will grow like the United States, and if it consumes English products it will become as industrious a nation as England. By importing French ideas, thinks the defeater of France, Mexico will become an erudite nation.

(142, 143, and 316)

1869: San Cristóbal de Las Casas
Neither Earth nor Time Is Dumb

The earth vibrates from all the talk among the dead below. The graveyard hums like a plaza on market day. The Mayas who fell in the old Chiapas rebellions are celebrating the latest news. Here they have fought with spear and ax since the remote day when the first usurper, son of woman and dog, swooped down upon the community lands. The dead chat happily among themselves, and through dreams congratulate the living and tell them truths that the ear does not know.

Again the Indians hereabouts have risen in rebellion. The Indians, debt-slaves, destroy haciendas and burn prisons and defend the last of their communal lands, which they work as a community despite the Juárez government.

The gods of the mountain also celebrate. They are the ones who deflect the gale when it carries disease or greed.

(155 and 274)

1869: Mexico City
Juárez and the Indians

For being a rebel, a bandit, a rabid socialist, Julio López was shot a year ago. At the head of Indians of the Chalco region, Julio López had vowed *war on the rich* and had rebelled to reclaim the stolen lands.

They have put soldiers' uniforms on Indian prisoners in Chalco and forced them to fight against the rebel Indians of Yucatán. Those "pacified" in each war become "pacifiers" in the next, rebels defeated and made to kill rebels; and thus the government of President Juárez keeps sending troops against the Mayas of Yucatán and the Mayas of Chiapas, the Coras of Nayarit and the Tarascans of Michoacán, the Yaquis of Sonora and the Apaches of the north.

To recover the lands of their communities, the Indians turn around hacienda signposts: the first dead fall and the air becomes nothing but gunsmoke. Juárez's Constitution seeks to turn the Indians into small proprietors and free workers. Juárez's laws ban the pillory and shackles, enslavement for debt and hunger wages. Reality, meanwhile, seizes lands the Indians still possess in common and makes them slaves of big estates or beggars in the cities.

Benito Juárez was born in the mountains, amid the rocks that resemble him, on the shores of Lake Guelatao. He learned to name the world in one of the hundred Indian languages of Mexico. Later, under the patronage of a pious man, he became a man of letters.

(142 and 274)

1869: London

Lafargue

When Paul Lafargue began laying siege to Laura Marx, the founder of scientific socialism was finishing the correction of the first volume of *Capital*. Karl Marx took a dim view of the Cuban's ardent assaults, and told him to court his green-eyed daughter with *quieter English manners*. He also asked him for economic guarantees. Ousted from Germany, France, and Belgium, Marx has gone through hard times in London, devoured by debt, sometimes without a penny to buy a newspaper. The miseries of exile have killed three of his children.

But he cannot scare off Lafargue. He always knew he couldn't. Lafargue was very young when he and Marx began to fight and to love each other. And now Marx's first grandson is born of the Cuban mestizo, great-grandson of a Haitian mulatta and an Indian from Jamaica.

(177 and 279)

1869: Acosta Ñú

Paraguay Falls, Trampled
Under Horses' Hooves

and, fallen, fights on. The last cannons are made of church bells and fire stones and sand, while the Triple Alliance armies press on to the north. The wounded tear off their bandages, because it is better to bleed to death than serve in the enemy army or march off to Brazilian coffee plantations with the brand of slavery.

Not even graves are spared in the sacking of Asunción. In Piribebuy, the invaders overrun trenches defended by women, the mutilated, and old people, and set fire to the hospital filled with wounded. In Acosta Ñú, the offensive is resisted by battalions of children disguised with beards of wool or grass.

And the butchery goes on. Those not killed by bullets are killed by plague. And every death hurts. Every death seems like the last, but is the first.

(61 and 254)

1870: Mount Corá

Solano López

This is a caravan of dead people who breathe. Paraguay's last soldiers tramp behind Marshal Francisco Solano López. No boots or harnesses are to be seen, because they have been eaten, but no sores or rags either: of mud and bone are these soldiers, wandering through the woods, masks of mud, carapaces of mud, pottery flesh that the sun has cooked with the mud of the swamps and the red dust of the deserts.

Marshal López does not surrender. Hallucinating, sword borne high, he heads this last march to nowhere. He discovers plots, or imagines them, and for the crime of treason or weakness has his brother and all his in-laws executed, and also the bishop and a minister and a general . . . For lack of powder, the executions are performed with a spear. Many die by López's order, many more from exhaustion, and they are left behind on the road. The earth recovers its own and bones mark the trail for the pursuer.

Enormous enemy hosts close the circle at Mount Corá. They bring López down on the banks of the River Aquidabán, wound him with a spear, kill him with a sword, and with one shot finish him off, because he still howls.

(291)

1870: Mount Corá

Elisa Lynch

Surrounded by the conquerors, Elisa digs with her nails a grave for Solano López.

Bugles no longer sound, nor do bullets whistle, nor grenades explode. Flies cover the marshal's face and attack his gashed body, but Elisa sees only a red mist. As her hands tear the ground open, she insults this accursed day; and the sun hesitates on the horizon because the day dares not withdraw before she finished cursing it.

This Irishwoman with golden hair, who has fought at the head of columns of women armed with hoes and sticks, has been López's most implacable adviser. Last night, after sixteen years and four children, he told her for the first time that he loved her.

(25)

Guaraní

Of annihilated Paraguay, the language survives.

Mysterious powers has Guaraní, language of Indians, language of the conquered which the conquerors made their own. In spite of bans and slights, Guaraní is still the national language of this land in ruins, and will be so although the law wills otherwise. Here the mosquito will continue to be called "Devil's fingernail" and the dragonfly, "Devil's little horse"; the stars, "fires of the moon," and dusk, "the mouth of night."

Paraguayan soldiers gave passwords and pep talks in Guaraní, while the war lasted, and in Guaraní they sang. Now the dead fall silent, in Guaraní.

(152)

1870: Buenos Aires

Sarmiento

Argentina's president, Domingo Faustino Sarmiento, receives the military communiqué of the victory in Paraguay. He orders the band to play serenades, and writes: *Providence decreed that a tyrant should cause the death of that Guaraní people. It was necessary to purge the earth of all that human excrescence.*

Sarmiento, founder of the Animal Protection Society, preaches pure unabashed racism and practices it with untrembling hand. He admires the North Americans, *free from any mixture of inferior races*, but from Mexico southward he sees only barbarism, dirt, superstitions, chaos, and madness. Those dark shadows terrify and fascinate him. He goes for them with sword in one hand and lamp in the other. As governor and president, he multiplies cemeteries and schools, and fosters the noble virtues of throat-cutting, saving, and reading. As a writer, he publishes prose works of great talent in favor of the extermination of gauchos, Indians, and blacks and their replacement by white laborers from northern Europe, and in defense of the frock coat and the English-style haircut.

(310 and 311)

1870: Rio de Janeiro
A Thousand Candelabra Proliferate
in the Mirrors

and silken shoes draw waltz circles on the lustrous floor of Baron de Itamaraty's palace. Through clouds of guests pass the imperial couple, from salon to salon, endless hand-kissing and tinkling of glass, and as they go, martial trumpetings and thunderous cheers interrupt the ball. The gentlemen look like penguins and the ladies like butterflies, tightly enclosed in their crinolines, unfurling laces; and more than one wear European breasts, imported by Mademoiselle Arthémise, which ripple in perfect accompaniment to their breathing. With champagne and music in the French fashion, Brazil celebrates the devastation of Paraguay.

Carriages rolling up to the fiesta cross paths with caravans of blacks toting fetid pots and barrels. Clouds of flies pursue the procession to the beaches of Rio de Janeiro. Every evening, slaves throw the masters' shit into the waters of the lovely bay.

(204)

1870: Rio de Janeiro
Mauá

While they celebrate the annihilation of Paraguay, the conquering countries fight over who will get the biggest bite of the conquered.

In Rio de Janeiro, someone observes the effervescent celebrations with furrowed brow and shrugs his shoulders at talk of new frontiers. Irineo Evangelista de Souza, baron of Mauá by grace of Emperor Pedro II, never wanted this war. From the start he had presentiments that it would be long and bloody, and also that whoever won it would lose it. Laurels for the empire of Brazil? Peace illuminated by glory? The empire prospering as if the war had never been? Baron de Mauá, Brazilian partner of the Rothschilds of London, knows that the exterminators now owe British banks twice as much as they did before. Mauá, owner of great plantations, knows that the coffee estates have lost many thousands of black slaves on the battlefields. Accustomed to financing the victorious countries' budgets and issuing their banknotes, Mauá also knows that they have papered themselves with valueless vouchers. And perhaps he knows—who knows?—that this just-ended war is the beginning of his personal ruin, that creditors will end up seizing even his gold eyeglasses and that, in his last years, he will again be that lonesome child some sailor had abandoned on the docks of Rio.

(109)

1870: Vassouras

The Coffee Barons

The southern Paraíba River valley produces most of the coffee the world consumes, and also produces the largest number of viscounts, barons, and marquises per square foot.

From the throne of Brazil, Emperor Pedro II now rewards with new titles of nobility the coffee slavers who have contributed so much money to the war against Paraguay.

No plantation has fewer than a hundred slaves. When it is still night, at the toll of the iron bell the slaves wash in the tank, offer loud thanks to Our Lord Jesus Christ, and march to work up the mountain, inspired by the cat-o'-nine-tails.

The masters' sons are brought into the world by black midwives, and black wet nurses suckle them. Black nurses teach them songs, legends, and tastes in food. With black children they learn to play and with black girls they discover love. But from early on they know who is proprietor and who is property. Marriage to a cousin or niece will fortify family unity and perpetuate the nobility of the lineage.

(327)

1870: São Paulo

Nabuco

Everyone eats off the black slave. Not only the coffee barons and the sugar lords, but every free Brazilian, no matter how poor, has at least one slave working for him.

Joaquim Nabuco denounces this deep infection in fiery speeches. Born of landowners and professional politicians, Nabuco proclaims that Brazil will not enter the modern world as long as land and politics belong to a handful of families, and as long as the whole country rests on the backs of slaves.

The poet José Bonifácio heads up a group of abolitionists from

São Paulo University. Working with him in addition to Nabuco are other brilliant orators such as Castro Alves, Rui Barbosa, and Luis Gama, who was sold by his own father in Bahia and managed to escape slavery to denounce it.

(74)

1870: Buenos Aires

The North Barrio

A blue-bloused horseman blows the bugle that warns of danger. Clatter of hooves, hubbub of bells, stampede of pedestrians: the new streetcar comes dashing on rails at the mad speed of six miles per hour. A Buenos Aires newspaper promises to reserve a column every day for the victims.

The streetcar manages a death or two to avoid disappointment, but in a short while no one talks of its homicidal furies. Yellow fever has invaded Buenos Aires and is killing off three hundred a day.

Because there is no place to bury so many paupers, the Chacarita cemetery is born of this plague, as is the North Barrio, because the rich flee from their traditional bastion. The ten blocks south of the Plaza de Mayo have always decided the fate of all Argentina, and have always prospered at its expense. There, until now, have lived the gentlemen who make politics and business in the Cafe de Paris and the ladies who shop at the London Store. Now they are chased out by the yellow fever, which feeds cruelly on the low district surrounded by garbage dumps and swamps, cradle of mosquitos, broth of plagues; and the mansions emptied by the exodus become tenements. Where one family lived before, two hundred will crowd in as best they can.

This city scattered over river banks has grown prodigiously. A couple of centuries ago, Buenos Aires was a sad, lost village. Today a hundred and eighty thousand people live here, half of them foreigners: masons, washerwomen, shoemakers, day laborers, cooks, night watchmen, carpenters, and other newcomers whom the trade winds have blown in from the Mediterranean.

(312)

1870: Paris

Lautréamont at Twenty-Four

He had speech impediments and got tired from nothing at all. He spent nights at the piano, spinning chords and words, and at dawn his eyes were pitifully feverish.

Isidoro Ducasse, the imaginary Count of Lautréamont, has died. The child born and raised in the Montevideo war, that child who asked questions of the river-sea, has died in a hotel in Paris. His publisher dared not send his "Cantos" to the bookshops.

Lautréamont had written hymns to the louse and to the pederast. He had sung to the red light of the brothels and to the insects that prefer blood to wine. He had scolded the drunken god who created us, and proclaimed it better to be born from the womb of a female shark. He had flung himself into the abyss, human scrapmeat capable of beauty and madness, and on his way down had discovered ferocious images and astounding words. Every page he wrote screams when you tear it.

(181)

1871: Lima

Juana Sánchez

Melgarejo the destroyer has fallen. Stoned by the Indians, he has fled from Bolivia, and suffers out his exile in a hovel in the Lima slums. All the power he has left is in his blood-red poncho. The Indians killed his horse Holofernes and cut off its ears.

He spends his nights howling before the home of the Sánchez family. Melgarejo's sad, booming voice sets Lima atremble. Juana doesn't open the door.

Juana was eighteen when she arrived at the palace. Melgarejo shut himself in with her for three days and three nights. His guards heard screams, blows, snorts, groans, never a word. On the fourth day Melgarejo emerged.

"I love her as much as my army!"

The banquet table was turned into an altar. In the center, surrounded by candles, reigned a nude Juana. Ministers, bishops, and generals paid homage to her beauty, falling to their knees when Melgarejo raised a glass of flaming cognac and sang verses of devotion.

She, an erect marble statue, with no more clothes than her hair, looked down and away.

And she said nothing. Juana said nothing. When Melgarejo went on a military campaign, he left her shut up in a La Paz convent. He returned to the palace with her in his arms and she said nothing, a virgin woman every night, every night born for him. Juana said nothing when Melgarejo seized the Indians' communal lands and gave her eighty properties and an entire province for her family.

Now, too, Juana says nothing. With the door of her mansion in Lima stoutly barricaded, she does not show herself or answer the desperate roarings of Melgarejo. She does not even say to him, *"You never had me. I wasn't there."*

Melgarejo weeps and bellows, his fists thundering on the door. In this shadow, shouting the name of this woman, he dies of two bullets.

(85)

1873: Camp Tempú

The Mambises

The blacks, lustrous from torches and other lights, undulate and spin and jump and talk to the gods howling with pain and pleasure. For the *New York Herald* correspondent this commotion is as incomprehensible as the seasons, which in Cuba come all at once within an endless summer. The journalist blinks hard when he discovers that the same tree has at the same time one branch bursting in full verdure and another yellowing in its death throes.

This is the land of the Mambí, in the forest of eastern Cuba. Mambí meant "bandit" or "rebel" back there in the Congo, but on this island Mambí is the slave who fights to become a person again.

Before joining the patriot army, the Mambises had been fugitive slaves in the mountains. The *Herald* correspondent calculates that in five years the colonial war has taken eighty thousand Spanish lives. Many soldiers have been felled by disease or bullet; and many more by Mambí machete. The war has turned sugar mills into fortresses armed against attacks by blacks from the outside and escapes by blacks inside.

In this camp of ragged, almost naked Mambises, everything is shared. The journalist drinks water with molasses for lack of coffee, and after a few days swears eternal hatred for sweet potatoes and hutia—a small animal that provides food for anyone who can catch it in the crannies of a tree or rock. This war could last forever, writes the journalist. Here, lianas give water when there is no nearby river, and the trees provide fruit, hammocks, sandals, and good shade for those who need to sit down and swap jokes and stories while their wounds heal.

(237)

1875: Mexico City
Martí

Recently his pointed mustache got a blunting in Havana when he started two short-lived newspapers, *The Lame Devil* and *Free Fatherland*; and for wanting independence for Cuba, a Spanish colony, he was sentenced to prison and forced labor. Earlier, when he was still a very young child, he had wanted to translate Shakespeare, and had set fire to words, and sworn vengeance before a black slave hanging from the gallows. He had guessed, in his earliest verses, that he would die in and for Cuba.

From prison they sent him into exile. The marks of the shackles have not disappeared from his ankles. No more patriotic Cuban than this son of a Spanish colonial sergeant; none more childlike than this inquisitive exile, so astonished and indignant at the world.

José Martí is twenty-two when he attends in Mexico his first joint demonstration of students and workers. The hat makers have gone on strike. They have the solidarity of the Fraternal and Constancy Society of Hairdressers, the Fraternal Society of Bookbinders, the typographers, the tailors, and the intellectuals, "workers of the Idea." At the same time, the first university strike erupts, against the expulsion of three medical students.

Martí organizes benefit recitals for the hat makers, and in his articles describes students marching with workers through the streets of Mexico City, arm-in-arm, all in their Sunday best. *These enthusiastic young people*, he observes, *are right. But even if they were wrong, we would love them.*

(129, 200, and 354)

1875: Fort Sill

The Last Buffalos of the South

The southern plains were carpeted with buffalos, which multiplied like the tall grasses, when the white man arrived from Kansas. Now the wind smells of decay. Skinned buffalos lie on the prairie. Millions of skins have gone to eastern Europe. The extermination of the buffalo not only brings in money, but, as General Sheridan explains, *it is the only way to bring lasting peace and allow civilization to advance.*

The Kiowa and Comanche Indians now find no buffalos within the Fort Sill reservation. In vain they invoke good hunting with dances to the sun god. On their federal government rations, pitiful rations, they cannot survive.

The Indians escape to far-off Palo Duro canyon, the last place with buffalos in the southern plains. There, they find food and all the rest: they use the skins for shelter, blankets, and clothing; the horns and bones for spoons, knives, and arrowheads; the nerves and tendons for ropes and nets, the bladders for water pitchers.

Soon the soldiers arrive, amid clouds of dust and gunpowder. They burn huts and provisions, kill a thousand horses and herd the Indians back into their enclosure.

A few Kiowas manage to escape. They wander the prairie until hunger defeats them. They surrender at Fort Sill. There the soldiers put them in a corral and every day throw them bits of raw meat.

(51 and 229)

Into the Beyond

The buffalos of the last southern herd hold a meeting. The discussion does not last long. Everything has been said and night continues. The buffalos know they are no longer able to protect the Indians.

When dawn rises from the river, a Kiowa woman sees the last herd passing through the mist. The leader walks with slow tread, followed by the females, the calves, and the few surviving males. Reaching the foot of Mount Scott, they pause, motionless, with their heads down. Then the mountain opens its mouth and the buffalos enter. There, inside, the world is green and fresh.

The buffalos have passed. The mountain closes.

(198)

1876: Little Big Horn
Sitting Bull

When he speaks, no word tires or falls.

No more lies, he says. Eight years ago, the United States government guaranteed to the Sioux, by solemn treaty, that they would forever be owners of the Black Hills, the center of their world, the place where warriors talk with the gods. Two years ago, gold was discovered in these lands. Last year, the government ordered the Sioux to leave the hunting grounds where miners were seeking gold in rocks and streams.

I have said enough. No more lies. Sitting Bull, chief of chiefs, has assembled thousands of warriors of the plains, Sioux, Cheyennes, Arapahos. He has danced for three days and three nights. He has fixed his eyes on the sun. He knows.

He wakes before dawn. He wets his bare feet in the dew and receives the heartbeat of the earth.

At dawn he raises his eyes beyond the hills. There comes General Custer. There comes the Seventh Cavalry.

(51 and 206)

1876: Little Big Horn
Black Elk

At the age of nine he heard the voices. He knew that all of us who have legs, wings, or roots are children of the same father sun and of the same mother earth, whose breasts we suck. The voices told him that he would make flowers bloom on the sacred cane, the tree of life planted in the center of the land of the Sioux, and that mounted on a storm cloud he would kill drought. They also announced wars and sufferings.

At ten, he met a white man for the first time. He thought the fellow must be ill.

At thirteen, Black Elk is bathing in Little Big Horn River when shouts warn him that soldiers are coming. He climbs a hill and from there sees an immense dust cloud full of hooves and yells, and from the cloud many horses stampeding with empty saddles.

(51 and 230)

1876: Little Big Horn

Custer

Black Kettle, the Cheyenne chief, had warned him of it when they smoked the peace pipe together. Custer would die if he betrayed his promises, and no Indian would dirty his hands scalping him. Afterwards Custer burned down that camp and Chief Black Kettle was riddled with bullets amid the flames.

Now, General George Armstrong Custer is just one more of the dead of the Seventh Cavalry, which the Indians have wiped out on the banks of the Little Big Horn River. Custer had had his golden hair shaved off the night before. His smooth cranium seems intact, and he still wears that rather stupid expression of men who have never been defeated.

(51, 91, and 198)

1876: War Bonnet Creek

Buffalo Bill

Shortly after the defeat at Little Big Horn, some soldiers descend upon the Cheyenne Indians camped on the banks of a brook, and in the shoot-out Chief Yellow Hand falls.

Buffalo Bill is first on the scene. At one slash he scalps the Cheyenne chief, and at one gallop flies to the footlights of distant cities. The history of the West is becoming a theatrical spectacle as it unfolds. The battle is not yet over and the scalper is already selling his epic feat in the theaters of Philadelphia, Baltimore, Washington, and New York. In memory and vengeance of General Custer, Buffalo Bill raises his arms before the packed auditorium: in one hand appears the knife and from the other, which clutches a scalp dyed with blood, hangs a cascade of multicolored feathers. The hero wears a heavily ornamented Mexican suit, with a pair of revolvers in his belt and his fifteen-shot Winchester slung from his shoulder. Soon the scene will adorn the covers of cowboy dime novels selling throughout the country.

Buffalo Bill, most famous of cowboys, has never herded a cow in his life. The living symbol of the winning of the West, the immortal superman, has earned his fame exterminating Indians and buffalos and talking endlessly about his own courage and marksmanship. They baptized him Buffalo Bill when he was working for the Kansas Pacific

Railroad: he says that in a year and a half he fired 4,280 shots and killed 4,280 buffalos although women prevented him from going all out.

(157)

1876: Mexico City
Departure

Eleven times General Santa Anna had been president of Mexico. He bought his generals' loyalty by selling bits of the country and imposing taxes on dogs, horses, and windows; but he often had to flee from the palace disguised as a pauper. Although he specialized in losing wars, he had many statues of himself erected galloping in bronze, sword on high, and by decree he turned his birthday into a national holiday.

When he returned from exile, all his friends had died, and all his enemies too. Buried deep in an armchair, always with a fighting cock in his arms, Santa Anna rubbed old medals or scratched his cork leg. He was blind, but thought he saw carriage-loads of princes and presidents drawing up at his door. He was deaf, but thought he heard supplicatory multitudes coming to plead for an audience, clemency, or a job.

"You wait!" Santa Anna would yell. *"Shut up!"*—while the last of his lackeys changed his wetted trousers.

Now from his house on Vergara Street, mortgaged, always empty, they take him out to the cemetery. The cocks march ahead of the coffin, confronting people and looking for a fight.

(227 and 266)

1877: Guatemala City
The Civilizer

Justo Rufino Barrios, president of Guatemala, closes his eyes and hears a din of railroads and steam engines violating the silence of the monasteries.

There is no stopping synthetic dyes in the world's markets, and no one buys the cochineal and indigo that Guatemala sells. It's time for coffee. The markets demand coffee and coffee demands lands and hands, trains and ports. *To modernize the country,* Barrios expels the parasitic monks, seizes from the Church its immense properties and gives them to his closest friends. He also expropriates the lands of Indian communities. Collective property is abolished by decree and compulsory peonage is imposed. *To integrate the Indian into the nation*, the liberal government makes him a serf of the new coffee plantations. The colonial system of forced labor returns.

Soldiers tour the plantations distributing Indians.

(59)

1879: Mexico City
The Socialists and the Indians

It is painful to say so, but we must. Colonel Alberto Santa Fe says it from Tlatelolco prison: the Indians were happier under Spanish rule. *Today they are pompously called free and they are slaves.*

According to the socialist Santa Fe, who has set off an Indian insurrection in the valley of Texmelucan, the ills of Mexico stem from the poverty of the people, which in turn stems from the concentration of land in a few hands and the lack of industry, *because everything comes from abroad when we could make it ourselves.* And he asks himself: *would we do better to lose independence and become a North American colony, or to change the social organization that has ruined us?*

In the newspaper *The Socialist*, Juan de Mata Rivera also proclaims that the Indians were better off in the colony, and demands that their lands be returned to them. There is no law granting rights to thieves over the fruits of violence and infamy.

At the same time, campesinos of Sierra Gorda publish their "Socialist Plan." They call the rapacious big estates and governments that have put the Indians at the landowners' service the root of all misfortune. They propose that haciendas become "townships," that community property in farmlands, waters, woods, and pastures be restored.

(129 and 274)

1879: Choele-Choel Island
The Remington Method

Argentine soldiers conquer twenty thousand leagues of Indian land.

The London market demands a multiplication of cattle; and the frontier explodes. For the southward and westward growth of the great estates of the pampas, repeating rifles empty out "empty spaces." Clearing savages out of Patagonia, burning villages, using Indians and ostriches for target practice, General Julio Argentino Roca winds up the brilliant military career which he began in the wars against gauchos and Paraguayans.

On the island of Choele-Choel in the Negro River, four thousand dusty soldiers attend Mass. They offer their victory to God. The desert campaign is over.

The survivors—Indian men, Indian women, frontier booty—are divided among estancias, forts, stables, kitchens, and beds. More than ten thousand of them, calculates Lieutenant Colonel Federico Barbará. Thanks to the generosity of Argentine ladies, says Barbará, the savage children change their chiripás for pants and come to look like human beings.

(353)

1879: Buenos Aires
Martín Fierro and the
Twilight of the Gaucho

José Hernández publishes in Buenos Aires the final part of "Martín Fierro," a song of the death-throes of the gaucho who made this country and ended up without a country. For some time the other half of this splendid poem has been circulating throughout the River Plata countryside, its stanzas basic necessities of life like meat, maté, and tobacco.

Sadly reciting couplets around the campfires, serfs on the big estates and conscripts in the forts evoke the ways of that wild brother, the man without ruler or rules, and thus resurrect the memory of their lost freedom.

(158)

1879: Port-au-Prince
Maceo

The exiled Antonio Maceo reaches the heights of Belle Air on the road to Santo Domingo when five assassins fall upon him. It is a night of full moon, but Maceo escapes from the shoot-out and at a gallop, buries himself in the brush. The Spanish consul in Haiti had promised the killers twenty thousand pesos in gold. Maceo is the most popular and dangerous of the fighters for the independence of Cuba.

He has lost his father and fourteen brothers in the war, and to the war he will return. In the thunder of cavalry, as clashing machetes advance into the mouths of cannons, Maceo charges ahead. He has won his promotions in combat, and certain white officers are not at all happy about a near-black being a major general.

Maceo fights for a real revolution. *It's not a matter of replacing the Spaniards*, he says. Independence is not the final goal, but the first one. After that, Cuba has to be changed. As long as the people don't command, the colony will not become a fatherland. The big Creole landowners are mistrustful, for good reasons, of this man who says there is nothing sacred about the right of property.

(262)

1879: Chinchas Islands
Guano

Pure shit were the hills that rose on these islands. For millennia, millions of birds had concluded their digestive process on the coast of southern Peru.

The Incas knew that this guano could revive any land, however dead it seemed; but Europe did not know the magical powers of the Peruvian fertilizer until Humboldt brought back the first samples.

Peru, which had gained worldwide prestige for silver and gold, perpetuated its glory thanks to the goodwill of the birds. Europeward sailed ships laden with malodorous guano, and returned bringing statues of pure Carrara marble to decorate Lima's boulevards. Their holds were also filled with English clothing, which ruined the textile mills of the southern sierra, and Bordeaux wines which bankrupted the national vineyards of Moquequa. Entire houses arrived at Callao from London. From Paris were imported whole luxury hotels complete with chefs.

After forty years, the islands are exhausted. Peru has sold twelve million tons of guano, has spent twice as much, and now owes a candle to every saint.

(43, 44, and 289)

1879: Atacama and Tarapacá Deserts

Saltpeter

No war breaks out over guano, of which little remains. It is saltpeter that throws the Chilean army into the conquest of the deserts, against the allied forces of Peru and Bolivia.

From the sterile Atacama and Tarapacá deserts comes the secret of the verdure of Europe's valleys. In these solitudes there are only lizards hiding under stones and herds of mules carting to Pacific ports loads of saltpeter, a lumpy snow which will restore enthusiasm to weary European lands. Nothing throws a shadow in this world of nothing, unless it be the sparkling mountains of saltpeter drying forsakenly in the sun or the wretched workers, desert warriors with ragged flour sacks for uniforms, pickaxes for spears, and shovels for swords.

The saltpeter, or nitrate, turns out to be indispensable for the businesses of life and of death. Not only is it the most coveted of fertilizers, mixed with carbon and sulphur it becomes gunpowder. Agriculture and the prosperous industry of war need it.

(35 and 268)

1880: Lima

The Chinese

Chile invades and devastates. With English uniforms and English weapons, the Chilean army levels the Lima beach towns of Chorrillos, Barranco, and Miraflores, leaving no stone on another. Peruvian officers send Indians into the slaughter and run off yelling, *"Long live the fatherland!"*

There are many Chinese, Chinese from Peru, fighting on the Chilean side. They are Chinese fugitives from the big estates, who now enter Lima singing the praises of the invading general Patricio Lynch, the Red Prince, the Savior.

Those Chinese were shanghaied a few years ago from the ports of Macao and Canton by English, Portuguese, and French merchants. Of every three, two reached Peru alive. In the port of Callao they were put up for sale. Lima newspapers advertised them *fresh off the boat*. Many were branded with hot irons. Railroads, cotton, sugar, guano, and coffee needed slave hands. On the guano islands the guards never took their eyes off them, because with the smallest negligence some Chinese kills himself by jumping into the sea.

The fall of Lima sets off chaos in all Peru. In the Cañete valley, blacks rise in rebellion. At the end of an Ash Wednesday carnival the hatred of centuries explodes. Ritual of humiliations: blacks, slaves until recently and still treated as such, avenge old scores killing Chinese, also slaves, with sticks and machetes.

(45 and 329)

1880: London

In Defense of Indolence

Run out by the French police and mortified by the English winter, which makes one piss stalactites, Paul Lafargue writes in London a new indictment of *the criminal system that makes man a miserable servant of the machine*.

Capitalist ethics, a pitiful parody of Christian ethics, writes Marx's Cuban son-in-law. Like the monks, capitalism teaches workers that they were born into this vale of tears to toil and suffer; and induces them to deliver up their wives and children to the factories, which grind them up for twelve hours a day. Lafargue refuses to join in *nauseating songs in honor of the god Progress, the eldest son of Work*, and claims the right to indolence and a full enjoyment of human passions. Indolence is a gift of the gods. Even Christ preached it in the Sermon on the Mount. Some day, announces Lafargue, there will come an end to the torments of hunger and forced labor, more numerous than the locusts of the Bible, and then the earth will tremble with joy.

(177)

1881: Lincoln City

Billy the Kid

"I'm gonna give you a tip, doc."

Until a minute ago, Billy the Kid was awaiting the gallows in a cell. Now he aims at the sheriff from the top of the stairs.

"I'm gettin' tired, doc."

The sheriff throws him the key to the handcuffs and when Billy bends down there is a burst of revolver fire. The sheriff topples with a bullet in his eye and his silver star in smithereens.

Billy is twenty-one and has twenty-one notches in the butt of his Colt, not counting a score of Apaches and Mexicans, who died unrecorded.

"I wouldn't do that if I was you, stranger."

He began his career at twelve, when a bum insulted his mother, and he took off at full gallop, brandishing a razor that dripped blood.

(131 and 292)

1882: Saint Joseph

Jesse James

Jesse and his lads, the "James Boys," had fought with the slaver army of the South and later were the avenging angels of that conquered land. To satisfy their sense of honor they have plucked clean eleven banks, seven mail trains, and three stage coaches. Full of braggadocio, reluctantly, without taking the trouble to draw his gun, Jesse has sent sixteen fellowmen to the other world.

One Saturday night, in Saint Joseph, Missouri, his best friend shoots him in the back.

"You, baby, dry them tears and set 'em up all around. And see if they can get that garbage out of the way. I'll tell you what he was. Know what he was? Stubbornest damn mule in Arizona."

(292)

1882: Prairies of Oklahoma

Twilight of the Cowboy

Half a century ago, the legendary wild horse of Oklahoma, amazed Washington Irving and inspired his pen. That untameable prince of the prairies, that long-maned white arrow, is now a meek beast of burden.

The cowboy, too, champion of the winning of the West, angel of justice or vengeful bandit, becomes a soldier or a peon observing regular hours. Barbed wire advances at a thousand kilometers a day and refrigerator trains cross the great prairies of the United States. Ballads and dime novels evoke the howls of coyotes and Indians, the good times of covered-wagon caravans, their creaking wooden axles greased with bacon; and Buffalo Bill is demonstrating that nostalgia can be turned into a very lucrative business. But the cowboy is another machine among the many that gin the cotton, thresh the wheat, or bale the hay.

(224 and 292)

1882: New York

You Too Can Succeed in Life

The happiness road no longer leads only to the prairies of the West. Now, it is also the day of the big cities. The whistle of the train, magic flute, awakens youth from its rustic drowsiness and invites it to join the new paradises of cement and steel. Any ragged orphan, promise the siren voices, can become a prosperous businessman if he works hard and lives virtuously in the offices and factories of the giant buildings.

A writer, Horatio Alger, sells these illusions by the millions of copies. Alger is more famous than Shakespeare and his novels have a bigger circulation than the Bible. His readers and his characters, tame wage earners, have not stopped running since they got off the trains or transatlantic ships. In reality, the track is reserved for a handful of business athletes, but North American society massively consumes the fantasy of free competition, and even cripples dream of winning races.

(282)

1882: New York

The Creation According to John D. Rockefeller

In the beginning I made light with a kerosene lamp. And the shadows, which mocked tallow or sperm candles, retreated. And the evening and the morning were the first day.

And on the second day God put me to the test and allowed the Devil to tempt me, offering me friends and lovers and other extravagances.

And I said: "Let petroleum come to me." And I founded Standard Oil. And I saw that it was good and the evening and the morning were the third day.

And on the fourth I followed God's example. Like Him, I threatened and cursed anyone refusing me obedience; and like Him I applied extortion and punishment. As God has crushed his competitors, so I pitilessly pulverized my rivals in Pittsburgh and Philadelphia. And to the repentant I promised forgiveness and eternal peace.

And I put an end to the disorder of the Universe. And where there was chaos, I made organization. And on a scale never before known I calculated costs, imposed prices, and conquered markets. And I distributed the force of millions of hands so that time would never again be wasted, nor energy, nor materials. And I banished chance and fate from the history of men. And in the space created by me I reserved no place for the weak or the inefficient. And the evening and the morning were the fifth day.

And to give my work a name I coined the word "trust." And I saw that it was good. And I confirmed that the world turned around my watchful eyes, while the evening and the morning were the sixth day.

And on the seventh day I did charity. I added up the money God had given me for having continued His perfect work and gave twenty-five cents to the poor. And then I rested.

(231 and 282)

1883: Bismarck City
The Last Buffalos of the North

The buffalo has become a curiosity in Montana and the Blackfeet Indians gnaw old bones and tree bark.

Sitting Bull heads the last hunt of the Sioux on the northern prairies. After traveling far they meet a few animals. For each one they kill, the Sioux ask forgiveness of the Great Invisible Buffalo, as tradition requires, and promise him they will not waste one hair of the body.

Soon afterwards, the Northern Pacific Railroad celebrates the completion of its coast-to-coast line. This is the fourth line to cross North American territory. Coal locomotives, with pneumatic brakes and Pullman coaches, advance behind the pioneers toward the prairies that belonged to the Indians. On all sides new cities spring up. The giant national market grows and coheres.

The Northern Pacific authorities invite Chief Sitting Bull to make a speech at the great inauguration party. Sitting Bull arrives from the reservation where the Sioux survive on charity. He mounts the rostrum covered with flowers and flags, and addresses himself to the president of the United States, the officials and personalities present, and to the general public: "*I hate all the white people,*" he says. "*You are thieves and liars . . .*"

The interpreter, a young officer, translates: "My red and gentle heart bids you welcome . . ."

Sitting Bull interrupts the clamorous applause of the audience: "*You have taken away our land and made us outcasts . . .*"

The audience gives the feather-headdressed warrior a standing ovation; and the interpreter sweats ice.

(224)

1884: Santiago de Chile

The Wizard of Finance
Eats Soldier Meat

"*Our rights are born of victory, the supreme law of nations,*" says the victorious governor.

The War of the Pacific, the nitrates war, has ended. By sea and by land Chile has crushed its enemies. The immense deserts of Atacama and Tarapacá become part of the map of Chile. Peru loses its nitrates and the exhausted guano islands. Bolivia loses its outlet to the sea and is bottled up in the heart of South America.

In Santiago de Chile they celebrate the victory. In London they collect on it. Without firing a shot or spending a penny, John Thomas North has become the nitrates king. With money borrowed from Chilean banks, North has bought for a song the bonds that the Peruvian State had given to the deposits' old proprietors. North bought them when the war was just beginning; and before it was over, the Chilean State had the kindness to recognize the bonds as legitimate property titles.

(268 and 269)

1884: Huancayo

The Fatherland Pays

Against the Chilean invaders of Peru, Marshal Andrés Avelino Cáceres and his Indian guerrillas have fought over two hundred mountain leagues without letup for three years.

The Indians of the communities call their marshal, a man with fierce whiskers, "Grandpa"; and many have lost their lives following him, shouting "vivas" for a fatherland that despises them. In Lima, too, Indians were cannon fodder, and the social chronicler Ricardo Palma blames the defeat on *that abject and degraded race.*

In contrast, Marshal Cáceres was saying until recently that Peru was defeated by its own merchants and bureaucrats. Until recently he also rejected the peace treaty that amputated a good piece of Peru. Now Cáceres has changed his mind. He wants to be president. He has to earn merits. He must demobilize the armed Indians, who have fought against the Chileans, but have also invaded haciendas and are threatening the sacred order of great estates.

The marshal summons Tomás Laimes, chief of the Colca guerrilla fighters. Laimes comes to Huancayo with fifteen hundred Indians. He comes to say, *"At your orders, my Grandpa."*

But no sooner does Laimes arrive than his troop is disarmed. When he has barely crossed the barracks threshold, he is felled by a rifle butt. Later they shoot him, blindfolded and sitting down.

(194)

1885: Lima

"The trouble comes from the top," says Manuel González Prada.

Peru groans under the domination of a few privileged beings. Those men would roll us flat between the crushers of a sugar mill, they would distill us in an alembic, they would burn us to a crisp in a smelting oven, if they could extract from our residuum just one milligram of gold . . . Like land with a curse on it, they receive the seed and drink the water without ever producing fruit . . .

In the war against Chile they proved their cowardice, not even having the guts to defend the guano and nitrate deposits . . .We were insulted, trodden on, and bloodied as no nation ever was; but the war with Chile has taught us nothing, nor corrected us of any vice.

(145)

1885: Mexico City

"All belongs to all,"

says Teodoro Flores, Mixtec Indian, hero of three wars.
"Repeat that!"
And the sons repeat: *"All belongs to all."*

Teodoro Flores has defended Mexico against North Americans, conservatives, and the French. President Juárez gave him three farms with good soil as a reward. He didn't accept.

"*Land, water, woods, houses, oxen, harvests. To all. Repeat that!*"

And the sons repeat it.

Open to the sky, the roof is almost immune to the smell of shit and frying, and it is almost quiet. Here, one can take the air and talk, while in the patio below, men fight with knives over a woman, someone calls loudly upon the Virgin, and dogs howl omens of death.

"*Tell us about the Sierra*," asks the youngest son.

And the father tells how people live in Teotitlán del Camino. There, those who can work do so and everyone gets what he needs. No one is allowed to take more than he needs. That is a serious crime. In the sierra, crimes are punished with silence, scorn, or expulsion. It was President Juárez who brought the jail, something that wasn't known there. Juárez brought judges and property titles and ordered the communal lands divided up. "*But we paid no attention to the papers he gave us.*"

Teodoro Flores was fifteen when he learned the Spanish language. Now he wants his sons to become lawyers to defend the Indians from the tricks of the doctors. For that purpose he brought them to the capital, that deafening pigsty, to squeak by, crammed among rowdies and beggars.

"*What God created and what man creates. All belongs to all. Repeat that!*"

Night after night, the children listen to him until sleep overcomes them.

"*We are all born equal, stark naked. We are all brothers. Repeat that!*"

(287)

1885: Colón

Prestán

The city of Colón was born thirty years ago, because a terminal station was needed for the train that crosses Panama from sea to sea. The city came to birth on the Caribbean Sea swamps, and offered fevers and mosquitos, seedy hotels, gambling dens, and brothels to adventurers who streamed through in pursuit of the gold of California, and miserable hovels for the Chinese workers who maintained the tracks and died of plague or sadness.

This year, Colón burned. The fire devoured wooden arcades, houses, and markets, and Pedro Prestán took the blame. Prestán, teacher and doctor, almost black, always wearing a derby hat and bow tie, always impeccable in the mud streets, had led a popular insurrection. A thousand U.S. Marines went into action on Panamanian territory, purportedly to protect the railroad and other North American properties. Prestán, who defended the humiliated people with life and soul and derby, hangs on the gallows.

The crime puts a curse on Colón. For expiation, the city will burn every twenty years from now on and forever.

(102, 151, and 324)

1886: Chivilcoy

The Circus

At dawn a circus trailer appears out of the mist, amid the leafy groves of Chivilcoy.

By afternoon, colored banners flutter over the tent.

A triumphal parade around the city. The Podesta Brothers' *Equestrian, Gymnastic, Acrobatic, and Creole Drama Company* has a Japanese juggler and a talking dog, trained doves, a child prodigy, and four clowns. The program claims that the harlequin, Pepino the 88th, and the trapeze team *have earned the admiration of audiences in London, Paris, Vienna, Philadelphia, and Rome.*

But the main dish the circus offers is *Juan Moreira*, the first Creole drama in Argentine history, a pantomime with duels of couplets and knives, which tells the misfortunes of a gaucho harassed by an officer, a judge, a mayor, and the grocer.

(34)

1886: Atlanta

Coca-Cola

John Pemberton, pharmacist, has won some prestige for his love potions and baldness cures.

Now he invents a medicine that relieves headaches and alleviates nausea. His new product is made from a base of coca leaves, brought from the Andes, and cola nuts, stimulant seeds that come from Africa. Water, sugar, caramel, and certain secrets complete the formula.

Soon Pemberton will sell his invention for two thousand three hundred dollars. He is convinced that it is a good remedy; and he would burst with laughter, not with pride, if some fortuneteller revealed to him that he had just created the symbol of the coming century.

(184)

1887: Chicago
Every May First, They Will Live Again

The gallows awaits them. They were five, but Lingg got death up early by exploding a dynamite capsule between his teeth. Fischer dresses himself unhurriedly, humming "La Marseillaise." Parsons, the agitator, who used words like a whip or knife, grips his comrades' hands before the guards tie them behind their backs. Engel, famous for his marksmanship, asks for port wine and makes everyone laugh with a joke. Spies, who has written so much *portraying anarchy as the entrance to life*, prepares in silence for the entrance to death.

The spectators, in theater seats, fasten their eyes on the scaffold. *A signal, a noise, the trap is sprung . . . There, in a horrible dance, they died spinning in the air*.

José Martí writes reportage of the anarchists' execution in Chicago. The world's working class will revive them every First of May. That is still not known, but Martí always writes as if hearing, where it is least expected, the cry of a newborn child.

(199)

1889: London
North

Twenty years ago, he jumped onto the pier at Valparaíso, eyes of blue stone, fuzzy red whiskers. He had ten pounds sterling in his pockets and a bundle of clothing on his back. In his first job he got to know saltpeter the hard way, in the cauldron of a small deposit in Tarapacá, and later he was a merchant in the port of Iquique. During the War of the Pacific, while Chileans, Peruvians, and Bolivians were disemboweling each other with bayonets, John Thomas North performed conjuring tricks that made him owner of the battlefields.

Now North, the nitrates king, makes beer in France and cement in Belgium, owns streetcars in Egypt and sawmills in black Africa, and exploits gold in Australia and diamonds in Brazil. In England, this Midas of plebeian stock and quick fingers has bought the rank of colonel in Her Majesty's army, heads the Masonic lodge of Kent county and is a prominent member of the Conservative Party; dukes, lords and ministers sit at his table. He lived in a palace whose big iron doors were, they say, lifted from the Cathedral in Lima by Chilean soldiers.

On the eve of a voyage to Chile, North gives a farewell ball in the Hotel Metropole. A thousand English people attend. The Metropole's salons gleam like suns, and so do the dishes and drinks. The letter *N* blazes in the center of immense chrysanthemum coats-of-arms. An ovation greets the almighty host as he descends the stairs disguised as Henry VIII. On his arm is his wife dressed as a duchess; and behind comes the daughter, as a Persian princess, and the son in Cardinal Richelieu costume.

The war correspondent of the *Times* is one of the great retinue that will accompany North to his Chilean kingdom. Turbulent days await him. There, in the deserts conquered with bullets, North is the master of saltpeter and coal and water and banks and newspapers and railroads; but in the city of Santiago there is a president who has the bad taste to refuse his gifts. His name is José Manuel Balmaceda. North is heading there to overthrow him.

(269 and 270)

1889: Montevideo

Football

In London, it is Queen Victoria's seventieth birthday. On the banks of the River Plata, they celebrate it with their feet.

The Buenos Aires and Montevideo teams vie for the ball on the little Blanqueada field under the disdainful scrutiny of the queen. At the center of the grandstand, between flags, hangs a portrait of this mistress of the world's seas and a good part of its lands.

Buenos Aires wins, 3-0. There are no dead to mourn, although the penalty has not yet been invented and anyone approaching the enemy goal risks his life. To get a close shot at the goal, one must penetrate an avalanche of legs that shoot out like axes; and every match is a battle requiring bones of steel.

Football is an Englishman's game. It is played by officials of the railway, the gas companies, and the Bank of London, and by visiting sailors; but already a few Creoles, infiltrators among the blond-mustachioed marksmen, are showing that craftiness can be an efficient weapon for bringing down goalkeepers.

(221)

1890: River Plata

Comrades

More than fifty thousand workers come each year to the River Plata, Europeans washed up by desperation on these coasts. Italian flags greet the visit of Edmundo de Amicis to the Piedmontese colonies of the Argentine coast, and at workers' meetings in Buenos Aires or Montevideo speeches are heard in Spanish, Italian, French, or German.

Eight of every ten workers or artisans are foreigners, and among them are Italian socialists and anarchists, Frenchmen of the Commune, Spaniards of the first republic, and revolutionaries from Germany and Central Europe.

Strikes break out on both banks of the river. In Montevideo, streetcar conductors work eighteen hours a day; mill and noodle-factory workers, fifteen. There are no Sundays, and a member of the government in Buenos Aires has published his discovery that idleness is the mother of all vice.

In Buenos Aires, Latin America's first May First is celebrated. The chief speaker, Joseph Winiger, salutes the Chicago martyrs in German and announces that the hour of socialism is approaching, while men of the gown, pen, sword or cassock clamor for the expulsion of alien enemies of order. The inspired writer Miguel Cané drafts a law to expel foreign agitators from Argentina.

(140 and 290)

1890: Buenos Aires

Tenements

Poor and rich pay the same price at the Colón theater at carnival time, but once past the door Hands go to their place and Brains to theirs, and no one commits the sacrilege of sitting in the wrong place. The lower-downs dance in the parterre, the higher-ups in boxes and lounges.

Buenos Aires is like its theater. High-class people sleep in two-or-three-story French palaces in the North barrio, and alone sleep the spinsters who would rather die as virgins than mix their blood with some foreigner of indeterminate hue. The top people decorate their lineage, or manufacture it, with torrents of pearls and initials engraved on silver tea sets, and show off Saxony or Sèvres or Limoges porcelains, Waterford crystal, Lyons tapestries, and Brussels tablecloths. From the secluded life of the Big Village they have moved on to the frenetic exhibitionism of the Paris of America.

In the south are huddled the beaten-down of the earth. In abandoned three-patioed colonial mansions, or in specially built tenements, the workers newly arrived from Naples or Vigo or Bessarabia sleep by turns. Never cold are the scarce beds in the nonspace invaded by braziers and washbasins and chests which serve as cradles. Fights are frequent in the long queues at the door to the only latrine, and silence is an impossible luxury. But sometimes, on party nights, the accordion or mandolin or bagpipes bring back lost voices to these washerwomen and dressmakers, servants of rich bosses and husbands, and ease the loneliness of these men who from sun to sun tan hides, pack meat, saw wood, sweep streets, tote loads, raise and paint walls, roll cigarettes, grind wheat, and bake bread while their children shine shoes and call out the crime of the day.

(236 and 312)

Man Alone

One fire less, they say in the villages of Galicia when someone emigrates.

Over there, he was excess population; and here, he doesn't want to exceed. Like a mule, he works and resists and keeps quiet, a man of few words, and in the foreign city he takes up less room than a dog.

Here, they make fun of him and treat him with contempt, because he can't even sign his name, and manual labor is for inferior species. On the other hand, here they worship anyone with a lot of arrogance and applaud the slicker who can deflate the most boastful swollen head with a stroke of cunning and luck.

He gets little sleep, the lonely immigrant, but no sooner does he close his eyes than some fairy or witch comes to love him on green mountains and snowy precipices. Sometimes he has nightmares. Then, he drowns in the river. Not in just any river, but a particular river over there. Whoever crosses it, they say, loses his memory.

Tangoing

The tango, wistful offspring of the gay milonga, has been born in the corrals at the city's edge and in tenement courtyards.

On the two banks of the River Plata, it is music of ill repute. Workers and malefactors dance it on earth floors, men of the hammer or the knife, male with male if the woman is not able to follow the very daring and broken step, or if such a body-to-body embrace seems more suitable for whores: the couple slides, rocks, stretches, and flowers in coupés and filigrees.

The tango comes from gaucho tunes of the interior and comes from the sea, the chanteys of sailors. It comes from the slaves of Africa and the gypsies of Andalusia. Spain contributes its guitar, Germany its concertina, Italy its mandolin. The driver of the horse-drawn streetcar contributed his trumpet, and the immigrant worker his harmonica, comrade of lonely moments. With hesitant step the tango spans barracks and dives, midways of traveling circuses and the patios of slum brothels. Now organ grinders parade it through shore streets on the outskirts of Buenos Aires and Montevideo, heading downtown; and ships take it to drive Paris wild.

(257, 293, and 350)

1890: Hartford

Mark Twain

The novelist's hands whisk Hank Morgan, an offical of the Colt arms factory, into the distant court of King Arthur. The telephone, the bicycle, and dynamite journey to the times of Merlin the magician and Sir Galahad in the vale of Camelot; there Hank Morgan publishes and sells a newspaper at the modest price of two cents, founds a West Point military academy and reveals that the world is not a dish supported on columns. Although he comes from a society that already knows monopolies, Hank brings to the feudal castles the good news of free competition, free trade, and the free ballot. In vain, he tries to replace mounted duels with baseball, hereditary monarchy with democracy, and the code of honor with the calculation of costs; and finally he burns up thirty thousand armor-and-lance English horsemen with electric wires already tried out against the Indians of the United States. The adventure speeds to a deadly climax and Hank falls, asphyxiated by the miasma of putrefaction from his victims.

Mark Twain finishes writing *A Connecticut Yankee in King Arthur's Court* at his home in Hartford. "It is my swan song," he announces. He has always lived by leaps and bounds, pursuing a fugitive million dollars. He has been journalist and explorer, publicity agent, miner of gold, ship's pilot, speculator, inventor of gadgets, director of an insurance company, and unsuccessful entrepreneur. Between bankruptcy and bankruptcy he managed to invent or recall Tom Sawyer and Huck Finn, and found a way to invite us all to float on a raft down the waters of the Mississippi. And he did it for the pure joy of going, not for the urgency of arriving.

(149 and 341)

1890: Wounded Knee
Wind of Snow

The Creator did not make the Indians: he sang them, he danced them.

Through songs and dances the Creator is now announcing that this old and dying earth will soon be demolished by the greenish whirlwind of a new earth. The prophet Wovoka brought word of it from the other world. In the new earth, buffalos will be revived, dead Indians will be reborn, and a ferocious flood will drown the whites. Not one of the usurpers will survive.

The prophet Wovoka's dances and songs come out of the West, cross the Rocky Mountains, and spread throughout the prairies. The Sioux, who were the most numerous and powerful of the tribes in these regions, celebrate the annunciation of paradise, the end of hunger and exile. They dance and sing from dawn to the depth of every night.

Four days after Christmas, the thunder of gunfire interrupts the ceremonies in the Sioux camp at Wounded Knee. The soldiers riddle women, children, and the few men with bullets like so many buffalos. The blizzard strikes the dead and freezes them on the smow.

(51, 91, and 230)

Prophetic Song of the Sioux

A thunder-being nation I am, I have said.
A thunder-being nation I am, I have said.
You shall live.
You shall live.
You shall live.
You shall live.

(38)

1891: Santiago de Chile

Balmaceda

José Manuel Balmaceda wanted to promote national industry, *to live and dress by ourselves*, intuiting that the nitrate era would pass leaving Chile nothing but remorse. He wanted to apply stimulants and protections similar to those that the United States, England, France, and Germany had practiced in their industrial infancy. He raised the workers' wages and sowed the country with public schools. He gave Chile's long body a spine of railways and roads. In his years as president, sacred British capital ran a grave risk of profanation. Balmaceda wanted to nationalize the railways and put an end to the usury of banks and the voracity of the nitrate companies.

Balmaceda wanted much and could do plenty; but the enormous budget that John Thomas North devoted to buying consciences and twisting justice could do more. The press let loose its thunder against *the Caesar drunk with power, despotic enemy of freedom, hostile to foreign enterprises*, and the clamor of bishops and parliamentarians was no less deafening. A military rising broke out like an echo, and then the blood of the people flowed.

The South American Journal announces the triumph of the coup

d'état: *Chile will return to the good times of yesterday.* The banker
Eduardo Matte also celebrates it: *We are the masters of Chile, we
owners of the capital and of the soil. All else is an influenceable and
saleable mass.*

Balmaceda shoots himself.

(270)

1891: Washington

The Other America

For ten years José Martí has been living in the United States. There
is much that he admires in this multifarious and vigorous country,
where no one is afraid of anything new; but he also denounces in his
articles the imperial ambitions of the young nation, the glorification
of avarice into a divine right, and the atrocious racism that exterminates Indians, humiliates blacks, and looks down on Latins.

South of the Rio Grande, says Martí, there is *another* America,
our America, land that stammers, that does not recognize its full
likeness either in the European or in the North American mirror. It
is the Hispanic American fatherland, he says, which reclaims Cuba
to complete itself, while in the north they claim it to devour it. One
America's interests don't coincide with the other's. *Does political and
economic union with the United States suit Hispanic America?* Martí
asks. And he replies: *Two condors, or two lambs, unite without so
much danger as a condor and a lamb.* Last year the first Pan-American
conference was held in Washington and now Martí sits in on the
continuation of the dialog as delegate of Uruguay. *Whoever says economic union, says political union. The people that buys gives the
orders. The people that sells, serves . . . The people that wants to
die sells to one people alone, and the people that wants to save itself,
sells to more than one . . . The people that wants to be free distributes
its business among equally strong peoples. If either is to be given
preference, prefer the one that needs less to the one that is less
disdainful . . .*

Martí has dedicated his life to that *other* America: he wants to
revive everything in it that has been killed from the conquest onward,
and wants to reveal it and make it rebel, because its hidden and
betrayed identity will not be revealed until it loosens its bonds.

What fault can my great mother America throw in my face?

Son of Europeans but son of America, Cuban patriot of the great
fatherland, Martí feels flowing in his veins the blood of the sorely

wounded peoples who were born of palm or corn seeds and who called the Milky Way *road of the soul* and the moon *sun of night* or *sun asleep*. So he writes, replying to Sarmiento, who is enamored of what is foreign: *This is no battle between civilization and barbarism, but between false learning and nature*.

(112 and 354)

1891: New York

The Thinking Begins to Be Ours, Believes José Martí

. . . *To know is to resolve. Knowing the country, and governing it according to our knowledge, is the only way to free it from tyrannies. The European university must yield to the American university. The history of America, from the Incas till now, must be put at our fingertips, even though that of the Greek Archons is not taught. Our Greece is preferable to the Greece that is not ours. It is more necessary for us. National politicians must replace exotic politicians. Let the world be grafted onto our republics; but the trunk must be that of our republics. And let the defeated pedant keep quiet; for there is no fatherland in which man can take more pride than our wounded American republics . . .*

We were a mask, with trousers from England, Parisian vest, jacket from North America, and cap from Spain . . .We were epaulettes and togas, in countries that came into the world with sandaled feet and banded hair . . . Neither the European book, nor the Yanqui book, has provided the key to the Hispanic American enigma . . .

The peoples stand and greet one another. "What are we like?" they ask; and they tell one another what they are like. When a problem arises in Cojímar, they don't go to Danzig for the solution. The frock coats are still French, but the thinking begins to be American . . .

(199)

1891: Guanajuato

34 Cantarranas Street. Instant Photography

The hooded gunner bends and takes aim. The victim, a highborn gentleman of Guanajuato, does not smile or blink or breathe. There is no escape. Behind him the curtain has fallen, leafy landscape of painted plaster, and the stage-prop staircase leads nowhere. Surrounded by paper flowers and cardboard columns and balustrades, the solemn personage rests his hand on the arm of a chair and with dignity confronts the cannon-mouth of the bellows camera.

All Guanajuato has itself shot in the studio at 34 Cantarranas Street. Romualdo García photographs gentlemen of the uppermost crust and their wives and children, boys who look like dwarves wrapped in large vests with pocket watches, and girls austere as grandmothers crushed by beribboned silken bonnets. He photographs plump friars and soldiers in full dress uniform, the first-communioned and the newly wed; and also some poor people who come from afar and give what they don't have just to pose, bountifully hairdressed and ironed, wearing their best clothes, before the camera of the Mexican artist who won a prize in Paris.

The magician Romualdo García turns persons into statues and sells eternity to mortals.

(158)

1891: Purísima del Rincón
Lives

He learned from no one; he paints for the love of it. Hermenegildo Bustos is paid in kind or at four pennies a portrait. The people of Purísima del Rincón have no photographer, but they have a painter.

Forty years ago Hermenegildo did a portrait of Leocadia López, the belle of the town, and it was very much her. Since then, the town of Purísima has seen successful burials and weddings, many serenades, and one or another disembowelment in the bars; some girl eloped with the clown of a traveling circus, the earth trembled more than once, and more than once a new political boss was sent from Mexico City; and as the slow days passed with their suns and downpours, Hermenegildo Bustos kept painting the live people he saw and the dead ones he remembered.

He is also a market gardener, an ice cream man, and a dozen more things. He plants corn and beans on his own land or by commission, and he keeps busy deworming crops. He makes ices with the frost he collects from maguey leaves; and when the cold spell lets up he makes orange preserves. He also embroiders national flags, fixes leaky roofs, directs the drumming during Holy Week, decorates screens, beds, and coffins, and with a very delicate touch paints Doña

Pomposa López giving thanks to the Most Holy Virgin, who pulled her from her deathbed, and Doña Refugio Segovia, highlighting her charms, not omitting a hair of the curls on her forehead and copying the gold brooch at her throat which says "Refugito."

He paints, and paints himself: freshly shaved and barbered, prominent cheekbones and frowning eyebrows, military uniform. And on the back of his image he writes: *Hermenegildo Bustos, Indian of this town of Purísima del Rincón, I was born on 13 April 1832 and I painted my portrait to see if I could on 19 June 1891.*

(333)

1892: Paris

The Canal Scandal

A French court has decreed the bankruptcy of the Panama Canal Company. Work is suspended and scandal explodes. Suddenly, the savings of thousands of French peasants and petty bourgeois disappear. The enterprise that was to open a swathe between the oceans, that passage the conquistadors sought and dreamed about, has been a colossal swindle. The multi-million-dollar squanderings to bribe politicians and silence journalists are published. From London, Friedrich Engels writes: *The Panama business could well become for the bourgeois republic a Pandora's box, this grand National Steeplechase of Scandals. The miracle has been performed of transforming a canal which has* not *been dug out, into an unfathomable abyss . . .*

No one mentions the Antillean, Chinese, and East Indian workers whom yellow fever and malaria have exterminated at the rate of seven hundred dead per kilometer of canal opened through the mountains.

(102, 201, and 324)

1892: San José, Costa Rica

Prophesy of a Young Nicaraguan Poet
Named Rubén Darío

The coming century will see the greatest of the revolutions that have bloodied the earth. Big fish eat little fish? So be it, but soon we will have our own back. Pauperism reigns, and the worker carries on his

*shoulders a mountainous curse. Nothing matters now but miserable
gold. The disinherited are the eternal flock for the eternal slaughterhouse . . .*

*No force will be able to contain the torrent of fatal vengeance.
We will have to sing a new Marseillaise which, like the trumpets of
Jericho, will bring down the dwellings of the wicked . . .The heavens
will see with fearful joy, amid the thunder of the redemptive catas-
trophe, the castigation of arrogant evildoers, the supreme and terrible
vengeance of drunken poverty.*

(308)

1893: Canudos

Antonio Conselheiro

For a long time prophets have roamed the burning lands of northeast
Brazil. They announce that King Sebastian will return from the island
of Las Brumas and punish the rich and turn blacks into whites and
old into young. When the century ends, they say, the desert will be
sea and the sea, desert; and fire will destroy the coastal cities, frenetic
worshipers of money and sin. On the ashes of Recife, Bahia, Rio, and
São Paulo will rise a new Jerusalem and in it Christ will reign for a
thousand years. The hour of the poor is approaching, announce the
prophets. In seven years' time the heavens will descend to earth.
Then there will be no disease or death; and in the new terrestrial
and celestial reign every injustice will be corrected.

The pious Antonio Conselheiro wanders from town to town, squalid
and dusty phantom, followed by a chorus of litanies. His skin is a
jaded armor of leather; his beard, a thicket of brambles; his tunic, a
ragged shroud. He does not eat or sleep. He distributes among the
unfortunate the alms he receives. He talks to women with his back
turned. He refuses obedience to the impious government of the republic and in the plaza of the town of Bom Conselho throws the tax
edicts on a fire.

Pursued by the police, he flees into the desert. With two hundred
pilgrims he founds the community of Canudos beside the bed of an
ephemeral river. Here, heat does not permit rain to touch the soil.
From bald hillsides rise the first huts of mud and straw. In the middle
of this sullen land, promised land, first stair up to heaven, Antonio
Conselheiro triumphantly raises the image of Christ and announces
the apocalypse: *The rich, the unbelieving, and the fickle will be wiped*

*out. The waters will be dyed with blood. There will be only one
shepherd and one flock. Many hats and few heads . . .*

(80 and 252)

1895: Key West
Freedom Travels in a Cigar

He never sleeps, eats little. José Martí collects people and money,
writes articles and letters, gives speeches, poetry readings, and lec-
tures; discusses, organizes, buys weapons. More than twenty years
of exile have not been able to put out his light.

He always knew that Cuba could not be itself without a revolution. Three years ago he founded the Cuban Revolutionary Party
on three Florida coasts. The party was born in the tobacco workshops
of Tampa and Key West, under the aegis of exiled Cuban workers
who have heard Martí in person and from the printed page.

The workshops are like labor universities. It is the tradition that
someone reads books or articles while the others work in silence, and
thus the tobacco workers daily receive ideas and news, and daily
travel through the world and history and the wonderful regions of
the imagination. Through the mouth of the "reader" the human word
shoots out and penetrates the women who strip tobacco and the men
who twist the leaves and shape cigars on thigh or table.

By agreement with generals Máximo Gómez and Antonio Maceo,
Martí gives the order to rise. The order travels from these Florida
workshops and reaches Cuba concealed within a Havana cigar.

(165, 200, and 242)

1895: *Playitas*
The Landing

Forty years from now, Marcos del Rosario will recall: "*General Gómez
didn't like me at first sight. He asked me, 'What are you going to
Cuba for? Did you lose something there?'* "

Marcos will clap his hands, knocking the dirt off them. "*General
Gómez was a fabulous little old guy, strong, strong, and very agile,
and talked very loud and sometimes would rear up and try to swallow
you. . .*"

He will cross the orchard looking for shade. *"Finally we found a ship that put us close to the coast of Cuba."*

He will show off the iron rings of his hammock. *"These are from that ship."*

Lying in the hammock, he will light a cigar. *"The ship left us in the sea and there was a terrific swell . . ."*

Two Dominicans and four Cubans in a boat. The storm plays with them. They have sworn that Cuba will be free.

"A dark night, you couldn't see a thing . . ."

A red moon rises, fights with the clouds. The boat fights with the hungry sea.

"The old guy was up in the prow. He was holding the wheel and Martí had the boat's compass. A big wave tore the wheel from the general . . . We were fighting the sea that wanted to swallow us and didn't want to let us reach land in Cuba . . ."

By some magic the boat does not shatter against the cliffs. The boat flies and plunges and surges back. Suddenly, it tacks about, the waves open up, and a little beach appears, a tiny horseshoe of sand.

"And General Gómez jumped onto the beach and when he stood on terra firma, he kissed the ground straight off and crowed like a rooster."

(258 and 286)

1895: Arroyo Hondo
In the Sierra

Not sadly but radiantly, festively, Marcos del Rosario will speak of Martí. *"When I saw him, I thought he was too weak. And then I saw he was a little live wire, who would jump here and land over there . . ."*

Martí teaches him to write. Martí puts his hand on Marcos's while he draws the letter A. *"He had gone to school and was a superb man."*

Marcos looks after Martí. He makes him good mattresses of dry leaves; he brings him coconut water to drink. The six men who landed at Playitas become a hundred, a thousand . . . Martí marches, knapsack on back, rifle over shoulder, climbing the sierra and stirring up people.

"When we were climbing the mountains, all loaded up, sometimes he'd fall. And I'd go to pick him up and right away he'd say, 'No,

*thanks, no.' He had a ring made out of the shackles the Spaniards
put on him when he was still a child."*

(286)

1895: Dos Rios Camp
Martí's Testament

In the camp, in his shirtsleeves, Martí writes a letter to the Mexican
Manuel Mercado, his intimate friend. He tells him that his life is in
danger every day, and that it is well worthwhile to give it for his
country, *and for my duty to prevent, in time, with the independence
of Cuba, the United States from extending itself into the Antilles and
from falling, with that extra force, upon our American lands. All I
have done until now, and all I will do, is for that. It has had to be
done in silence* . . . Shedding blood, writes Martí, the Cubans are
preventing *the annexation of the peoples of our America by the turbulent and brutal North which despises them . . . I lived within the
monster and I know its entrails—and my sling is the sling of David.*
And further on: *This is death or life, and there is no room for error.*

Later his tone changes. He has other things to tell about. *And
now, I will talk to you about myself.* But the night stops him, or
maybe modesty, as soon as he starts to offer his friend those depths
of his soul. *There is an affection of such delicate honesty . . .* he
writes, and that is the last thing he writes.

At noon the next day, a bullet tumbles him from his horse.

(199)

1895: Niquinohomo
His Name Will Be Sandino

At the doors of this adobe house people gather, drawn by the cry.
Like an upside-down spider the newborn baby moves his arms and
legs. No Magi Kings come from afar to welcome him, but a farm
laborer, a carpenter, and a passing market woman leave gifts.

The godmother offers lavender water to the mother and to the
child a pinch of honey, which is his first taste of the world.

Later the godmother buries the placenta, which looks so like a
root, in a corner of the garden. She buries it in a good spot, where
there is plenty of sun, so that it will become soil here in Niquinohomo.

Within a few years, the child that just came from that placenta will become soil too, the rebellious soil of all Nicaragua.

(8 and 317)

1896: Port-au-Prince
Disguises

According to the Constitution of Haiti, the republic of free blacks speaks French and professes the Christian religion. The doctors are mortified because, despite laws and punishments, "Creole" continues as the language of nearly all Haitians and nearly all continue believing in the voodoo gods who wander at large through woods and bodies.

The government demands that peasants publicly swear an oath: *"I swear to destroy all fetishes and objects of superstition, if I carry them with me or have them in my house or on my land. I swear never to lower myself to any superstitious practice . . ."*

(68)

1896: Boca de Dos Rios
Requiem

"Was it here?"

A year has passed, and Máximo Gómez is telling the story to Calixto García. The old warriors for Cuba's independence lead the way from the Contramaestre River. Behind come their armies. General Gómez tells, that midday, how Martí had eaten with a good appetite and afterwards recited some verses, as was his custom, and how they then heard some shots. Everyone ran looking for a horse.

"Was it here?"

They come to a thicket, at the entrance to the road to Palo Picado.

"Here," someone says.

Machete wielders clear the little patch of ground.

"I never heard him complain or saw him give in," says Gómez. Grumbling and getting angry, he adds, *"I ordered him . . . I advised him to stay behind."*

A patch of ground the size of his body.

General Máximo Gómez drops a stone. General Calixto García another stone. And officers and soldiers keep filing past, and one after another stones fall with a sharp click, stones on top of stones, as

Martí's memorial mound rears toward the sky, and only those clicks can be heard in the immense silence of Cuba.

(105)

1896: Papeete
Flora Tristán

The canvas, bare and immense, offers itself challengingly. Paul Gauguin paints, hunts around, throws on color as if bidding farewell to the world; and his desperate hand writes: *Where do we come from, what are we, where are we going?*

Over half a century ago, Gauguin's grandmother asked the same question in one of her books, and died finding out. The Peruvian family of Flora Tristán never mentioned it, as if it were bad luck or as if she were crazy or a ghost. When Paul asked about his grandmother, in the remote years of his childhood in Lima, they answered him:

"Time to go to bed, it's late."

Flora Tristán had burned up her short life preaching revolution, the proletarian revolution and the revolution of women enslaved by father, employer, and husband. Illness and the police finished her off. She died in France. The workers of Bordeaux paid for her coffin and carried her on a bier to the cemetery.

(21)

1896: Bogotá
José Asunción Silva

He loves his sister Elvira, aroma of lavender, balsam incense, furtive kisses of the palest sylph in Bogotá, and for her he writes his best verses. Night after night he goes to visit her in the cemetery. At the foot of her grave he feels better than in literary coteries.

José Asunción Silva had been born dressed in black, with a flower in his buttonhole. Thus has he lived for thirty years, through blow after blow, this languid founder of modernism in Colombia. The bankruptcy of his father, a silk and perfume merchant, has taken the bread from his mouth; and his complete works have been lost at sea in a shipwreck.

Far into the night he discusses, for the last time, the cadence of an alexandrine verse. From the door, lamp in hand, he bids goodnight to his guests. Then he smokes his last Turkish cigarette and for the last time pities himself before the mirror. No letter arrives from Paris to save him. Tormented by his creditors and by the spiteful who call him Chaste Susan, the poet unbuttons his shirt and presses the revolver against the ink cross that a doctor friend has drawn over his heart.

(319)

1896: Manaos

The Tree That Weeps Milk

The Indians call it "caucho." They slash it and the milk flows. In plantain leaves folded like bowls, the milk is collected and hardens in the heat of sun or smoke, while the human hand gives it shape. Since very ancient times the Indians have made from this wild milk long-lasting torches, pots that don't break, roofs that laugh at the rain, and balls that bounce and fly.

Over a century ago, the king of Portugal received from Brazil syringes without plungers and waterproof clothing; and before that the French sage La Condamine had studied the virtues of the scandalous gum that paid no attention to the law of gravity.

Thousands and thousands of shoes traveled from the Amazonian jungle to the port of Boston, until Charles Goodyear and Thomas Hancock, half a century ago, discovered how to keep the gum from breaking and softening. Then the United States started producing five million shoes a year, shoes invulnerable to cold, damp, and snow; and great factories arose in England, Germany, and France.

And not only shoes. The gum multiplies products and creates needs. Modern life turns giddily about the immense tree that weeps milk when you wound it. Eight years ago, in Belfast, the son of John Dunlop won a tricycle race using the pneumatic tires his father had invented to replace solid wheels; and last year Michelin created removable pneumatic tires for automobiles racing from Paris to Bordeaux.

Amazonia, fantastic jungle that seemed to be a reserve for monkeys, Indians, and lunatics, is now a game preserve for the United States Rubber Company, the Amazon Rubber Company, and other distant enterprises that suck its milk.

(334)

1896: Manaos
The Golden Age of Rubber

The curtain rises, parsimoniously, as the first chords of Ponchielli's opera *La Gioconda* are struck up. It is a night of great pomp and gala and mosquitos in the city of Manaos. Italian opera stars are inaugurating the Amazonas Theater, an immense nave of marble brought, like them, from Europe to the heart of the jungle.

Manaos and Belem do Pará are the rubber capitals of Brazil. Along with Iquitos in the Peruvian thickets, the three Amazonian cities lay out their streets with European paving stones and enliven their nights with horizontal girls from Paris, Budapest, Baghdad, or the local jungle. Gold batons conduct orchestras and ingots serve as paperweights; a hen's egg costs an arm and a leg. Extremely important people drink extremely imported drinks, recuperate in the thermal baths of Vichy, and send their children to study in Lisbon or Geneva on Booth Line ships which ply the muddy waters of the Amazon.

Who does the work in the rubber forests? In Brazil, victims of the droughts in the northeast. From those deserts peasants come to these swamps where one would be better off as a fish. This green prison shuts them in under contract; and soon death comes to rescue them from slavery and appalling solitude. In Peru, the hands are Indian. Many tribes are annihilated in this age of rubber which seems so eternal.

(299, 325, and 334)

1897: Canudos
Euclides da Cunha

During the day the earth smokes, flames, expands. When night falls, ax of ice, the earth shivers and contracts; by dawn, it has split apart.

Debris of earthquakes, Euclides da Cunha writes in his notebook. *Landscape that seems made to run away*, he notes. He observes the wrinkles of the earth and the curves of the river, a twisting strip of dried mud that the Indians call "Red Honey," and vainly seeks shade among the rachitic bushes. Here, the air turns all it touches to stone. A soldier lies face up with arms outstretched. A black scab disfigures his forehead. They killed him three months ago in hand-to-hand fighting, and now he is his own statue.

From afar, from the sacred village of Canudos, shots ring out. The monotonous staccato lasts for days, months, varied at times by cannon fire and machine-gun bursts, and Euclides would like to understand what kind of strength enables these mystical peasants to resist so fearlessly the assault of thirty battalions. Many thousands of them are letting themselves be killed out of devotion to the Messiah Antonio Conselheiro. The chronicler of this holy war asks himself how they can confuse these barren plains with heaven and this visionary, who only escaped the madhouse because it had no room for him, with Jesus Christ.

Hesitating between disgust and admiration, Euclides da Cunha describes what he sees, from bewilderment to bewilderment, for the readers of a São Paulo newspaper. A European-style socialist, mestizo who despises mestizos, Brazilian ashamed of Brazil, Euclides is among the most brilliant intellectuals of the republic that displays on its newly born flag the motto "Order and Progress." While the slaughter lasts, he strives to comprehend the mystery of the northeastern hinterland, land of fanatics where animosities and loyalties are inherited, where the "melancholia" of squalid cattle is cured with prayers and the deaths of children are celebrated with guitars.

(80)

1897: Canudos

The Dead Contain More Bullets Than Bones

but the last defenders of Canudos sing behind an enormous wooden cross, still expecting the arrival of archangels.

The commander of the first column has the horrifying corpse of Antonio Conselheiro photographed, *so that his death may be confirmed.* He too needs to be sure. Out of the corner of his eye the commander glances at that handful of rags and little bones.

Wretched peasants of all ages and colors had raised a rampart of bodies around this battered Methuselah, enemy of the republic and of the sinful cities. Five military expeditions have been necessary: five thousand soldiers surrounding Canudos, twenty cannons bombarding from the hillsides, incredible war of blunderbuss against Nordenfeldt machine gun.

The trenches have been reduced to graves of dust, and still the Canudos community does not surrender, this utopia without property or law where the poor shared the miserly land, the paltry bread, and faith in the immensity of heaven.

They fight house by house, inch by inch.
The four last survivors fall. Three men, one child.

(80)

1897: Rio de Janeiro
Machado de Assís

Brazilian writers, divided into sects that loathe each other, celebrate communions and consecrations at the Colombo and other cafes and bookshops. There they bid farewell, in the odor of sanctity, to colleagues journeying to lay flowers on Maupassant's grave in Paris; and in those temples, to the clink of glasses blessed by sacred liquors, is born the Brazilian Academy of Letters. Its first president is Machado de Assís.

He is the great Latin American novelist of this century. His books lovingly and humorously unmask the high society of drones that he, son of a mulatto father, has conquered and knows better than anyone. Machado de Assís tears off the fancy wrapping, false frames of false windows with a European view, and winks at the reader as he strips the mud wall.

(62 and 190)

1898: Coasts of Cuba
This Fruit Is Ready to Fall

The three hundred and twenty-five pounds of General William Shafter land on the eastern coast of Cuba. They come from cold northern climes where the general was busy killing Indians, and here they melt inside his overpowering wool uniform. Shafter sends his body up some steps to the back of a horse, and from there scans the horizon with a telescope.

He has come to command. As one of his officers, General Young, puts it, *the insurgents are a lot of degenerates, no more capable of self-government than the savages of Africa*. When the Spanish army begins to collapse before the patriots' implacable assault, the United States decides to take charge of the freedom of Cuba. If they come in, no one will be able to get them out, Martí and Maceo had warned. And they come in.

Spain had declined to sell this island *for a reasonable price*, and the North American intervention found its pretext in the opportune explosion of the battleship *Maine*, sunk in Havana harbor with its many guns and crewmen.

The invading army invokes the protection of North American citizens and the rescue of their interests threatened by devastating war and economic disaster. But in private, the officers explain that they must prevent the emergence of a black republic off the coasts of Florida.

(114)

1898: Washington

Ten Thousand Lynchings

In the name of the Negroes of the United States, Ida Wells protests to President McKinley that ten thousand lynchings have occurred in the past twenty years. If the government does not protect North American citizens within its borders, asks Ida Wells, by what right does it invoke that protection to invade other countries? Are not Negroes citizens? Or does the Constitution only guarantee them the right to be burned to death?

Mobs of fanatics, stirred up by press and pulpit, drag blacks from jails, tie them to trees, and burn them alive. Then the executioners celebrate in bars and broadcast their feats through the streets.

As a pretext, nigger-hunters use the rape of white women, in a country where a black woman's violation by a white is considered normal, but in the great majority of cases the burned blacks are guilty of no greater crime than a bad reputation, suspicion of robbery, or insolence.

President McKinley promises to look into the matter

(12)

1898: San Juan Hill

Teddy Roosevelt

Brandishing his Stetson, Teddy Roosevelt gallops at the head of his "Rough Riders"; and when he descends San Juan Hill he carries, crumpled in his hand, a Spanish flag. He will take all the glory for this battle which opens the way to Santiago de Cuba. Of the Cubans who also fought, no journalist will write a word.

Teddy believes in the grandeur of imperial destiny and in the power of his fists. He learned to box in New York, to save himself from beatings and humiliations he suffered as a sickly, asthmatic, and very myopic child. As an adult, he puts on the gloves with champions, hunts lions, lassos bulls, writes books, and roars speeches. On the printed page and from platforms he exalts the virtues of the strong races, born to rule, warlike races like his own, and proclaims that in nine out of ten cases there is no better Indian than a dead Indian (and the tenth, he says, must be more closely examined). A volunteer in all wars, he adores the supreme qualities of the soldier, who in the euphoria of battle feels himself in his heart to be a wolf, and despises soft generals who anguish over the loss of a couple of thousand men.

To make a quick end to the Cuban war, Teddy has proposed that a North American squadron should flatten Cadiz and Barcelona with its guns; but Spain, exhausted from so much warfare against the Cubans, surrenders in less than four months. From San Juan Hill, the victorious Teddy Roosevelt gallops at top speed to the governorship of New York State and on to the presidency of the United States. This fanatical devotee of a God who prefers gunpowder to incense takes a deep breath and writes: *No triumph of peace is quite so great as the supreme triumph of war.*

Within a few years, he will receive the Nobel Peace Prize.

(114 and 161)

1898: Coasts of Puerto Rico
This Fruit Is Falling

Ramón Emeterio Betances, long white beard, eyes of melancholy, is dying in Paris, in exile.

"*I do not want a colony,*" he says. "*Not with Spain, nor with the United States.*"

While the patriarch of Puerto Rico's independence approaches death, General Miles's soldiers sing as they land on the Guánica coast. With guns slung from shoulders and toothbrushes stuck in hats, the soldiers march before the impassive gaze of the peasants of sugarcane and coffee.

And Eugenio María de Hostos, who also wanted a fatherland, contemplates the hills of Puerto Rico from the deck of a ship, and feels sad and ashamed to see them pass from one master to another.

(141 and 192)

1898: Washington

President McKinley Explains
That the United States Should Keep
the Philippines by Direct Order of God

I walked the floor of the White House night after night until midnight; and I am not ashamed to tell you, gentlemen, that I went down on my knees and prayed Almighty God for light and guidance more than one night. And one night late it came to me this way—I don't know how it was but it came; first, that we could not give [the Philippines] back to Spain—that would be cowardly and dishonorable; second, that we could not turn them over to France or Germany—our commercial rivals in the Orient—that would be bad business and discreditable; third, we could not leave them to themselves—they were unfit for self-government, and they would soon have anarchy and misrule over there worse than Spain's was; and fourth, that there was nothing left for us to do but to take them all, and to educate the Filipinos, and uplift and civilize and Christianize them, and by God's grace do the very best we could by them, as our fellow men for whom Christ also died. And then I went to bed, and went to sleep and slept soundly.

(168)

1899: New York

Mark Twain Proposes Changing the Flag

I lift my lamp beside the golden door. The Statue of Liberty welcomes innumerable pilgrims, Europeans in search of the Promised Land, while it is announced that the center of the world, which took millennia to shift from the Euphrates to the Thames, is now the Hudson River.

In full imperial euphoria, the United States celebrates the conquest of the Hawaiian islands, Samoa and the Philippines, Cuba, Puerto Rico, and some little islands eloquently named the Ladrones (Thieves).* Now the Pacific and Caribbean are North American lakes, and the United Fruit Company is coming to birth; but novelist Mark Twain, the old spoilsport, proposes changing the national flag: the

---

* Former name of the Marianas in the Western Pacific.

white stripes should be black, he says, and the stars should be skulls and crossbones.

Trade union leader Samuel Gompers demands recognition of Cuba's independence and denounces those who throw freedom to the dogs at the moment of choosing between freedom and profit. For the great newspapers, on the other hand, the Cubans wanting independence are ingrates. Cuba is an occupied country. The United States flag, without black bars or skulls, flies in place of the Spanish flag. The invading forces have doubled in a year. The schools are teaching English; and the new history books speak of Washington and Jefferson and do not mention Maceo or Martí. There is no slavery any more; but in Havana cafes signs appear that warn: "Whites Only." The market is opened without conditions to capital hungry for sugar and tobacco.

(114 and 224)

1899: Rome

Calamity Jane

They say she sleeps with her revolvers hung from the bedpost and that she still beats the men at poker, drinking, and blasphemy. She has felled many men, they say, with a hook to the jaw, since the time when she is said to have fought with General Custer in Wyoming, and killed Indians to protect miners in the Black Hills of the Sioux. They say that they say that she rode a bull down the main street of Rapid City, and that she held up trains, and that in Fort Laramie she got the handsome sheriff Wild Bill Hickok to fall for her, and that he gave her a daughter and a horse named Satan that knelt to help her dismount. She always wore pants, they say, and often took them off, and there was no more generous woman in the saloons, nor more barefaced in loving and lying.

They say. Maybe she never was. Maybe, tonight, she isn't really in the arena of the Wild West Show, and old Buffalo Bill is having us on again. If it were not for the applause of the audience, not even the real Calamity Jane would be sure that she is this woman of forty-four, overweight and plain, who sends her Stetson flying and turns it into a colander.

(169)

1899: Rome

The Nascent Empire Flexes Its Muscles

In an ostentatious ceremony Buffalo Bill receives a gold watch encrusted with diamonds from the hands of the king of Italy. The Wild West Show is touring Europe. The conquest of the West has ended and the conquest of the world has begun. Buffalo Bill has under his orders a multinational army of five hundred men. Not only cowboys work in his circus; but also authentic lancers of the Prince of Wales, light cavalrymen of the French republican guard, cuirassiers of the emperor of Germany, Russian Cossacks, Arab horsemen, Mexican charros, and gauchos from the River Plata. Soldiers of the Fifth Cavalry act out their role as conquerors and conquered Indians, torn from the reservations, appear as extras repeating their defeats on the sands of the arena. A herd of buffalos, rare museum pieces, add realism to the blue uniforms and plumed helmets. Teddy Roosevelt's Rough Riders dramatize for the audience their recent conquest of Cuba and squads of Cubans, Hawaiians, and Filipinos pay servile homage to the victorious flag.

The program of the spectacle explains the winning of the West with Darwin's words: *It is the inevitable law of survival of the fittest.* In epic phrases, Buffalo Bill exalts the civic and military virtues of his nation, which has digested half of Mexico and numerous islands and now enters the twentieth century striding the world with the strut of a great power.

(157)

1899: Saint Louis

Far Away

Fire sprouts from mouths and rabbits from top hats; from the magic horn come little glass horses. A car runs over a prostrate woman, who gets up with one jump; another dances with a sword stuck in her belly. An enormous bear obeys complicated orders given in English.

Geronimo is invited to enter a little house with four windows. Suddenly the house moves and rises into the air. Startled, Geronimo leans out: down there the people look the size of ants. The keepers laugh. They give him some binoculars, like those he took from officers fallen in battle. Through the binoculars the far away comes close.

Geronimo aims at the sun and the violent light hurts his eyes. The keepers laugh; and since they laugh, he laughs too.

Geronimo, prisoner of war of the United States, is one of the attractions at the Saint Louis fair. Crowds come to see the tamed beast. The chief of the Apaches of Arizona sells bows and arrows, and for a few cents poses for snapshots, or prints as best he can the letters of his name.

(24)

1899: Rio de Janeiro
How to Cure by Killing

Sorcerous hands play with the price of coffee, and Brazil cannot pay the London and River Plate Bank and other very important creditors.

It is the hour of sacrifice, announces Finance Minister Joaquim Murtinho. The minister believes in the *natural laws* of economics, which by *natural selection* condemn the weak, that is to say the poor, that is to say almost everyone. Should the State take the coffee business out of the speculators' hands? That, says an indignant Murtinho, would be a violation of *natural laws* and a dangerous step toward socialism, that fearsome plague that European workers are bringing to Brazil: socialism, he says, denies freedom and turns man into an ant.

National industry, Murtinho believes, is not *natural*. Small as it is, national industry is taking labor from the plantations and raising the price of hands. Murtinho, guardian angel of the great-estate order, will see to it that the crisis is not paid for by the owners of men and lands, who have survived intact the abolition of slavery and the proclamation of the republic. To pay off the English banks and balance the books, the minister burns in an oven any banknote that comes his way, suppresses any public service that is handy, and lets loose a hail of taxes on the poor.

Economist by vocation and physician by profession, Murtinho also makes interesting experiments in the field of physiology. In his laboratory he extracts the encephalic mass of rats and rabbits and decapitates frogs to study the convulsions of the body, which continues moving as if it had a head.

(75)

1900: Huanuni

Patiño

The horseman comes from desolation and rides across desolation, through icy winds, at a slow gait over the nakedness of the planet. A mule loaded with rocks follows him.

The horseman has spent much time boring into rocks and opening up caves with dynamite charges. He has never seen the sea, nor known even the city of La Paz, but suspects that the world is living an industrial era and that industry eats hitherto disdained minerals. He has not gone into the mountains after silver, as so many have. Searching for tin, as no one else is, he has penetrated to the heart of the mountain, to its very soul, and has found it.

Simón Patiño, the horseman stung through with cold, the miner mortified by solitude and debt, reaches the town of Huanuni. In his mule's saddlebags he has pieces of the world's richest vein of tin. These rocks will make him king of Bolivia.

(132)

1900: Mexico City

Posada

He illustrates verses and news. His broadsheets sell in the markets and at the doors of churches and wherever a balladeer sings the prophesies of Nostradamus, the horrifying details of the train derailment at Temamatla, the last appearance of the Virgin of Guadalupe, or the tragedy of the woman who gave birth to four lizards in a barrio of this city.

By the magical hand of José Guadalupe Posada, *corrido* ballads never lose their spontaneity, topicality, and popularity. In his drawings, the knives of loudmouths and tongues of gossips will always be sharp, the Devil will keep dancing and flaming, Death laughing, pulque moistening mustaches, *the unhappy Eleuterio Mirafuentes crushing with an enormous stone the cranium of the ancient author of his days*. This year, a Posada drawing celebrated the appearance of the first electric streetcar in the streets of Mexico. Now, another shows the streetcar crashing into a funeral procession in front of the cemetery, with a tremendous scattering of skeletons. They sell for one centavo a copy, printed on brown paper, with verses for anyone who knows how to read and weep.

His workshop is a mess of rolls and receptacles and zinc plates and wooden wedges, all piled around the press and beneath a rain of newly printed papers hung up to dry. Posada works from morning till night, engraving marvels. "Little drawings," he says. From time to time he goes to the door to smoke a restful cigar, not forgetting to cover his head with a derby and his great belly with a dark woolen vest.

Every day, past Posada's workshop door go the professors of the neighboring Fine Arts Academy. They never look in or greet him.

(263 and 357)

1900: Mexico City
Porfirio Díaz

He grew up in the shadow of Juárez. *The man who weeps as he kills,* Juárez called him.

"Weeping, weeping, he'll kill me if I'm not careful."

Porfirio Díaz has been ruling Mexico for a quarter of a century. The official biographers record for posterity his yawns and his aphorisms. They do not note it down when he says:

"The best Indian is six feet underground."

"Kill them on the spot."

"Don't stir up the herd on me."

"The herd" are the legislators, who vote Yes when their heads nod from sleepiness, and who call Don Porfirio *the Unique, the Indispensable, the Irreplaceable*. The people call him "Don Perfidy" and make fun of his courtiers:

"What time is it?"

"Whatever you say, Señor President."

He displays his little finger and says: *"Tlaxcala hurts me."* He points to his heart and says: *"Oaxaca hurts me."* With his hand on his liver, he says: *"Michoacán hurts me."* In a flash he has three governors trembling before him.

The shot-while-trying-to-escape law is applied to the rebellious and the curious. At the height of Pax Porfiriana, Mexico makes progress. Messages that previously went by mule, horse, or pigeon now fly over seventy thousand kilometers of telegraph wires. Where stagecoaches used to go, there are fifteen thousand kilometers of railway. The nation pays its debts punctually and supplies minerals and food to the world market. On every big estate a fortress rises. From the battlements guards keep watch over the Indians, who may not even change masters. There are no schools of economics but Don Porfirio rules surrounded by "scientists" specializing in the purchase of lands precisely where the next railway will pass. Capital comes from the United States and ideas and fashions are bought secondhand in France. Mexico City likes to call itself "the Paris of the Americas," although more white peasant pants than trousers are seen in the streets; and the frock-coated minority inhabit Second Empire–style palaces. The poets have baptized its evenings as "the green hour," not because of the light through the trees, but in memory of De Musset's absinthe.

(33 and 142)

1900: Mexico City
The Flores Magón Brothers

The people sail on rivers of pulque as bells ring out and rockets boom and knives glint under the Bengal lights. The crowd invades the Alameda and other prohibited streets, the zone sacred to corseted ladies and jacketed gentlemen, with the Virgin on a portable platform. From that lofty ship of lights, the Virgin's wings protect and guide.

This is the day of Our Lady of the Angels, which in Mexico lasts for a week of balls; and on the margin of the violent joy of people, as if wishing to merit it, a new newspaper is born. It is called *Regeneration*. It inherits the enthusiasms and debts of *The Democrat*, closed down by the dictatorship. Jesús, Ricardo, and Enrique Flores Magón write it, publish it, and sell it.

The Flores Magón brothers grow with punishment. Since their father died, they have taken turns between jail, law studies, occasional small jobs, combative journalism, and stones-against-bullets street demonstrations.

All belongs to all, they had been told by their father, the Indian Teodoro Flores, that bony face now up among the stars. A thousand times he had told them: *Repeat that!*

(287)

1900: Mérida, Yucatán
Henequén

One of every three Mayas in Yucatán is a slave, hostage of henequén, and their children, who inherit their debts, will be slaves too. Lands are sold complete with Indians, but the great henequén plantations use scientific methods and modern machinery, receive orders by telegraph and are financed by New York banks. Steam-driven scraping machines separate the fibers; and International Harvester trains run them to a port called Progress. Meanwhile guards shut the Indians into barracks when night falls, and at dawn mount horses to herd them back to the rows of spiny plants.

With sisal yarn, henequén yarn, everything on earth can be tied up, and every ship on the ocean uses henequén ropes. Henequén brings prosperity to Yucatán, one of Mexico's richest regions: in Mérida, the capital, golden grilles keep mules and Indians from trampling gardens badly copied from Versailles. The bishop's carriage is almost identical to the one the pope uses in Rome, and from Paris come architects who imitate French medieval castles, although today's heroes venture forth not for captive princesses but for free Indians.

General Ignacio Bravo, eyes like knives, white moustache, mouth clamped tight, has arrived in Mérida to exterminate the Mayas who still beat the drums of war. The guns of San Benito salute the redeemer of henequén. In the Plaza de Armas, beneath leafy laurels, the masters of Yucatán offer General Bravo the silver sword that awaits the conqueror of Chan Santa Cruz, the rebels' sacred city in the jungle.

And then falls the slow lid of night.

(273)

From the Mexican Corrido of the Twenty-Eighth Battalion

I'm on my way, on my way,
on my way with great delight,
because the Maya Indians
are dying, they say, of fright.

I'm on my way, on my way,
to the other side of the sea,
for the Indians no longer
have any way to flee.

I'm on my way, on my way,
God keep you warm, my jewel,
because the Maya Indians
will make a lovely fuel.

I'm on my way, on my way,
for the winter there to dwell,
because the Maya Indians
are going straight to hell.

(212)

1900: Tabi
The Iron Serpent

In the forefront the cannons thunder, overturning barricades and crushing the dying. Behind the cannons the soldiers, almost all Indians, set fire to the communities' cornfields and fire repeating Mausers against old weapons loaded by the barrel. Behind the soldiers, peons, almost all Indians, lay tracks for the railway and raise posts for the telegraph and the gallows.

The railway, snake without scales, has its tail in Mérida and its long body grows toward Chan Santa Cruz. The head reaches Santa María and jumps to Hobompich and from Hobompich to Tabi, double tongue of iron, swift, voracious. Breaking jungle, cutting earth, it pursues, attacks, and bites. On its gleaming march it swallows free Indians and shits slaves.

The Chan Santa Cruz sanctuary is doomed. It had come into being half a century ago, born of that little mahogany cross that appeared in the thicket and said, *"My father has sent me to speak with you, who are earth."*

(273)

The Prophet

Here it came to pass, more than four centuries ago. Lying on his mat, on his back, the priest-jaguar of Yucatán heard the message of the gods. They spoke to him through the roof, squatting on his house, in a language no one understood any more.

Chilam Balam, he who was the mouth of the gods, remembered what had not yet happened and announced what would be:

"Stick and stone will rise up for the struggle . . . Dogs will bite their masters . . . Those with borrowed thrones must throw up what they swallowed. Very sweet, very tasty was what they swallowed, but they will vomit it up. The usurpers will depart to the limits of the

waters . . . Then there will be no more devourers of man . . . When greed comes to an end, the face of the world will be set free, its hands will be set free, its feet will be set free."

(23)

(End of the second volume of
Memory of Fire)

The Sources

1. Abreu y Gómez, Ermilo. *Canek. Historia y leyenda de un héroe maya.* Mexico City: Oasis, 1982.
2. Acevedo, Edberto Oscar. *El ciclo histórico de la revolución de mayo.* Seville: Escuela de Estudios Hispanoamericanos, 1957.
3. Acuña de Figueroa, Francisco. *Nuevo mosaico poético*, (prologue by Gustavo Gallinal). Montevideo: Claudio García, 1944.
4. Adoum, Jorge Enrique. "Las Galápagos: el origen de *El origen* . . ." (and articles by Asimov, Pyke, and others) in *Darwin,* El Correo de la Unesco, Paris, May 1982.
5. Aguirre, Nataniel. *Juan de la Rosa.* La Paz: Gisbert, 1973.
6. Ajofrín, Francisco de. *Diaro de viaje.* Madrid: Real Academia de la Historia, 1958.
7. Alcáraz, Ramón, *et al. Apuntes para la historia de la guerra entre México y los Estados Unidos.* Mexico City: Siglo XXI, 1970.
8. Alemán Bolaños, Gustavo. *Sandino, el libertador.* Mexico City and Guatemala: Ed. del Caribe, 1951.
9. Anderson Imbert, Enrique. *Historia de la literatura hispanoamericana.* Mexico City: FCE, 1974.
10. Anson, George, *Voyage autour du monde,* Amsterdam and Leipzig, 1751.
11. Antonil, André João. *Cultura e opulencia do Brasil por suas drogas e minas,* (annotated by A. Mansuy). Paris: Université, 1968.
12. Aptheker, Herbert (ed.). *A Documentary History of the Negro People in the United States.* New York: Citadel, 1969.
13. Arciniegas, Germán, *Los comuneros.* Mexico City: Guarania, 1951.
14. Arnold, Mayer. *Del Plata a los Andes. Viaje por las provincias en la época de Rosas.* Buenos Aires: Huarpes, 1944.
15. Arriaga, Antonio. *La patria recobrada.* Mexico City: FCE, 1967.
16. Arzáns de Orsúa y Vela, Bartolomé. *Historia de la Villa Imperial de Potosí* (Lewis Hanke and Gunnar Mendoza, eds.). Providence: Brown University Press, 1965.
17. Astuto, Philip Louis. *Eugenio Espejo, reformador ecuatoriano de la Ilustración.* Mexico City: FCE, 1969.
18. Atl, Dr. *Las artes populares en México.* Mexico City: Instituto Nacional Indigenista, 1980.
19. Aubry, Octave. *Vie privée de Napoléon.* Paris: Tallandier, 1977.
20. Ayestarán, Lauro. *La música en el Uruguay.* Montevideo: SODRE, 1953.
21. Baelen, Jean. *Flora Tristán: Feminismo y socialismo en el siglo XIX.* Madrid: Taurus, 1974.
22. Barnet, Miguel. *Akeké y la jutía.* Havana: Unión, 1978.

23. Barrera Vásquez, Alfredo, and Silvia Rendón (eds.). *El libro de los libros de Chilam Balam*. Mexico City: FCE, 1978.
24. Barrett, S. M. (ed.). *Gerónimo, historia de su vida* (notes by Manuel Sacristán). Barcelona: Grijalbo, 1975.
25. Barrett, William E. *La amazona*. Barcelona: Grijalbo, 1982.
26. Basadre, Jorge. *La multitud, la ciudad y el campo en la historia del Perú*. Lima: Treintaetrés y Mosca Azul, 1980.
27. Bastide, Roger. *Les religions africaines au Brésil*. Paris: Presses Universitaires, 1960.
28. ———. *Les Amériques noires*. Paris: Payot, 1967.
29. Bazin, Germain. *Aleijadinho et la sculpture baroque au Brésil*. Paris: Du Temps, 1963.
30. Beck, Hanno. *Alexander von Humboldt*. Mexico City: FCE, 1971.
31. Benítez, Fernando. *Los indios de México* (Vol. 2). Mexico City: Era, 1968.
32. ———. *Los indios de México* (Vol. 4). Mexico City: Era, 1972.
33. ———. *El porfirismo. Lázaro Cárdenas y la revolución mexicana*. Mexico City: FCE, 1977.
34. Benítez, Rubén A. *Una histórica función de circo*. Buenos Aires: Universidad, 1956.
35. Bermúdez, Oscar. *Historia del salitre, desde sus orígenes hasta la guerra del Pacífico*. Santiago de Chile: Universidad, 1963.
36. Bermúdez Bermúdez, Arturo. *Materiales para la historia de Santa Marta*. Bogotá: Banco Central Hipotecario, 1981.
37. Beyhaut, Gustavo. *American centrale e meridionale. Dall'indipendenza alla crisis attuale*. Roma: Feltrinelli, 1968.
38. Bierhorst, John. *In the Trail of the Wind. American Indian Poems and Ritual Orations*. New York: Farrar, Straus and Giroux, 1973.
39. Bilbao, Francisco. *La revolución en Chile y los mensajes del proscripto*. Lima: Imprenta del Comercio, 1853.
40. Bolívar, Simón. *Documentos*. (Selected by Manuel Galich.) Havana: Casa de las Américas, 1975.
41. Boorstin, Daniel J. *The Lost World of Thomas Jefferson*. Chicago: University of Chicago Press, 1981.
42. Bonilla, Heraclio, *et el*. *La independencia del Perú*. Lima: Instituto de Estudios Peruanos, 1981.
43. ———. *et al*. *Nueva historia general del Perú*. Lima: Mosca Azul, 1980.
44. ———. *Guano y burguesía en el Perú*. Lima: Instituto de Estudios Peruanos, 1974.
45. ———. *Un siglo a la deriva. Ensayos sobre el Perú, Bolivia y la guerra*. Lima: Instituto de Estudios Peruanos, 1980.
46. Botting, Douglas. *Humboldt and the Cosmos*. London: Sphere, 1973.
47. Box, Pelham Horton. *Los orígenes de la guerra de la Triple Alianza*. Buenos Aires and Asunción: Nizza, 1958.

48. Boxer, C. R. *The Golden Age of Brazil (1695–1750)*. Berkeley: University of California Press, 1969.
49. Brading, D. A., *Mineros y comerciantes en el México borbónico (1763–1810)*. Mexico City: FCE, 1975.
50. Brooke, Frances. *The History of Emily Montague*. Toronto: McClelland and Stewart, 1961.
51. Brown, Dee. *Bury My Heart at Wounded Knee. An Indian History of The American West*. New York: Holt, Rinehart and Winston, 1971.
52. Brunet, Michel. *Les canadiens après la conquête (1759–1775)*. Montreal: Fides, 1980.
53. Busaniche, José Luis. *Bolívar visto por sus contemporáneos*. Mexico City: FCE, 1981.
54. ———. *San Martín vivo*. Buenos Aires: Emecé, 1950.
55. ———. *Historia argentina*. Buenos Aires: Solar/Hachette, 1973.
56. Cabrera, Lydia. *El monte*. Havana: CR, 1954.
57. Calderón de la Barca, Frances Erskine de. *La vida en México durante una residencia de dos años en ese país*. Mexico City: Porrúa, 1959.
58. Canales, Claudia. *Romualdo García. Un fotógrafo, una ciudad, una época*. Guanajuato: Gobierno del Estado, 1980.
59. Cardoza y Aragón, Luis. *Guatemala: las líneas de su mano*. Mexico City: FCE, 1965.
60. Cardozo, Efraím. *Breve historia del Paraguay*. Buenos Aires: EUDEBA, 1965.
61. ———. *Hace cien años. Crónicas de la guerra de 1864–1870*, Asunción, Emasa, 1967/1976.
62. Carlos, Lasinha Luis. *A Colombo na vida do Rio*. Rio de Janeiro: n.p., 1970.
63. Carpentier, Alejo. *El reino de este mundo*. Barcelona: Seix Barral, 1975.
64. Carrera Damas, Germán. *Bolívar*. Montevideo: Marcha, 1974.
65. Carvalho-Neto, Paulo de. *El folklore de las luchas sociales*. Mexico City: Siglo XXI, 1973.
66. ———. "Contribución al estudio de los negros paraguayos de Acampamento Loma," in *América Latina*, Rio de Janeiro, Centro Latinoamericano de Pesquisas em Ciencias Sociais, January/June 1962.
67. Casarrubias, Vicente. *Rebeliones indígenas en la Nueva España*. Mexico City: Secretaría de Educación Pública, 1945.
68. Casimir, Jean. *La cultura oprimida*. Mexico City: Nueva Imagen, 1980.
69. Catton, Bruce. *Reflections on the Civil War*. New York: Berkley, 1982.
70. ———. *Short History of the Civil War*. New York: Dell, 1976.
71. Césaire, Aimé. *Toussaint Louverture*. Havana: Instituto del Libro, 1967.
72. Clastres, Hélène. *La terre sans mal. Le prophetisme tupi-guarani*. Paris: Seuil, 1975.
73. Clavijero, Francisco Javier. *Historia antigua de México*. Mexico City: Editora México, 1958.

74. Conrad, Robert. *Os últimos anos da escravatura no Brasil*. Rio de Janeiro: Civilização Brasileira, 1975.
75. Corrêa Filho, Virgilio. *Joaquim Murtinho*. Rio de Janeiro: Imprensa Nacional, 1951.
76. Cortesão, Jaime. *Do Tratado de Madri à conquista dos Sete Povos*. Rio de Janeiro: Biblioteca Nacional, 1969.
77. Coughtry, Jay. *The Notorious Triangle. Rhode Island and the African Slave Trade, 1700–1807*. Philadelphia: Temple University Press, 1981.
78. Craton, Michael. *Testing the Chains. Resistance to Slavery in the British West Indies*. Ithaca: Cornell University Press, 1982.
79. Crowther, J. G. *Benjamin Franklin y J. Willard Gibbs*. Buenos Aires: Espasa-Calpe, 1946.
80. Cunha, Euclides da. *Os sertões*. São Paulo: Alves, 1936.
81. Current, Richard N. *The Lincoln Nobody Knows*. New York: Hill and Wang, 1981.
82. Cháves, Julio César. *El Supremo Dictador*. Buenos Aires: Difusam, 1942.
83. ———. *El presidente López. Vida y govierno de don Carlos*. Buenos Aires: Ayacucho, 1955.
84. ———. *Castelli, el adalid de Mayo*. Buenos Aires: Ayacucho, 1944.
85. Daireaux, Max. *Melgarejo*. Buenos Aires: Andina, 1966.
86. Dallas, Robert Charles. *Historia de los cimarrones*. Havana: Casa de las Américas, 1980.
87. Dalton, Roque. *Las historias prohibidas del Pulgarcito*. Mexico City: Siglo XXI, 1974.
88. Darwin, Charles. *Mi viaje alrededor del mundo*. Valencia: Sampere, n.d.
89. Davidson, Basil. *Black Mother: Africa and the Atlantic Slave Trade*. London: Pelican, 1980.
90. Debien, Gabriel. "Le marronage aux Antilles Français au XVIIIe. siècle," in *Caribbean Studies*, Vol. 6, No. 3, Río Piedras, Institute of Caribbean Studies, October 1966.
91. Debo, Angie. *A History of the Indians of the United States*. Oklahoma: University of Oklahoma Press, 1979.
92. Defoe, Daniel. *Aventuras de Robinsón Crusoe*. Mexico City: Porrúa, 1975.
93. Descola, Jean. *La vida cotidiana en el Perú en tiempos de los españoles (1710–1820)*. Buenos Aires: Hachette, 1962.
94. Díaz, Lilia. "El liberalismo militante," in *Historia general de México*. Mexico City: El Colegio de México, 1977.
95. Doucet, Louis. *Quand les français cherchaient fortune aux Caraïbes*. Paris: Fayard, 1981.
96. Douville, Raymond, and Jacques-Donat Casanova. *La vie quotidienne en Nouvelle-France. Le Canada, de Champlain a Montcalm*. Paris: Hachette, 1964.

97. ———. *Des indiens du Canada a l'époque de la colonisation française*. Paris: Hachette, 1967.
98. Duchet, Michèle. *Antropología e historia en el Siglo de las Luces*. Mexico City: Siglo XXI, 1975.
99. Dugran, J. H. *Edgar A. Poe*. Buenos Aires: Lautaro, 1944.
100. Dujovne, Marta (with Augusto Roa Bastos *et al.*). *Cándido López*. Parma: Ricci, 1976.
101. Dumas, Alejandro. *Montevideo o una nueva Troya*. Montevideo: Claudio García, 1941.
102. Duval, Miles P., Jr. *De Cádiz a Catay*. Panama: Editorial Universitaria, 1973.
103. Echagüe, J. P. *Tradiciones, leyendas y cuentos argentinos*. Buenos Aires: Espasa-Calpe, 1960.
104. Echeverría, Esteban. *La cautiva/El matadero*. (Prologue by Juan Carlos Pellegrini.) Buenos Aires: Huemul, 1964.
105. Escalante Beatón, Aníbal. *Calixto García. Su campaña en el 95*. Havana: Ciencias Sociales, 1978.
106. Eyzaguirre, Jaime. *Historia de Chile*. Santiago de Chile: Zig-Zag, 1977.
107. ———. *Chile y Bolivia. Esquema de un proceso diplomático*. Santiago de Chile: Zig-Zag, 1963.
108. Fals Borda, Orlando. *Historia doble de la costa*. Bogotá: Carlos Valencia, 1980/1981.
109. Faria, Alberto de. *Irenêo Evangelista de Souza, barão e visconde de Mauá 1813–1889*. São Paulo: Editora Nacional, 1946.
110. Felce, Emma, and León Benarós. *Los caudillos del año 20*. Buenos Aires: Nova, 1944.
111. Fernández de Lizardi, José Joaquín. *El Periquillo Sarniento*. Buenos Aires: Maucci, n.d.
112. Fernández Retamar, Roberto. *Introducción a José Martí*. Havana: Casa de las Américas, 1978.
113. Fohlen, Claude. *La vie quotidienne au Far West*. Paris: Hachette, 1974.
114. Foner, Philip S. *La guerra hispano-cubano-norteamericana y el surgimiento del imperialismo yanqui*. Havana: Ciencias Sociales, 1978.
115. Franco, José Luciano. *Historia de la revolución de Haití*. Havana: Academia de Ciencias, 1966.
116. Frank, Waldo. *Nacimiento de un mundo. Bolívar dentro del marco de sus propios pueblos*. Havana: Instituto del Libro, 1967.
117. Freitas, Décio. *O socialismo missioneiro*. Porto Alegre: Movimento, 1982.
118. Freitas, Newton. *El Aletjadinho*. Buenos Aires: Nova, 1944.
119. Freyre, Gilberto. *Sobrados e mucambos*. Rio de Janeiro: José Olympio, 1951.
120. Friedemann, Nina S. de (with Richard Cross). *Ma Ngombe: Guerreros y ganaderos en Palenque*. Bogotá: Carlos Valencia, 1979.

121. ——— (with Jaime Arocha). *Herederos del jaguar y la anaconda*. Bogotá: Carlos Valencia, 1982.

122. Frieiro, Eduardo. *Feijão, agua e couve*. Belo Horizonte: Itatiaia, 1982.

123. Frota, Lélia Coelho. *Ataíde*. Rio de Janeiro: Nova Fronteira, 1982.

124. Furst, Peter T., and Salomón Nahmad. *Mitos y arte huicholes*. Mexico City: SEP/Setentas, 1972.

125. Fusco Sansone, Nicolás. *Vida y obras de Bartolomé Hidalgo*. Buenos Aires: n.p., 1952.

126. Gantier, Joaquín, *Doña Juana Azurduy de Padilla*. La Paz: Icthus, 1973.

127. García Cantú, Gastón. *Utopías mexcianas*. Mexico City: FCE, 1978.

128. ———. *Las invasiones norteamericanas en México*. Mexico City: Era, 1974.

129. ———. *El socialismo en México, siglo XIX*. Mexico City: Era, 1974.

130. Garraty, John A., and Peter Gay. *Columbia History of the World*. New York: Harper and Row, 1972.

131. Garrett, Pat. *La verdadera historia de Billy the Kid*. Mexico City: Premiá, 1981.

132. Geddes, Charles F. *Patiño, the Tin King*. London: Hale, 1972.

133. Gendrop, Paul. "La escultura clásica maya," in *Artes de México*, No. 167, Mexico.

134. Gerbi, Antonello. *La disputa del Neuvo Mundo*. Mexico City: FCE, 1960.

135. Gibson, Charles. *Los aztecas bajo el dominio español (1519–1810)*. Mexico City: Siglo XXI, 1977.

136. Girod, François. *La vie quotidienne de la société créole (Saint-Domingue au 18e. siècle)*. Paris: Hachette, 1972.

137. Gisbert, Teresa. *Iconografía y mitos indígenas en el arte*. La Paz: Gisbert, 1980.

138. ——— (with José de Mesa). *Historia de la pintura cuzqueña*. Lima: Banco Wiese, 1982.

139. Gisler, Antoine. *L'esclavage aux Antilles français (XVIIe.–XIXe. siècle)*. Paris: Karthala, 1981.

140. Godio, Julio. *Historia del movimiento obrero latinoamericano*. Mexico City: Nueva Imagen, 1980.

141. González, José Luis. *La llegada*. San Juan: Mortiz/Huracán, 1980.

142. González, Luis. "El liberalismo triunfante," in *Historia General de México*. Mexico City: El Colegio de México, 1977.

143. ——— et al. *La economía mexicana en la época de Juárez*. Mexico City: Secretaría de Industria y Comerdio, 1972.

144. González Navarro, Moisés. *Raza y tierra. La guerra de castas y el henequén*. Mexico City: El Colegio de México, 1979.

145. González Prada, Manuel. *Horas de lucha*. Lima: Universo, 1972.

146. González Sánchez, Isabel. "Sistemas de trabajo, salarios, y situación de los trabajadores agrćolas (1750–1810)," in *Las clase obrera en la historia de México*. *1. De la colonia al imperio*. Mexico City: Siglo XXI, 1980.

147. Granada, Daniel. *Supersticiones del río de la Plata*. Buenos Aires: Kraft, 1947.

148. Gredilla, A. Federico. *Biografía de José Celestino Mutis y sus observaciones sobre las viglias y sueños de algunas plantas*. Bogotá: Plaza y Janés, 1982.

149. Green, Martin. *Dreams of Adventure, Deeds of Empire*. New York: Basic Books, 1979.

150. Grigulévich, José. *Francisco de Mirana y la lucha por la liberación de la América Latina*. Havana: Casa de las Américas, 1978.

151. Griswold, D. C. *El istmo de Panamá y lo que vi en él*. Panama: Ed. Universitaria, 1974.

152. Guasch, Antonio. *Diccionario castellano-guaraní y guaraní-castellano*. Seville: Loyola, 1961.

153. Guerrero Guerrero, Raúl. *El pulque*. Mexico City: Instituto Nacional de Antropología e Historia, 1980.

154. Guier, Enrique. *William Walker*. San José, Costa Rica: n.p., 1971.

155. Guiteras Holmes, Cali. *Los peligros del alma*. *Visión del mundo de un tzotzil*. Mexico City: FCE 1965.

156. Guy, Christian. *Almanach historique de la gastronomie française*. Paris: Hachette, 1981.

157. Hassrick, Peter H., *et al*. *Buffalo Bill and the Wild West*. New York: The Brooklyn Museum, 1981.

158. Hernández, José. *Martín Fierro*. Buenos Aires: EUDEBA, 1963.

159. Hernández Matos, Román. *Micaela Bastidas, la precursora*. Lima: Atlas, 1981.

160. Herrera Luque, Francisco. *Boves, el Urogallo*. Caracas: Fuentes, 1973.

161. Hofstadter, Richard. *The American Political Tradition*. New York: Knopf, 1948.

162. Huberman, Leo. *We, the People*. *The Drama of America*. New York: Monthly Review Press, 1970.

163. Humboldt, Alejandro de. *Ensayo político sobre el reino del la Nueva España*. Mexico City: Porrúa, 1973.

164. Ibañez Fonseca, Rodrigo, *et al*. *Literatura de Colombia aborigen*. Bogotá: Instituto Colombiano de Cultura, 1978.

165. Ibarra, Jorge. *José Martí, dirigente político e ideólogo revolucionario*. Havana: Ciencias Sociales, 1980.

166. Irazusta, Julio. *Ensayo sobre Rosas*. Buenos Aires: Tor, 1935.

167. Isaacs, Jorge. *María* (introduction by Germán Arciniegas). Barcelona: Círculo de Lectores, 1975.

168. Jacobs, Paul (with Saul Landau and Eve Pell). *To Serve the Devil*. A

Documentary Analysis of America's Racial History and Why It Has
Been Kept Hidden. New York: Random House, 1971.

169. Jane, Calamity. Cartas a la hija (1877–1902). Barcelona: Anagrama,
1982.

170. Juan, Jorge, and Antonio de Ulloa. Noticias secretas de América. Caracas: Ayacucho, 1979.

171. Kaufmann, William W. British Policy and the Independence of
Latin American (1804–1828). Hamden, Connecticut: Shoe String Press,
1967.

172. Klein, Herbert S. Bolivia. The Evolution of a Multiethnic Society. New
York and Oxford: Oxford University Press, 1982.

173. Kom, Anton de. Nosotros, esclavos de Surinam. Havana: Casa de las
Américas, 1981.

174. Konetzke, Richard. Colección de documentos para la historia de la
formación social de Hispanoamérica. Madrid: Consejo Superior de
Investigaciones Científicas, 1962.

175. Kossok, Manfred. El virreynato del río de la Plata. Su estructura
económico-social. Buenos Aires: Futuro, 1959.

176. Lacoursière, J. (with J. Provencher and D. Vaugeois). Canada/Quebec.
Synthèse historique. Montreal: Renouveau Pedagogique, 1978.

177. Lafargue, Pablo (Paul). Textos escogidos. (Selection and introduction
by Salvador Morales.) Havana: Ciencias Sociales, 1976.

178. Lafaye, Jacques. Quetzalcóatl y Guadalupe. La formación de la conciencia nacional en México. Mexico City: FCE, 1977.

179. Lanuza, José Luis. Coplas y cantares argentinos. Buenos Aires: Emecé,
1952.

180. Lara, Oruno. La Guadeloupe dans l'histoire. Paris: L'Harmattan, 1979.

181. Lautréamont, Conde de. Oeuvres complètes. (Prologue by Maurice
Saillet.) Paris, Librairie Générale Française, 1963. Spanish trans: Obras completas. (Prologue by Aldo Pellegrini.) Buenos Aires: Argonauta,
1964.

182. Laval, Ramon. Oraciones, ensalmos y conjuros del pueblo chileno.
Santiago de Chile: n.p., 1910.

183. Lewin, Boleslao. La rebelión de Túpac Amaru y los orígenes de la
emancipación americana. Buenos Aires: Hachette, 1957.

184. Liedtke, Klaus. "Coca-Cola über alles," in the newspaper El País.
Madrid, 30 July 1978.

185. Liévano Aguirre, Indalecio. Los orandes conflictos sociales y económicos de nuestra historia. Bogotá: Tercer Mundo, 1964.

186. Lima, Heitor Ferreira. "Os primeiros empréstimos externos," in Ensaios de Opinião, No. 2/1, Rio de Janeiro, 1975.

187. López Cámara, Francisco. La estructura económica y social de México
en la época de la Reforma. Mexico City: Siglo XXI, 1967.

188. Ludwig, Emil. Lincoln. Barcelona: Juventud, 1969.

189. Lugon, Clovis. *A república "comunista" cristã dos quaranis (1610–1768)*. Rio de Janeiro: Paz e Terra, 1977.
190. Machado de Assís. *Obras completas*. Rio de Janeiro: Jackson, 1961.
191. Madariaga, Salvador de. *El auge y el ocaso del imperio español en América*. Madrid: Espasa-Calpa, 1979.
192. Maldonado Denis, Manuel. *Puerto Rico: una interpretación histórico-social*. Mexico City: Siglo XXI, 1978.
193. Mannix, Daniel P., and M. Cowley. *Historia de la trata de negros*. Madrid: Alianza, 1970.
194. Manrique, Nelson. *Las guerrillas indígenas en la guerra con Chile*. Lima: CIC, 1981.
195. Maria, Isidoro de. *Montevideo antiguo. Tradiciones y recuerdos*. Montevideo: Ministerio de Educación y Cultura, 1976.
196. Marmier, Xavier. *Buenos Aires y Montevideo en 1850*. Buenos Aires: El Ateneo, 1948.
197. Marmolejo, Lucio. *Efemérides guanajuatenses*. Guanajuato: Universidad, 1973.
198. Marriott, Alice, and Carol K. Rachlin. *American Indian Mythology*. New York: Mentor, 1972.
199. Martí, José. *Letras fieras*. (Selection and prologue by Roberto Fernández Retamar.) Havana: Letras Cubanas, 1981.
200. Martínez Estrada, Ezequiel. *Martí: el heroe y su acción revolucionaria*. Mexico City: Siglo XXI, 1972.
201. Marx, Karl, and Friedrich Engels. *Materiales para la historia de América Latina*. (Selection and commentaries by Pedro Scarón.) Mexico City: Pasado y Presente, 1979.
202. Masur, Gerhard. *Simón Bolívar*. Mexico City: Grijalbo, 1960.
203. Matute, Álvaro. *México en el siglo XIX. Fuentes e interpretaciones históricas* (anthology). Mexico City: UNAM, 1973.
204. Mauro, Frédéric. *La vie quotidienne au Brésil au temps de Pedro Segundo (1831–1889)*. Paris: Hachette, 1980.
205. Maxwell, Kenneth. *A devassa da devassa. A Inconfidência Mineira, Brasil-Portugal, 1750–1808*. Rio de Janeiro: Paz e Terra, 1978.
206. McLuhan, T. C. (ed.). *Touch the Earth. A Self-Portrait of Indian Existence*. New York: Simon and Schuster, 1971.
207. Medina Castro, Manuel. *Estados Unidos y América Latina, siglo XIX*. Havana: Casa de las Américas, 1968.
208. Mejía Duque, Jaime. *Isaacs y María*. Bogota: La Carreta, 1979.
209. Mello e Souza, Laura de. *Declassificados do ouro: a pobreza mineira no século XVIII*. Rio de Janeiro: Graal, 1982.
210. Meltzer, Milton (ed.). *In Their Own Words. A History of the American Negro (1619–1865)*. New York: Crowell, 1964.
211. Melville, Herman. *Moby Dick*. (Trans. by José María Valverde.) Barcelona: Bruguera, 1982

212. Mendoza, Vicente T. *El corrido mexicano*. Mexico City: FCE, 1976.
213. Mercader, Martha. *Juanamanuela, mucha mujer*. Buenos Aires: Sudamericana, 1982.
214. Mercado Luna, Ricardo. *Los coroneles de Mitre*. Buenos Aires: Plus Ultra, 1974.
215. Mesa, José de, (with Teresa Gisbert). *Holguín y la pintura virreinal en Bolivia*. La Paz: Juventud, 1977.
216. Mir, Pedro. *El gran incendio*. Santo Domingo: Taller, 1974.
217. Miranda, José. *Humboldt y México*. Mexico City: UNAM, 1962.
218. Mitchell, Lee Clark. *Witnesses to a Vanishing America. The Nineteenth-Century Response*. Princeton: Princeton University Press, 1981.
219. Molina, Enrique. *Una sombra donde sueña Camila O'Gorman*. Barcelona: Seix-Barral, 1982.
220. Montes, Arturo Humberto. *Morazán y la federación centroamericana*. Mexico: Libro Mex, 1958.
221. Morales, Franklin. "Los albores del futbol uruguayo," in *Cien años de futbol*. No. 1, Montevideo, Editores Reunidos, November 1969.
222. Moreno Fraginals, Manuel. *El ingenio*. Havana: Ciencias Sociales, 1978.
223. Morin, Claude. *Michoacán en la Nueva España del siglo XVIII. Crecimiento y desigualdad en una economía colonial*. Mexico City: FCE, 1979.
224. Morison, Samuel Eliot, (with Henry Steele Commager and W. E. Leuchtenburg). *Breve historia de los Estados Unidos*. Mexico City: FCE, 1980.
225. Mörner, Magnus. *La mezcla de razas en la historia de América Latina*. Buenos Aires: Paidós, 1969.
226. Mousnier, Roland, and Ernest Labrousse. *Historia general de las civilizaciones. El siglo XVIII*. Barcelona: Destino, 1967.
227. Muñoz, Rafael F. *Santa Anna. El que todo lo oanó y todo lo perdió*. Madrid: Espasa-Calpe, 1936.
228. Museo Nacional de Culturas Populares. *El maíz, fundamento de la cultura popular mexicana*; and *Nuestro maíz. Treinta monografías populares*. Mexico City: SEP, 1982.
229. Nabokov, Peter. *Native American Testimony. An Anthology of Indian and White Relations: First Encounter to Dispossession*. New York: Harper and Row, 1978.
230. Neilhardt, John G. *Black Elk Speaks*. New York: Washington Square, 1972.
231. Nevins, Allan. *John D. Rockefeller: The Heroic Age of American Business*. New York: Scribner's, 1940.
232. Nimuendajú, Curt. *Los mitos de creación y de destrucción del mundo*. Lima: Centro Amazónico de Antropología, 1978.
233. Nino, Bernadino de. *Etnografía chiriguana*. La Paz: Argote, 1912.
234. Núñez, Jorge. *El mito de la independencia*. Quito: Universidad, 1976.

235. Ocampo López, Javier, *et al*. *Manual de historia de Colombia*. Bogotá: Instituto Colombiano de Cultura, 1982.

236. Oddone, Juan Antonio. *La formación del Uruguay moderno. La inmigración y el desarrollo económico-social*. Buenos Aires: EUDEBA, 1966.

237. O'Kelly, James J. *La tierra del mambí*. Havana: Instituto del Libro, 1968.

238. O'Leary, Daniel Florencio. *Memorias*. Madrid: América, 1919.

239. Ortega Peña, Rodolfo, and Eduardo Duhalde. *Felipe Varela contra el Imperio británico*. Buenos Aires: Peña Lillo, 1966.

240. Ortiz, Fernando. *Los negros esclavos*. Havana: Ciencias Sociales, 1975.

241. ———. *Los bailes y el teatro de los negros en el folklore de Cuba*. Havana: Letras Cubanas, 1981.

242. ———. *Contrapunteo cubano del tabaco y el azúcar*. Havana: Consejo Nacional de Cultura, 1963.

243. Paine, Thomas. *Complete Writings*. New York: Citadel, 1945.

244. Palacio, Ernesto. *Historia de la Argentina (1515–1943)*. Buenos Aires: Peña Lillo, 1975.

245. Palma, Ricardo. *Tradiciones peruanas*. Lima: Peisa, 1969.

246. Palma de Feuillet, Milagros. *El cóndor: dimensión mítica del ave sagrada*. Bogotá: Caja Agraria, 1982.

247. Paredes, M. Rigoberto. *Mitos, supersticiones y supervivencias populares de Bolivia*. La Paz: Burgos, 1973.

248. Paredes-Candia, Antonio. *Leyendas de Bolivia*. La Paz and Cochabamba: Amigos del Libro, 1975.

249. Pareja Diezcanseco, Alfredo. *Historia del Ecuador*. Quito: Casa de la Cultura Ecuatoriana, 1958.

250. Parienté, Henriette, and Geneviève de Ternant. *La fabuleuse histoire de la cuisine française*. Paris: Odil, 1981.

251. Pereda Valdés, Ildefonso. *El negro en el Uruguay. Pasado y presente*. Montevideo: Instituto Histórico y Geográfico, 1965.

252. Pereira de Queiroz, Maria Isaura. *Historia y etnología de los movimientos mesiánicos*. Mexico City: Siglo XXI, 1978.

253. Pereyra, Carlos. *Historia de América española*. Madrid: Calleja, 1924.

254. ———. *Solano López y su drama*. Buenos Aires: Patria Grande, 1962.

255. Pérez Acosta, Juan F. *Francia y Bonpland*. Buenos Aires: Peuser, 1942.

256. Pérez Rosales, Vicente. *Recuerdos del pasado*. Havana: Casa de las Américas, 1972.

257. Petit de Murat, Ulyses. *Presencia viva del tango*. Buenos Aires: Reader's Digest. 1968.

258. Pichardo, Hortensia. *Documentos para la historia de Cuba*. Havana: Ciencias Sociales, 1973.

259. Plath, Oreste. *Geografía del mito y la leyenda chilenos*. Santiago de Chile: Nascimiento, 1973.

260. Poe, Edgar Allan. *Selected Prose and Poetry*. (Prologue by W. H. Auden.) New York: Rinehart, 1950.

261. Ponce de León, Salvador. *Guanajuato en el arte, en la historia y en la leyenda*. Guanajuato: Universidad, 1973.

262. Portuondo, Jose A. (ed.) *El pensamiento vivo de Maceo*. Havana: Ciencias Sociales, 1971.

263. Posada, Jose Guadalupe. *La vida mexicana*. Mexico City: Fondo Editorial de la Plástica Mexicana, 1963.

264. Price, Richard (ed.). *Sociedades cimarronas*. Mexico City: Siglo XXI, 1981.

265. Price-Mars, Jean. *Así habló el Tío*. Havana: Casa de las Américas, 1968.

266. Prieto, Guillermo. *Memorias de mis tiempos*. Mexico City: Patria, 1964.

267. Puiggros, Rodolfo. *La época de Mariano Moreno*. Buenos Aires: Partenon, 1949.

268. Querejazu Calvo, Roberto. *Guano, salitre, sangre. Historia de la guerra del Pacífico*. La Paz and Cochabamba: Amigos del Libro, 1979.

269. Ramírez Necochea, Hernan. *Historia del imperialismo en Chile*. Havana: Revolucionaria, 1966.

270. ———. *Balmaceda y la contrarrevolución de 1891*. Santiago de Chile: Universitaria, 1958.

271. Ramos, Jorge Abelardo. *Revolución y contrarrevolución en la Argentina*. Buenos Aires: Plus Ultra, 1965.

272. Ramos, Juan P. *Historia de la instrucción primaria en la Argentina*. Buenos Aires: Peuser, 1910.

273. Reed, Nelson. *La Guerra de Castas de Yucatán*. Mexico City: Era, 1971.

274. Reina, Leticia. *Las rebeliones campesinas en México (1819–1906)*. Mexico City: Siglo XXI, 1980.

275. Renault, Delso. *O Rio antigo nos anúncios de jornais*. Rio de Janeiro: José Olympio, 1969.

276. Revista *Signos*, Santa Clara, Cuba, July/December, 1979.

277. Reyes Abadie, W. (with Oscar H. Bruschera and Tabaré Melogno). *El ciclo artiquista*. Montevideo: Universidad, 1968.

278. ——— (with A. Vásquez Romero). *Crónica general del Uruguay*. Montevideo: Banda Oriental, 1979–1981.

279. Riazanov, David. *Karl Marx and Friedrich Engels. An Introduction to their Lives and Work*. New York: Monthly Review Press, 1973.

280. Rippy, J. Fred. *La rivalidad entre Estados Unidos y Gran Bretaña por América Latina (1808–1830)*. Buenos Aires: EUDEBA, 1967.

281. Roa Bastos, Augusto. *Yo el Supremo*. Buenos Aires: Siglo XXI, 1974.

282. Robertson, James Oliver. *American Myth, American Reality*. New York: Hill and Wang, 1980.

283. Robertson, J. P., and G. P. Robertson. *Cartas de Sud-América*. (Prologue by Jose Luis Busaniche.) Buenos Aires: Emecé, 1950.

284. Rodrigues, Nina. *Os africanos no Brasil*. São Paulo: Editora Nacional, 1977.

285. Rodríguez, Simón. *Sociedades americanas*. (Facsimile edition with prologues by Germán Carrera Damas and J. A. Cora.) Caracas: Catalá/ Centauro, 1975.

286. Rodríguez, Demorizi, Emilio. *Martí en Santo Domingo*. Havana: Ucar Garcia, 1953.

287. Roeder, Ralph. *Hacia el México moderno: Porfirio Díaz*. Mexico City: FCE, 1973.

288. Rojas-Mix, Miguel. *La Plaza Mayor. El urbanismo, instrumento de dominio colonial*. Barcelona: Muchnik, 1978.

289. Romero, Emilio. *Historia económica del Perú*. Lima: Universo, 1949.

290. Romero, José Luis. *Las ideas políticas en Argentina*. Mexico City and Buenos Aires: FCE, 1956.

291. Rosa, José María. *La guerra del Paraguay y las montoneras argentinas*. Buenos Aires: Huemul, 1965.

292. Rosenberg, Bruce A. *The Code of the West*. Bloomington, Indiana: Indiana University Press, 1982.

293. Rossi, Vicente. *Cosas de negros*. Buenos Aires: Hachette, 1958.

294. Rubin de la Barbolla, Daniel F. *Arte popular mexicano*. Mexico City: FCE, 1974.

295. Rumazo González, Alfonso. *Manuela Sáenz. La libertadora del Libertador*. Caracas and Madrid, Mediterráneo, 1979.

296. ———. *Sucre*. Caracas: Presidencia de la República, 1980.

297. ———. *Ideario de Simón Rodríguez*. Caracas: Centauro, 1980.

298. ———. *Simón Rodríguez*. Caracas: Centauro, 1976.

299. Rumrrill, Roger, and Pierre de Zutter. *Amazonia y capitalismo. Los condenados de la selva*. Lima: Horizonte, 1976.

300. Sabogal, José. *El desván de la imaginería peruana*. Lima: Mejía Baca y Villanueva, 1956.

301. Salazar, Sonia (compiler). "Testimonio sobre el origen de la leyenda del Señor de Ccoyllorithi," in *Sur*, No. 52, Cuzco, July 1982.

302. Salazar Bondy, Sebastian. *Lima la horrible*. Havana: Casa de las Américas, 1967.

303. Salomon, Noel. "Introducción a José Joaquín Fernández de Lizardi," in *Casa del Tiempo*, Vol. 2, No. 16, Mexico City, December 1981.

304. Sánchez, Luis Alberto. *La Perricholi*. Lima: Nuevo Mundo, 1964.

305. Sanford, John. *A More Godly Country. A Personal History of America*. New York: Horizon Press, 1975.

306. Sanhueza, Gabriel. *Santiago Arcos, comunista, millonario y calavera*. Santiago de Chile: Pacífico, 1956.

307. Santos, Joaquim Felício dos. *Memórias do Distrito Diamantino*. Belo Horizonte: Itatiaia, 1976.

308. Santos Rivera, José (compiler). *Rubén Darío y su tiempo*. Managua: Nueva Nicaragua, 1981.

309. Sarabia Viejo, María Justina. *El juego de gallos en Neuva España*. Seville: Escuela de Estudios Hispano-Americanos, 1972.

310. Sarmiento, Domingo Faustino. *Vida de Juan Facundo Quiroga*. Barcelona: Bruguera, 1970.

311. ———. *Conflicto y armonías de las razas en América*. Buenos Aires: La Cultura Argentina, 1915.

312. Scobie, James R. *Buenos Aires del centro a los barrios (1870–1910)*. Buenos Aires: Hachette, 1977.

313. Scott, Anne Firor. "Self-Portraits," in *Women's America*. Linda Kerber and Jane Mathews, eds. New York: Oxford University Press, 1982.

314. Scroggs, William O. *Filibusteros y financieros. La historia de William Walker y sus asociados*. Managua: Banco de America, 1974.

315. Schinca, Milton. *Boulevard Sarandí. 250 años de Montevideo; anécdotas, gentes, sucesos*. Montevideo: Banda Oriental, 1976.

316. Scholas, Walter V. *Política mexicana durante el régimen de Juárez (1855–1872)*. Mexico City: FCE, 1972.

317. Selser, Gregorio. *Sandino, general de hombres libres*. Buenos Aires: Triangulo, 1959.

318. Servando, Fray (Servando Teresa de Mier). *Memorias*. (Prologue by Alfonso Reyes.) Madrid: América, n.d.

319. Silva, José Asunción. *Prosas y versos*. (Prologue by Carlos García Prada.) Madrid: Eisa, 1960.

320. Silva Santisteban, Fernando. *Los obrajes en el Virreinato del Perú*. Lima: Museo Nacional de Historia, 1964.

321. Simpson, Lesley Byrd. *Muchos Méxicos*. Mexico City: FCE, 1977.

322. Solano, Francisco de. *Los mayas del siglo XVIII*. Madrid: Cultura Hispánica, 1974.

323. Soler, Ricaurte. "Formas ideológicas de la nación panameña," in *Tareas*, Panama City, October/November 1963.

324. Sosa, Juan B., and Enrique J. Arce. *Compendio de historia de Panamá*. Panama City: Editorial Universitaria, 1977.

325. Souza, Márcio. *Gálvez, Imperador do Acre*. Rio de Janeiro: Civilização Brasileira, 1981.

326. Sozina, S. A. *En el horizonte está El Dorado*. Havana: Casa de las Américas, 1982.

327. Stein, Stanley J. *Grandeza e decadência do café no vale do Paraíba*. São Paulo: Brasiliense, 1961.

328. Stern, Milton R. *the Fine Hammered Steel of Herman Melville*. Urban: University of Illinois Press, 1968.

329. Stewart, Watt. *La servidumbre china en el Peru*. Lima: Mosca Azul, 1976.

330. Syme, Ronald. *Fur Trader of the North*. New York: Morrow, 1973.

331. Taylor, William B. *Drinking, Homicide and Rebellion in Colonial Mexican Villages*. Stanford: Stanford University Press, 1979.
332. Teja Zabre, Alfonso. *Morelos*. Buenos Aires: Espasa-Calpe, 1946.
333. Tibol, Raquel. *Hermenegildo Bustos, pintor de pueblo*. Guanajuato: Gobierno del Estado, 1981.
334. Tocantins, Leandro. *Formação histórica do Acre*. Rio de Janeiro: Civilização Brasileira, 1979.
335. Touron, Lucía Sala de (with Nelson de la Torre and Julio C. Rodríguez). *Artigas y su revolución agraria (1811–1820)*. Mexico City: Siglo XXI, 1978.
336. Trías, Vivian. *Juan Manuel de Rosas*. Montevideo: Banda Oriental, 1970.
337. Tristán, Flora. *Les pérégrinations d'une paria*. Paris: Maspero, 1979.
338. Tulard, Jean (compiler). *L'Amérique espagnole en 1800 vue par un savant allemand: Humboldt*. Paris: Calmann-Lévy, 1965.
339. Tuñón de Lara, Manuel. *La España del siglo XIX*. Barcelona: Laia, 1973.
340. Turner, Frederick W., III. *The Portable North American Indian Reader*. London: Penguin, 1977.
341. Twain, Mark. *Un yanqui en la corte del rey Arturo*. Barcelona: Bruguera, 1981.
342. Un inglés ("An Englishman"). *Cinco años en Buenos Aires (1820–1825)*. Buenos Aires: Solar/Hachette, 1962.
343. Uslar, Pietri, Arturo. *La isla de Robinson*. Barcelona: Seix Barral, 1981.
344. Valcarcel, Carlos Daniel. *La rebelión de Túpac Amaru*. Mexico City: FCE, 1973.
345. ———, (ed.). *Colección documental de la independencia del Perú*, Book II, Vol. 2. Lima: Comisión Nacional del Sesquicentenario, 1971.
346. Valle-Arizpe, Artemio de. *Fray Servando*. Buenos Aires: Espasa-Calpe, 1951.
347. Vargas, José Santos. *Diario de un comandante de la independencia americana (1814–1825)*. Mexico City: Siglo XXI, 1982.
348. Vargas Martínez, Ubaldo. *Morelos, siervo de la nación*. Mexico City: Porrúa, 1966.
349. Velasco, Cuauhtemoc. "Los trabajadores mineros en la Nueva España (1750–1810)," in *La clase obrera en la historia de Mexico. 1. De la colonia al imperio*. Mexico City: Siglo XXI, 1980.
350. Vidart, Daniel. *El tango y su mundo*. Montevideo: Tauro, 1967.
351. Vieira, Antonio. *Obras várias*. Lisbon: Sá da Costa, 1951/1953.
352. Villarroel, Hipólito. *Enfermedades políticas que padece la capital de esta Nueva España*. Mexico City: Porrúa, 1979.
353. Viñas, David. *Indios, ejército y frontera*. Mexico City: Siglo XXI, 1983.
354. Vitier, Cintio. *Temas martianos*. Havana: Centro de Estudios Martianos, 1969 and 1982.

355. Von Hagen, Víctor W. *Culturas preincaicas*. Madrid: Guadarrama, 1976.
356. Walker, William. *La guerra de Nicaragua*. San José, Costa Rica: Educa, 1975.
357. Westheim, Paul, *et al. José Guadalupe Posada*. Mexico City: Instituto Nacional de Bellas Artes, 1963.
358. Whitman, Walt. *Hojas de hierba*. (Translation by Jorge Luis Borges.) Barcelona: Lumen, 1972.
359. Williams Garcia, Roberto. *Mitos tepehuas*. Mexico City: SEP/Setentas, 1972.
360. Wissler, Clark. *Indians of the United States*. New York: Doubleday, 1967.
361. Ziegler, Jean. *Les vivants et la mort*. Paris: Seuil, 1975.

Index

About the Author

Eduardo Galeano is one of the world's most distinguished writers. He is the author of *Mirrors: Stories of Almost Everyone; Voices of Time; Upside Down; Soccer in Sun and Shadow; The Book of Embraces; We Say No; Days and Nights of Love and War; Walking Words; Open Veins of Latin America;* and the three volumes of this trilogy: *Genesis, Faces and Masks,* and *Century of the Wind*. His work has served as inspiration around the world to cultural historians, political organizers, composers, and artists alike; it has been translated into twenty-eight languages.

Born in Montevideo in 1940, Galeano lived for years in Argentina and Spain, in exile from the Uruguayan military dictatorship, before returning to Montevideo, where he lives today. He is the recipient of many international prizes, including the inaugural Lannan Prize for Cultural Freedom, the American Book Award, the Casa de las Américas Prize, and the First Distinguished Citizen of the region by the countries of Mercosur.

About the Translator

Born in London in 1904, Cedric Belfrage came to the U.S. in 1925 and began writing about movies in Hollywood. He was a cofounder of the *National Guardian* in 1948 and its editor until 1955, when a brush with McCarthy led to his deportation. He wrote ten books and novels published in this country, including *Away from It All; Abide with Me; My Master Columbus;* and *The American Inquisition, 1945–1960*. He lived with his wife, Mary, in Cuernavaca, Mexico, until his death in 1990.

Made in the USA
Coppell, TX
08 October 2022

84259767R00185